IMAGES
of America

SOUTHSIDE PLACE

"THOU SHALT LOVE THY GOD

WITH ALL THY HEART

—and—

THY NEIGHBOR AS THYSELF"

A CHALLENGE

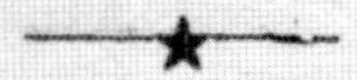

WE PASS THIS WAY BUT ONCE AS A TRAVELER AMONG TRAVELERS ON THIS ONE-WAY JOURNEY. MAY WE EVER BE KIND, PATIENT AND CONSIDERATE OF OUR FELLOW TRAVELLERS AND IN SO DOING BECOME TEACHERS BY EXAMPLE.........OUR CHILDREN WILL CARRY ON THE TRADITION .... RESULT ....A HEAP' O' LIVIN' IN SOUTHSIDE PLACE.

This poem appeared in the 1945–1946 Yearbook of Southside Place. (Courtesy of City of Southside Place.)

ON THE COVER: Ed (left) and Bob Judson swing from a Chinese tallow tree on Auden Street near their home in 1932. (Courtesy of Roger Judson.)

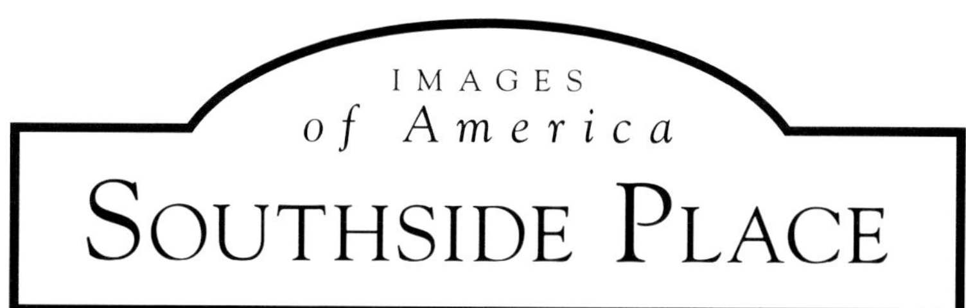

Kate McCormick and Kris Holt

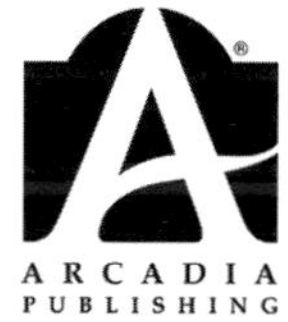

ISBN 978-1-4671-3174-2

Published by Arcadia Publishing
Charleston, South Carolina

Printed in the United States of America

Library of Congress Control Number: 2014932939

For all general information, please contact Arcadia Publishing:
Telephone 843-853-2070
Fax 843-853-0044
E-mail sales@arcadiapublishing.com
For customer service and orders:
Toll-Free 1-888-313-2665

Visit us on the Internet at www.arcadiapublishing.com

We dedicate this book to the residents of Southside Place who shape the community and continue its wonderful legacy.

Contents

ACKNOWLEDGMENTS

Southside Place was made possible by current and former residents who generously shared their photographs and memories with us. We are indebted to current residents Florine Carr, Robert Gray, Maurice and Sandy Lewis, Vicki Little, Lisa Roy, Martha Strawn, Liz Wood, and Seth and Ann Young and past residents Harriett Bevil, Gayle Bowyer, Mary Brandt, Paul Brewer, Ashley Bryan, Jackie Duffie, Annalea Flam, Henri Gadbois, Bert Graham, Thomas McWhorter, Mark Montgomery, Edward Rose, Cynthia Suhler, and Jim Williams. We are grateful to the descendants of former residents Lillie Mae Cameron, Rhonda Harrington, Arthur Hirdler, Mary Ethel Ireson, Kathy Kokas, J'Lynn Proctor, and Dena Wagner who kindly invited us into their homes, shared their family histories, and answered our relentless inquiries.

For contributing historical information and photographs, we thank Gene Crain; Celestine and Rudy Darelik; Susan Smith Finn; Stephen Fox; Sandy Peterson; Val Glitch, FAIA; Karen Lantz, AIA; Mike McCorkle; and Jim Wolf at Charter Title Company. We are also indebted to David Moss and Chief Mike Pack of the City of Southside Place; Dara Flinn at the Woodson Research Center, Fondren Library at Rice University; Annie Golden at the Harris County Archives; Tim Ronk at the Houston Metropolitan Research Center; contributors to *Southside Place USA, Our Heritage Past to Present*; Preservation Houston; St. Mark's Episcopal Church; Story Sloane's Gallery; Texas A&M Cushing Memorial Library and Archives; West University Baptist Church; and West University United Methodist Church.

For their professional help we recognize Michelle Garza, photographer Joe Gayle, and proofreaders Carolyn Covault, Ginny Crosthwait, Cynthia Lokken, and Jim Parsons.

Finally, we express our heartfelt appreciation to former residents Roger Judson and Kelly Mears. We had no idea what we were getting into when we penned the book's first word. Their generous contributions became our good fortune and the reason we were able to assemble a photographic timeline of life in Southside Place. The appreciation both Roger and Kelly have for their own family histories, along with an amazing wealth of family photographs and personal accounts, allowed us the opportunity to tell this story.

KEY TO ABBREVIATIONS

HCA	Harris County Archives
HMRC	Houston Metropolitan Research Center
Rice	Woodson Research Center, Fondren Library, Rice University
SSP	City of Southside Place

INTRODUCTION

In 1920, San Antonio was Texas's largest city, with Houston a distant third. In the decade that followed, Houston surpassed San Antonio as the state's largest city, and Harris County became the state's largest county. Fueled by the maturing oil industry and the growth of the Port of Houston, the city limits doubled every 10 years from 1910 to 1930. The growing population needed housing, and would-be developers responded by creating new subdivisions for all income levels in and around Houston. Southside Place was one such subdivision established during this time on the soggy barren prairie just three miles outside of Houston proper.

E.L. Crain began his real estate career in 1913 buying individual lots and building small, speculative residential homes in Montrose and other subdivisions. By the early 1920s, Crain had expanded into the prefabricated housing business and real estate and was establishing 100-lot subdivisions owned, planned, and marketed by the Crain Ready-Cut House Company. By the time Crain established Southside Place in 1924, he had successfully developed three such subdivisions: Cherryhurst, Brady Home, and Pineview Place. Although suburban neighborhoods of speculatively built, uniformly designed homes are common today, Crain was at the forefront of this trend.

Crain's business model alone did not ensure that Southside Place would be a success. He sited Southside Place between Bellaire and West University Place to take advantage of existing infrastructure improvements. In 1910, W.W. Baldwin, the founder of Westmoreland Farms (now Bellaire), had constructed Bellaire Boulevard to link his development to Houston's Main Street. He also created the Westmoreland Railroad Company and built an electric trolley line on Bellaire Boulevard to provide transportation to and from Houston for those without automobiles. Crain was keenly aware that the success of his development was also dependent on convenient access to streetcar transportation and purchased acreage along Bellaire Boulevard to create Southside Place's southern border. In 1920, A.D. Foreman, president of the West End Realty Company, reportedly spent $100,000 to bring electricity, water, and telephone service to West University Place after Houston deemed it economically infeasible to bring utilities so far away from downtown. It seems likely that an existing utility infrastructure in a neighboring community would have made it easier for Crain to offer modern amenities when he established Southside Place four years later.

While Crain may have built Southside Place on infrastructure laid by other developers, his vision of a community was qualitatively different than what had come before, and he took great pains to distinguish Southside Place from its neighbors. Westmoreland Farms sought buyers still tied to farming whether as an occupation or a means of self-sufficiency. It attracted these buyers by offering parcels ranging from 4.5 to 20 acres suitable for small truck farms and an agricultural trading center with access to downtown Houston. West University Place, on the other hand, catered to an untapped market of middle-class city dwellers who sought an escape from the bustle of downtown Houston. Southside Place, it seemed, sought to offer the best of both worlds by highlighting in its early marketing materials the subdivision's proximity to downtown and suitability for the "gentleman farmer:"

> How many times have you wished for a REAL HOME, one that wasn't crowded onto a 50 foot by 100 foot lot. A place with plenty of room for the growing children to play and work AT HOME.
>
> Southside Place fulfills your ideals, your needs—room for flower gardens, vegetable gardens, pet, poultry and fruit trees—close enough "in" to be convenient to the City, just far enough from downtown to make the ideal home.

What would ultimately differentiate Southside Place from neighboring communities, however, was Crain's decision to invest a reported $50,000 in a park at the center of his new subdivision that featured a pool, clubhouse, tennis court, and play equipment. This early attempt at city planning made Southside Place likely the first Houston subdivision to offer such amenities for the private use of its residents. Ninety years later, Crain's vision remains intact. Southside Place's park, now known as Fire Truck Park, continues to be the heart and soul of the community.

As Southside Place prepares to celebrate the anniversary of its founding, this book traces its history through family photographs and oral histories of its citizens, past and present. What is clear from these images and stories is that much has changed, yet so much remains the same. While the external features of the city have evolved with changing tastes and styles, the connection residents feel to their community and each other, irrespective of when they lived in Southside Place, endures.

One

The Early Years

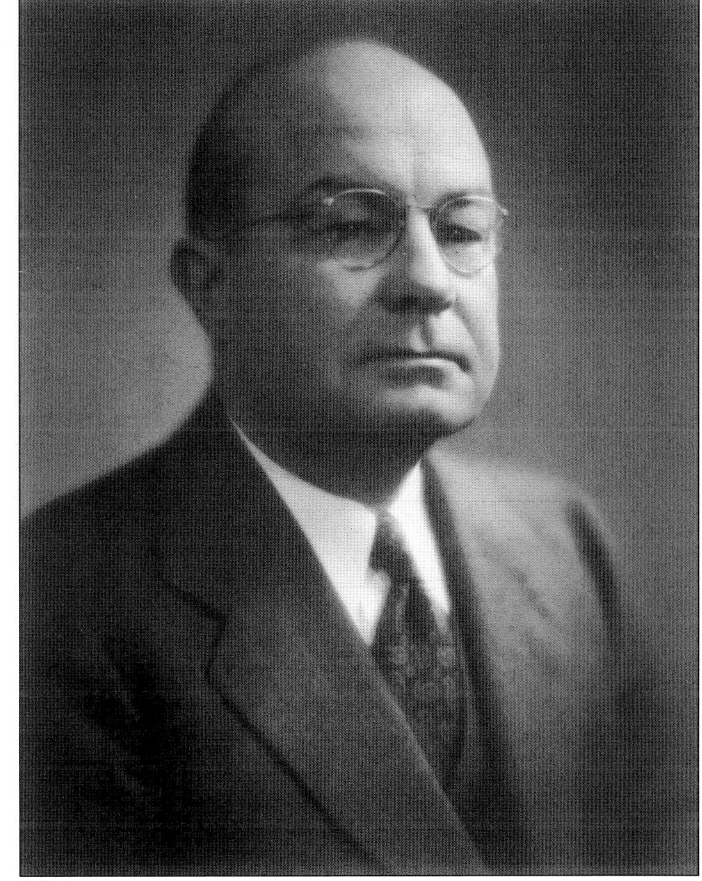

Edward Lillo Crain, founder of Southside Place, was born in Longview, Texas, in 1885. As a young man, Crain moved to Houston, Texas, and in 1913 began buying lots and building speculative homes in Montrose. By the early 1920s, Crain had expanded into the prefabricated home business and began developing subdivisions. Ahead of his time, Crain later combined the roles of investor, developer, and builder and filled the neighborhoods he established with uniformly designed prefabricated homes. Crain is reported to have built 10,000 such homes over his career. (Courtesy of Gene Crain.)

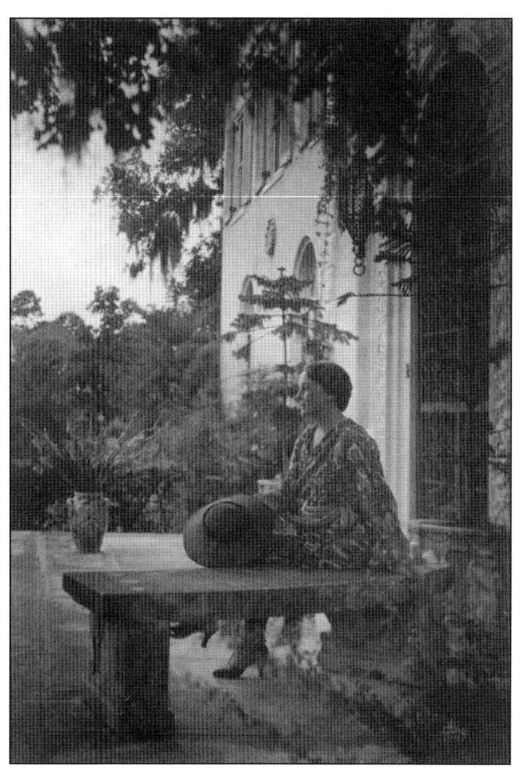

E.L. Crain married Annie Vive Carter in 1915, and they had three sons: Edward Lillo Crain Jr., after whom Edloe Street, which runs through Southside Place, was named; Carter F. Crain; and John Richard Crain. The couple did not live in any of the neighborhoods Crain developed, and none of their personal homes were prefabricated designs. This undated photograph shows the Crains' home on North MacGregor Drive in Houston, Texas, designed by architect William Ward Watkin in 1928. (Courtesy of Gene Crain.)

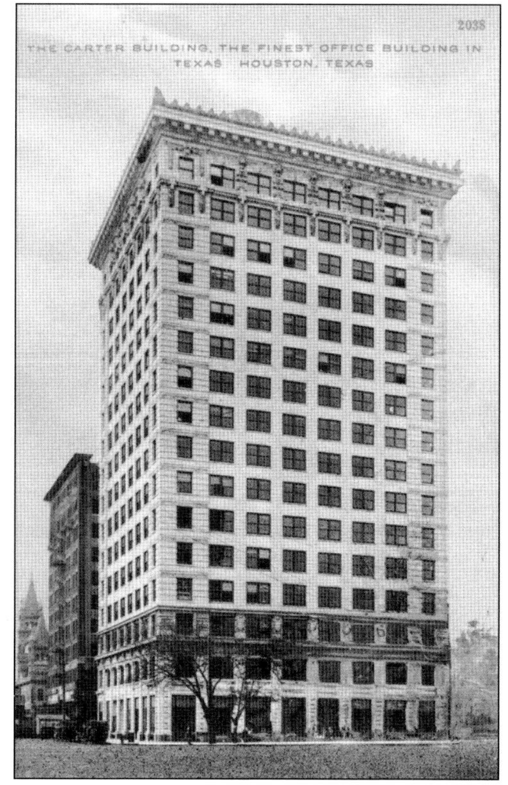

Crain's marriage to Annie Carter benefited him both socially and financially. She was the daughter of lumberman, banker, and promoter Samuel Fain Carter. Carter is credited with developing one of Houston's first skyscrapers, the 16-story Carter Building (later known as the Second National Bank Building) at 806 Main Street in 1910. Carter's claim to having the tallest building in Houston, however, was short-lived. In 1912, his uncle, philanthropist Jesse Jones, began construction of the Rice Hotel, which, when completed, stood 17 stories. In an effort to maintain its status as the tallest building, Carter later added six stories to the Carter Building, bringing the total number of floors to 22. (Courtesy of Kate McCormick.)

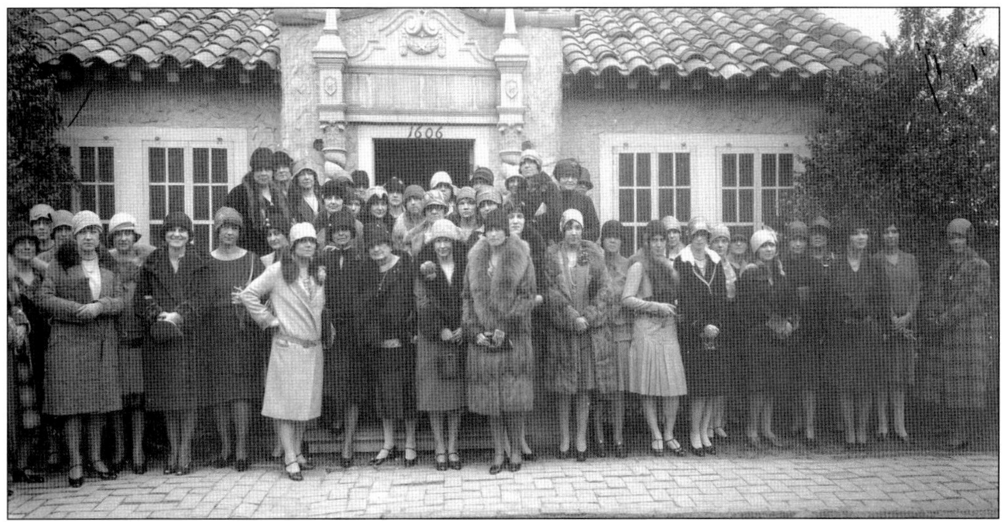

The Crains' philanthropic legacy in Houston is significant. Annie Crain was one of 15 charter members of the Blue Bird Circle, the oldest women's charitable organization in Houston. Founded in 1923 as a nondenominational service organization at the First Methodist Church in Houston, the Blue Bird's initial charitable projects included providing aid to the Young Women's Cooperative Home at 1808 Wheeler Street and a day nursery for the children of working mothers. In 1927, the Blue Bird Circle opened a small gift shop and held rummage sales to fund its charitable endeavors. Today, the group still operates the Blue Bird Circle Resale Shop on West Alabama Street in Houston. (Courtesy of Story Sloane's Gallery.)

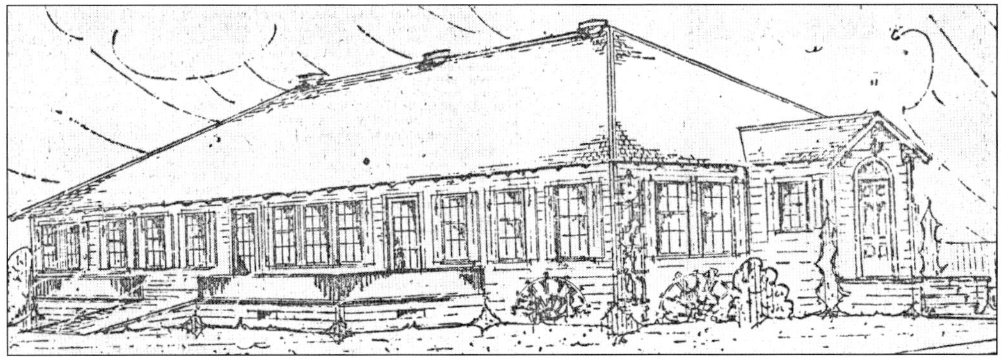

In 1934, Methodist Hospital asked the group to help it provide additional hospital space for crippled children because it wards were overflowing. The "Little Hospital" was designed by C.O. Bovee, chief architect of the Crain Ready-Cut House Company, and built by the Blue Bird Circle on the grounds of Methodist Hospital at a cost of $7,400. The 30-bed hospital had separate wards to accommodate boys and girls, as well as a day clinic. In 1939 alone, the Little Hospital served over 800 patients. When Annie Crain's youngest son died of appendicitis during her tenure as president of the Blue Bird Circle, the group founded the Richard Crain Memorial Fund (now known as the Blue Bird Memorial Fund), which continues to support pediatric neurological clinics and research today. (Courtesy of the John P. McGovern Historical Collections and Research Center.)

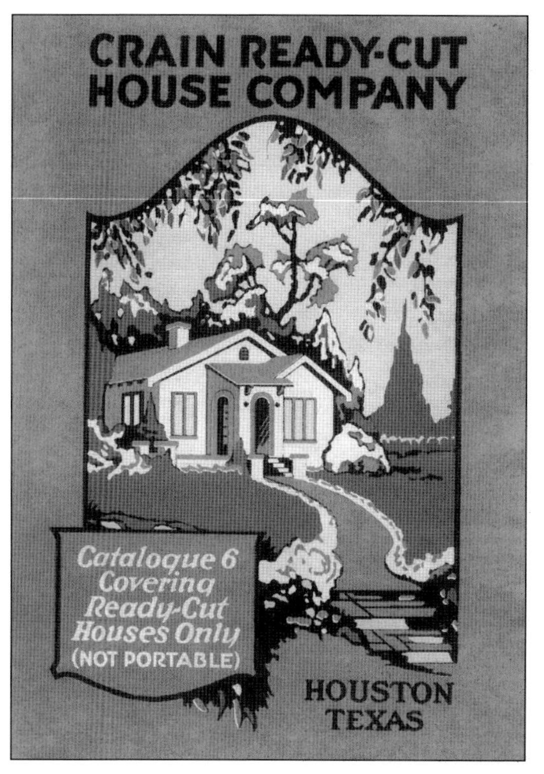

In 1917, E.L. Crain purchased the T.J. Williams House Manufacturing Company and renamed it the Crain Ready-Cut House Company. In doing so, he was able to build his speculative homes more cheaply and later expand into the business of selling his prefabricated homes through catalogues. The company maintained an architecture department that produced hundreds of canned design plans featured in its sales catalogues. (Courtesy of HCA.)

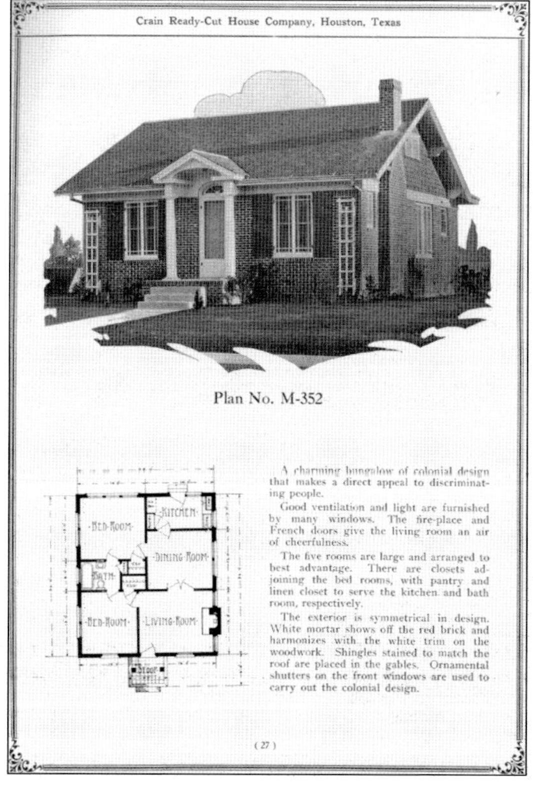

Crain Ready-Cut House Company, Houston, Texas

Plan No. M-352

A charming bungalow of colonial design that makes a direct appeal to discriminating people.

Good ventilation and light are furnished by many windows. The fire-place and French doors give the living room an air of cheerfulness.

The five rooms are large and arranged to best advantage. There are closets adjoining the bed rooms, with pantry and linen closet to serve the kitchen and bath room, respectively.

The exterior is symmetrical in design. White mortar shows off the red brick and harmonizes with the white trim on the woodwork. Shingles stained to match the roof are placed in the gables. Ornamental shutters on the front windows are used to carry out the colonial design.

(27)

Plan No. M-352 from Crain Ready-Cut House Catalogue No. 6 is an example of Crain's Ready-Cut House designs used in residential neighborhoods. This design was built at 3709 Garnet Street in Southside Place in 1924. The two-bedroom Colonial home featured a fireplace and French doors between the living room and dining room. Although modified over the years, it remains one of the few remaining Ready-Cut homes in Southside Place. (Courtesy of HCA.)

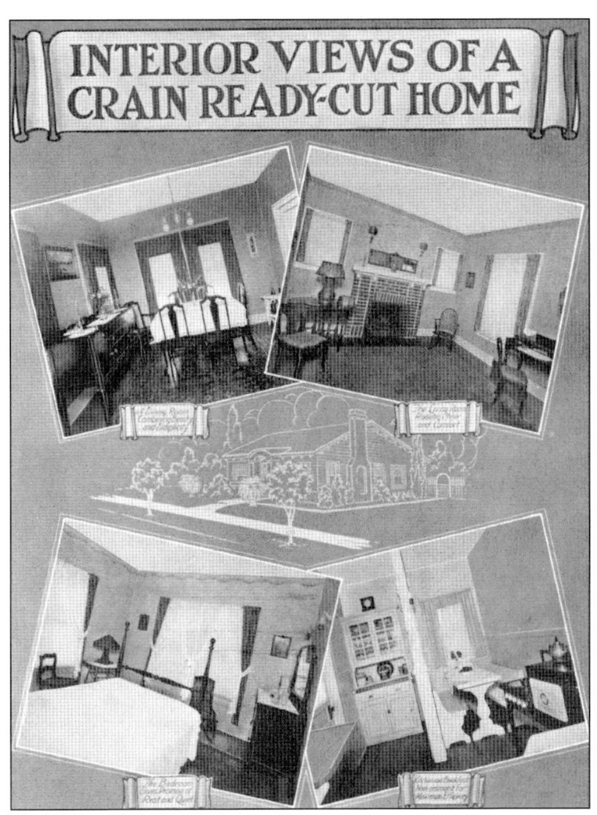

A Ready-Cut House package included everything from pre-cut lumber, windows, and doors, to nails, hardware, and wallpaper. Even where similar plans were used, each design showed individual characteristics and offered some opportunity for customization. Once a design was chosen, all the materials necessary to build the home were manufactured in Crain's Houston plant and delivered by truck or train to the buyer's home site for assembly. Careful manufacturing methods minimized waste, and the rapid handling of materials resulted in reduced labor costs. (Both courtesy of HCA.)

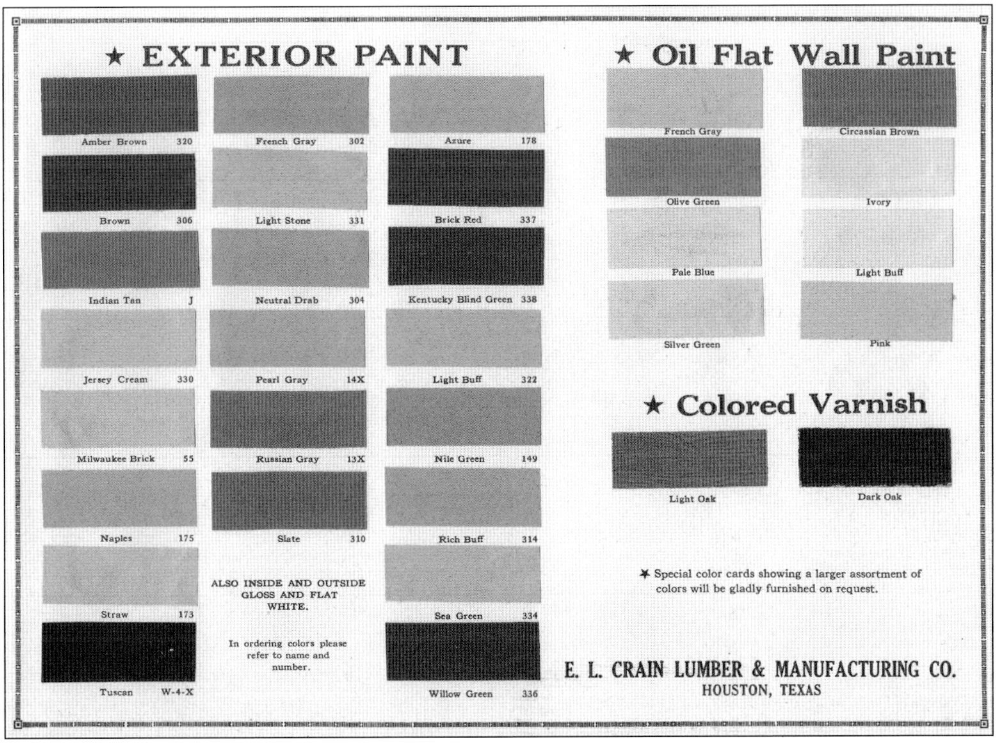

★ EXTERIOR PAINT

Amber Brown	320	French Gray	302	Azure	178
Brown	306	Light Stone	331	Brick Red	337
Indian Tan	J	Neutral Drab	304	Kentucky Blind Green	338
Jersey Cream	330	Pearl Gray	14X	Light Buff	322
Milwaukee Brick	55	Russian Gray	13X	Nile Green	149
Naples	175	Slate	310	Rich Buff	314
Straw	173			Sea Green	334
Tuscan	W-4-X			Willow Green	336

ALSO INSIDE AND OUTSIDE GLOSS AND FLAT WHITE.

In ordering colors please refer to name and number.

★ Oil Flat Wall Paint

French Gray	Circassian Brown
Olive Green	Ivory
Pale Blue	Light Buff
Silver Green	Pink

★ Colored Varnish

Light Oak	Dark Oak

★ Special color cards showing a larger assortment of colors will be gladly furnished on request.

E. L. CRAIN LUMBER & MANUFACTURING CO.
HOUSTON, TEXAS

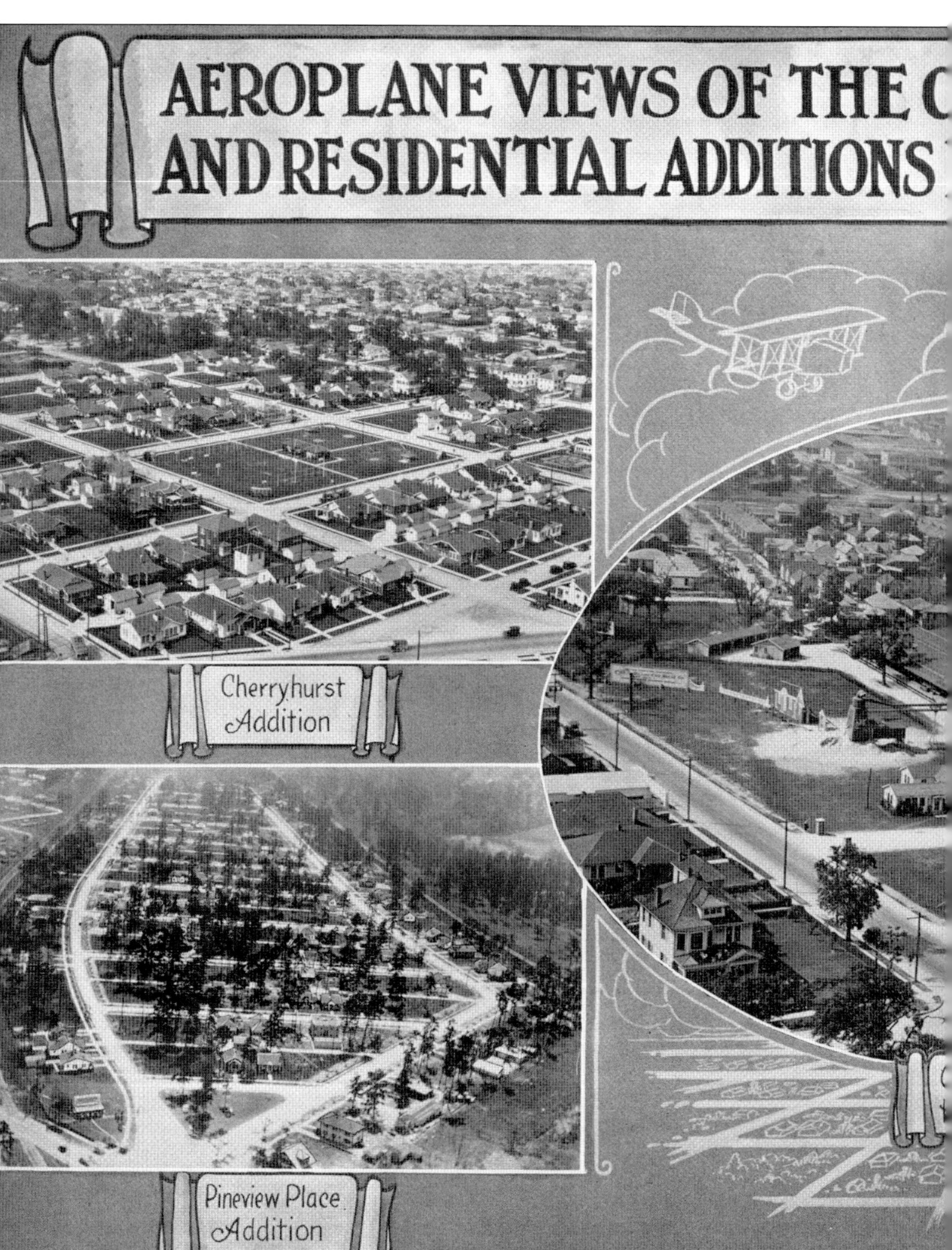

A few years after his acquisition of the T.J. Williams House Manufacturing Company, E.L. Crain began the first step in vertically integrating his business by establishing a real estate department. This allowed him to buy land and begin developing subdivisions. It also provided a built-in demand

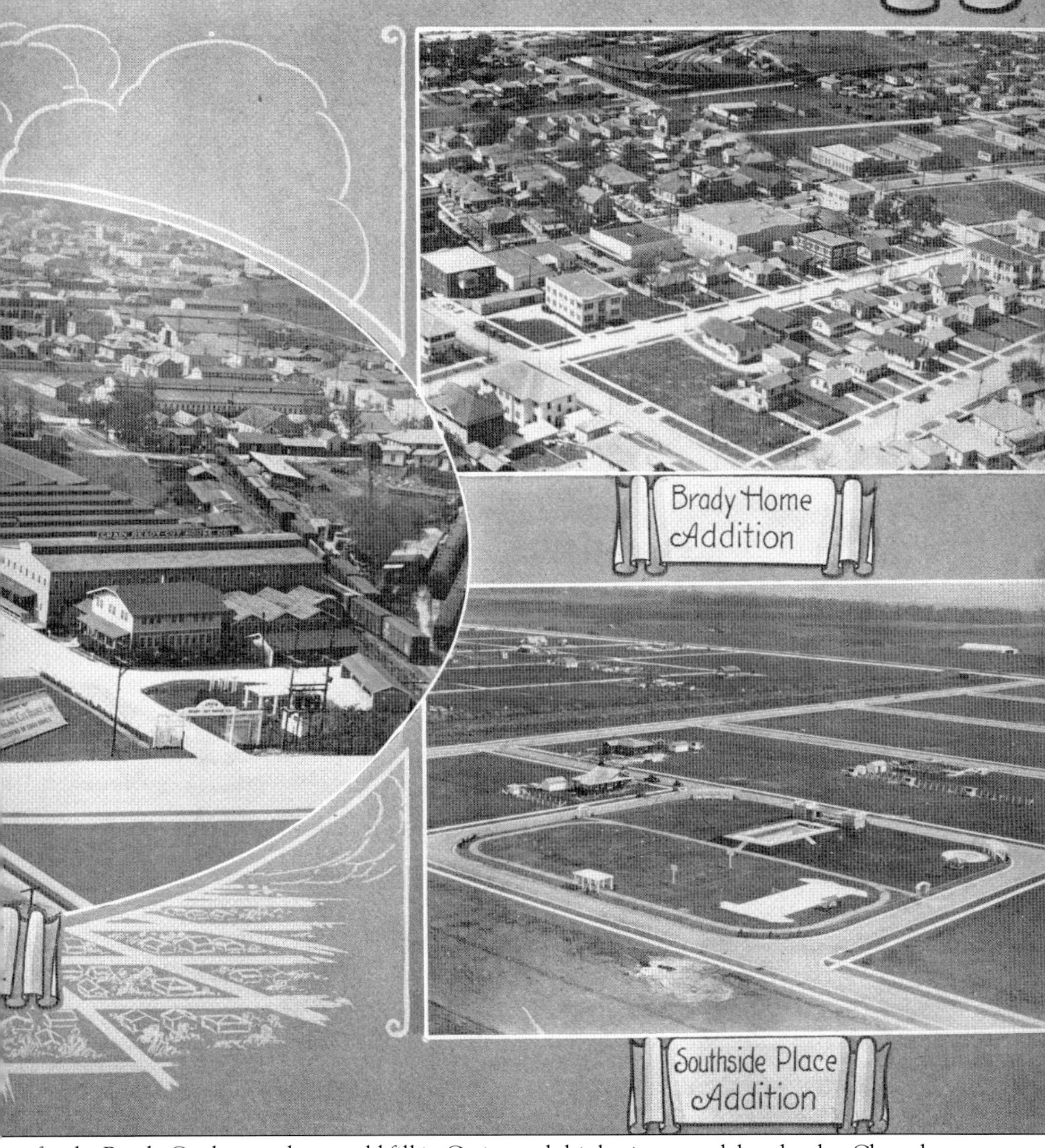

for the Ready-Cut homes that would fill it. Crain used this business model to develop Cherryhurst (1921), southwest of downtown Houston, and Brady Home (1922) and Pineview Place (1923), east of downtown. (Courtesy of HCA.)

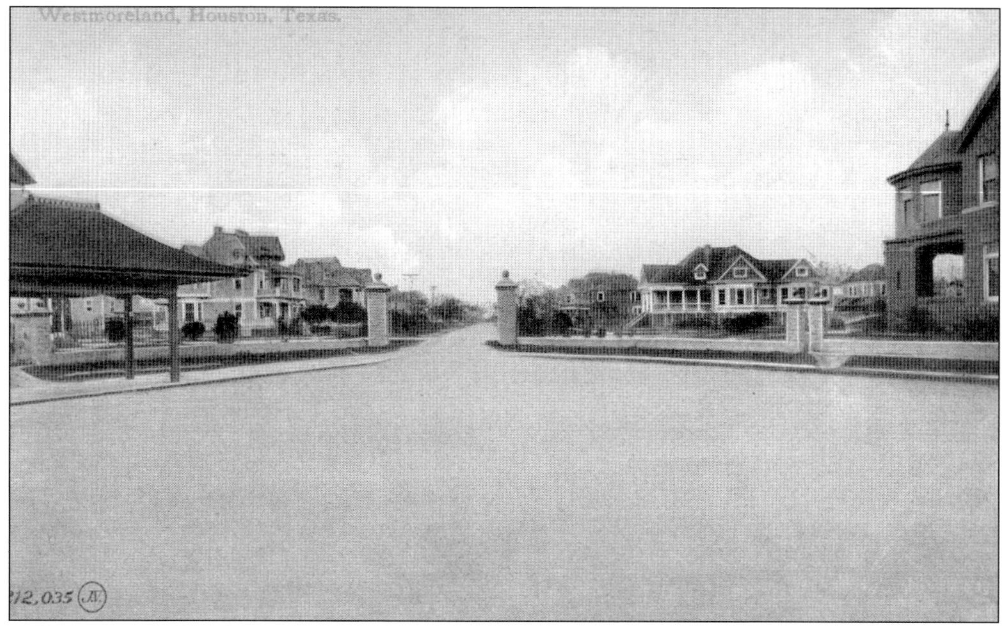

In creating Pineview Place and Southside Place, E.L. Crain may have been influenced by the development of "private places" made popular in St. Louis, Missouri, in the mid- to late 1800s. "Private places" are private residential enclaves where the streets and common areas are owned by the residents, and services are provided by private entities. The development of a subdivision as a "private place" allowed its residents to enforce and maintain property standards in an era before zoning laws. While Westmoreland Place (1902), pictured above, was inspired by private place neighborhoods, Courtlandt Place (1906), below, was the first private place in Houston. (Both courtesy of Kate McCormick.)

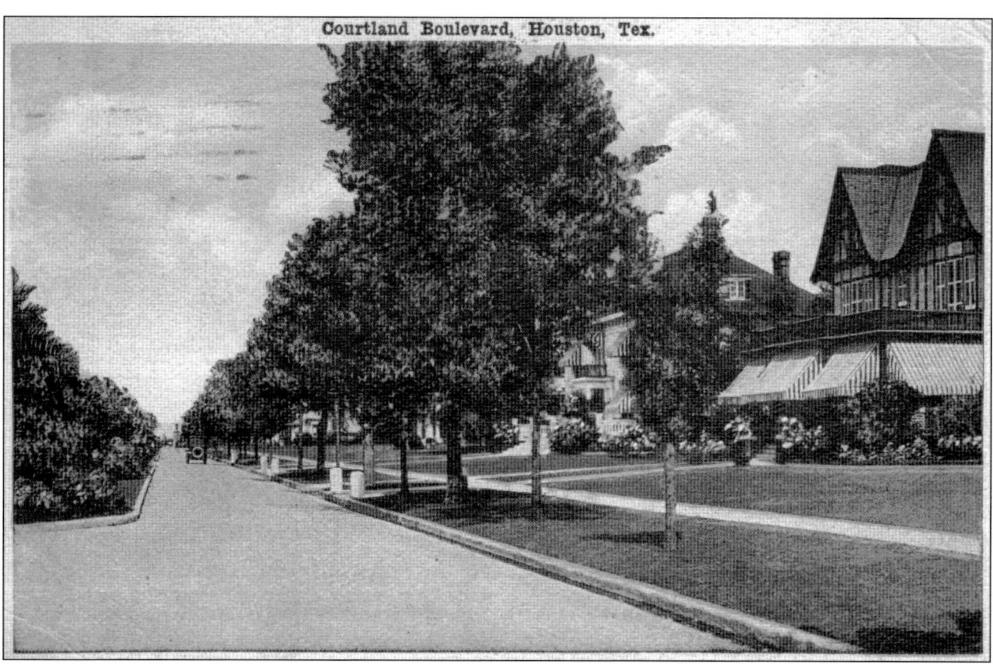

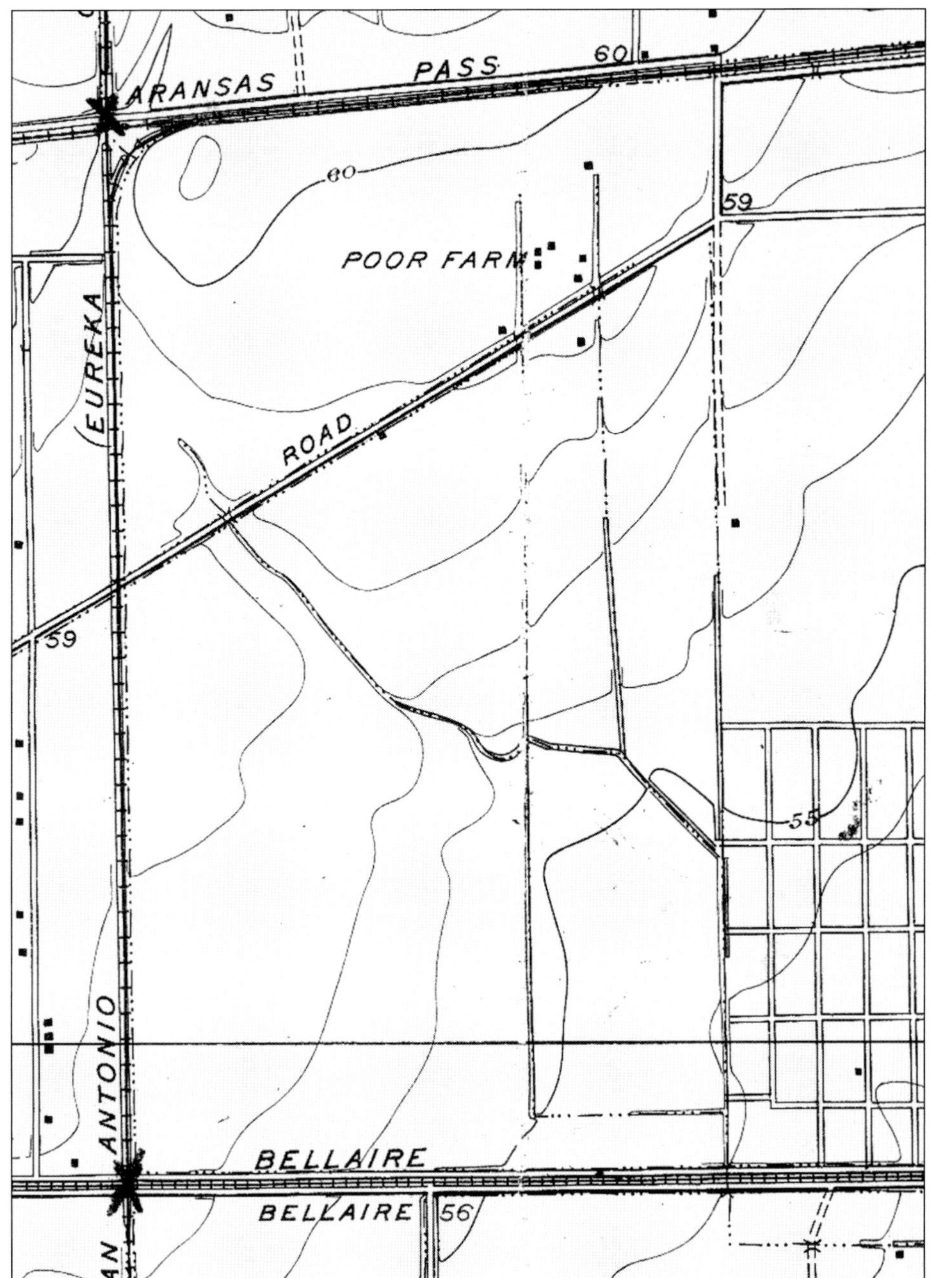

Southside Place was E.L. Crain's first development located outside of Houston proper in what was either the prairie or the suburbs, depending on one's point of view. Southside Place sits on the site of the former Harris County Poor Farm. In 1894, Harris County purchased the 200-acre plot for $6,000 and relocated the poor farm from its original setting on White Oak Bayou. The Harris County Poor Farm began 462.6 feet north of Bellaire Boulevard, roughly in the backyards of the homes on the north side of Carlon Street. It continued north past Richmond Road (now Bissonnet Street) and ended just north of Childress Street in Sunset Terrace. Its eastern boundary was the site of the current Poor Farm Ditch near Edloe Street, and its western boundary was just inside the Southern Pacific railroad tracks. (Courtesy of Roger Judson.)

198

Admitted in Aug 1922

NAME	Age	NATIONALITY	COMPLAINTS	Admitted		Discharged	REMARKS
C. R. Kelsey	66	American	Down & out	Aug	1	1922	Sister Mrs Mosher 1346 Harvest St
Jim Buttler	77	French	Simple & sick	Aug	3	1922	
J B Eliott	82	American	Old Age	"	8	"	Has no one
Pat Cassidy	83	Irish		"	9		
E.D. Dandy				"	13	"	
Geo Cummings		Negro	Bad eyes Sore foot	"	13	"	
Mary Johnson		Negro	Kidney trouble	"	18	"	
Mrs Lillie Ford	64	American	Weak in body & mind	"	22	"	a brother
Louis Witt	70	German	Cancer	"	24	"	Wife at Katie
C. R. Kelsey	66	American	Stomach trouble		24		
Mrs Sarah Chambers	67	American	Stomach trouble	"	25		
Henry Smith	76	Irish	Weak mind		26	Has no one	
Henry Nowesky		Polander	Old	"	1		
James Ervin		Negro	Stomach trouble	"	30		

Admitted in Aug 14 discharged 7 88 end of Aug

September

NAME	Age	NATIONALITY	COMPLAINTS	Admitted		Discharged	REMARKS
Allen Clark	87	Irish	Old age	Sept	1	1922	[Jacksonville
J C Pope	62	American	cripple leg	Sept	9	"	Brother J B Pope
D. C. Ray	80	American	Old age	Sept	14,	1922	Has no one
Hugh Moore	85	Irish	Weak mind	"	25	"	Has no one
Ed Brown	70	American	Cripple	"	27	"	
Marlin Bennett	72	American	Down & out	"	27	"	Has no one
Gustave Truman	81	German	Stomach Trouble	"	16	"	
Sam Solomon		Negro	Weak mind	"	30	"	From insane ward
Andrew King	82	German	Weak Mind	"	30	"	" insane ward

Admitted in Sept 9 discharged 6 83 at end

Admitted in Oct

NAME	Age	NATIONALITY	COMPLAINTS	Admitted		Discharged	REMARKS
John Edmonson		Negro	Kidney trouble	Oct	2	1922	[Kemp, Tex.
John Williamson	61	American		Oct	2	"	Has a brother A. C. Williamson
A. M. Tompson	72	American	T. B.	"	17	"	Has no one
P.S. Foxworthy			Weak mind	"	17	"	
Miles Roach	88	American	Old Age	"	27	"	
Chas Gartner	80	American	Old Age	"	27	"	
Mrs Stackhouse	80	American	Old age		27	"	Has no one
M S Woods	63	American	cripple		26	"	Has a nephew McKinney Woods
James Newel		American	Crazy		26	"	Has no one
Mrs Grace Millican		American	Weak mind		30	"	

Admitted in Oct. 18 discharged 8. 85 at end of Oct.

Although most Harris County Poor Farm inhabitants were elderly, the admission and discharge records on these facing pages reflect that it was a dumping ground for the disabled and mentally ill. The poor farm operated for almost 30 years until Houston began expanding outside its city limits and the land became valuable for development. (Courtesy of HMRC.)

Discharged in Aug 1922

NAME	Age	NATIONALITY	COMPLAINTS	Admitted	Discharged	REMARKS
Kelsey	66	American		Aug 18, 1922		to Infirmary
sh Ward		Negro		" 22	"	Ran away
ie Mae Faust	32	American	Deaf & Dum	" 24	"	Went to her sister
is Witt	70	German	Cancer	" 26		Sent back to hosp
ry Wesnesky		Polander	Old	" 25		Sent away
Cassidy	83	Irish	Old	" 19		
Kelley	34	Negro	Blind	" 28		Went to live with

End of Aug. 82

Discharged in Sept

NAME	Age	NATIONALITY	COMPLAINTS	Admitted	Discharged	REMARKS
es Roach	88	American	Weak mind	Sept 3		Discharged for disob
Jessie Hornes		American	Crazy & blind	" 6		Sent back to jail
ry Smith	76	Irish		7		Left without noti
s Billie Ford	64	American	Weak	" 16		Left of own acc
hram Nichols	83	Negro	Old and deaf	" 21		Killed by train
stave Trigman	81	German	Stomach trouble	" 30		

Discharged in Sept. 6 85 at end

Discharged in Oct

NAME	Age	NATIONALITY	COMPLAINTS	Admitted	Discharged	REMARKS
Smith	74	American	Down & out	Oct 2 1922		Left to hunt work
drew King	82	German	weak mind	" 8	"	
Buttler	77	French	weak mind	" 7	"	
as J. Gartner	80	American	Old age & grippe	" 19	"	To Hospital
McNerney	70	Canadian	Grippe	" 21	"	
gh More	85	Irish	weak mind	" 10		Went to town & never came back
m Edmonson		Negro	Kidney trouble	" 26		Went to work
as Donovan	83	American	Old Age	"		Went to Kansas

In 1923, the Harris County Commissioners disbanded the poor farm and sold the property in two tracts at auction. The southern tract was sold for $47,053. Just three months later, after multiple transfers, the Crain Ready-Cut House Company purchased the land for $75,424 and used it as the site of Southside Place. (Courtesy of HMRC.)

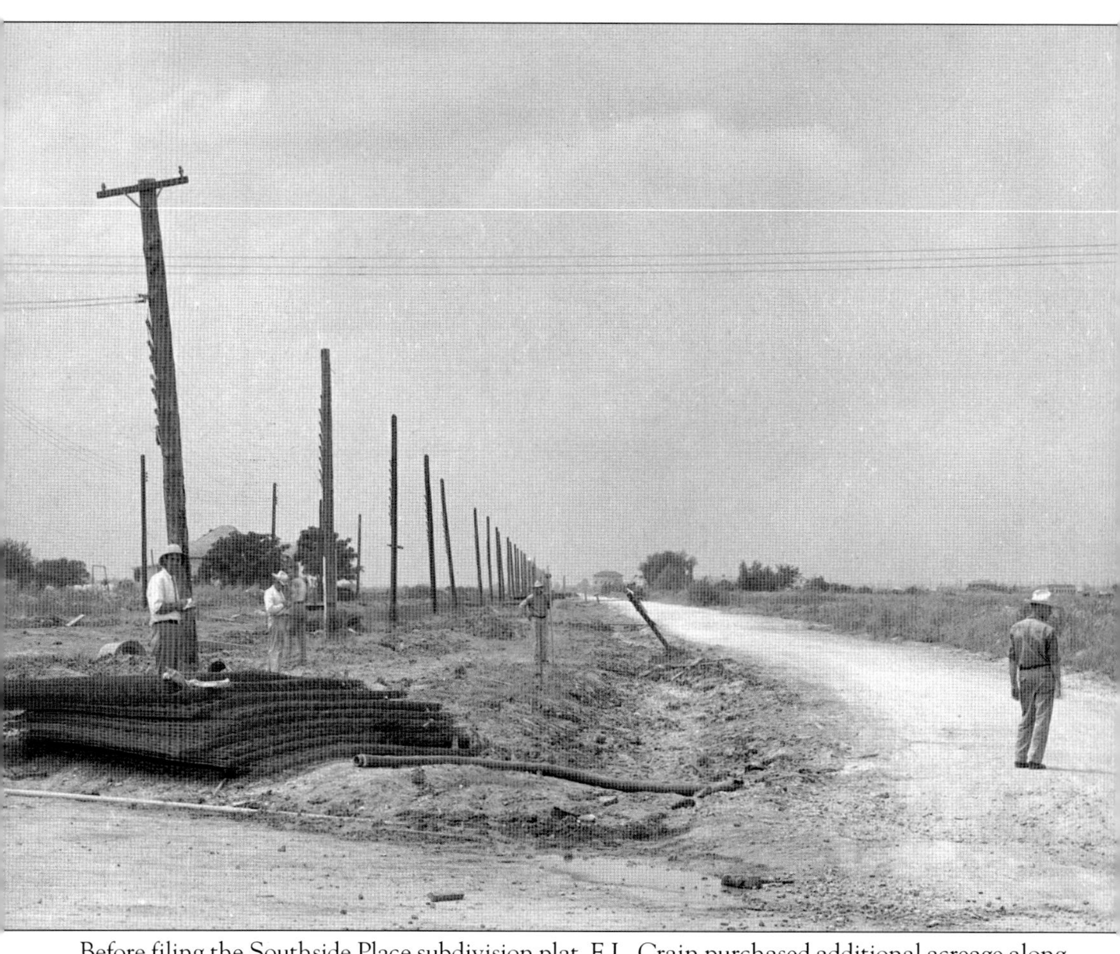

Before filing the Southside Place subdivision plat, E.L. Crain purchased additional acreage along the north side of Bellaire Boulevard from the Boulevard Land Company to combine with the former Harris County Poor Farm property. At the time, Bellaire Boulevard (pictured above in 1928 looking west from Main Street in Houston) was a crushed oyster-shell road with a single-track streetcar that had been built in 1910 by W.W. Baldwin, the founder of Westmoreland Farms. Baldwin was a railroad executive who built Bellaire Boulevard, and later the streetcar line, in order to promote the sale of real estate in his developments. Prior to the construction of the road, these communities were accessible only via old Richmond Road (now Bissonnet Street). By situating Southside Place on Bellaire Boulevard, Crain could ensure, at least for a time, that its residents had easy access to streetcar transportation to and from downtown Houston. (Courtesy of Story Sloane's Gallery.)

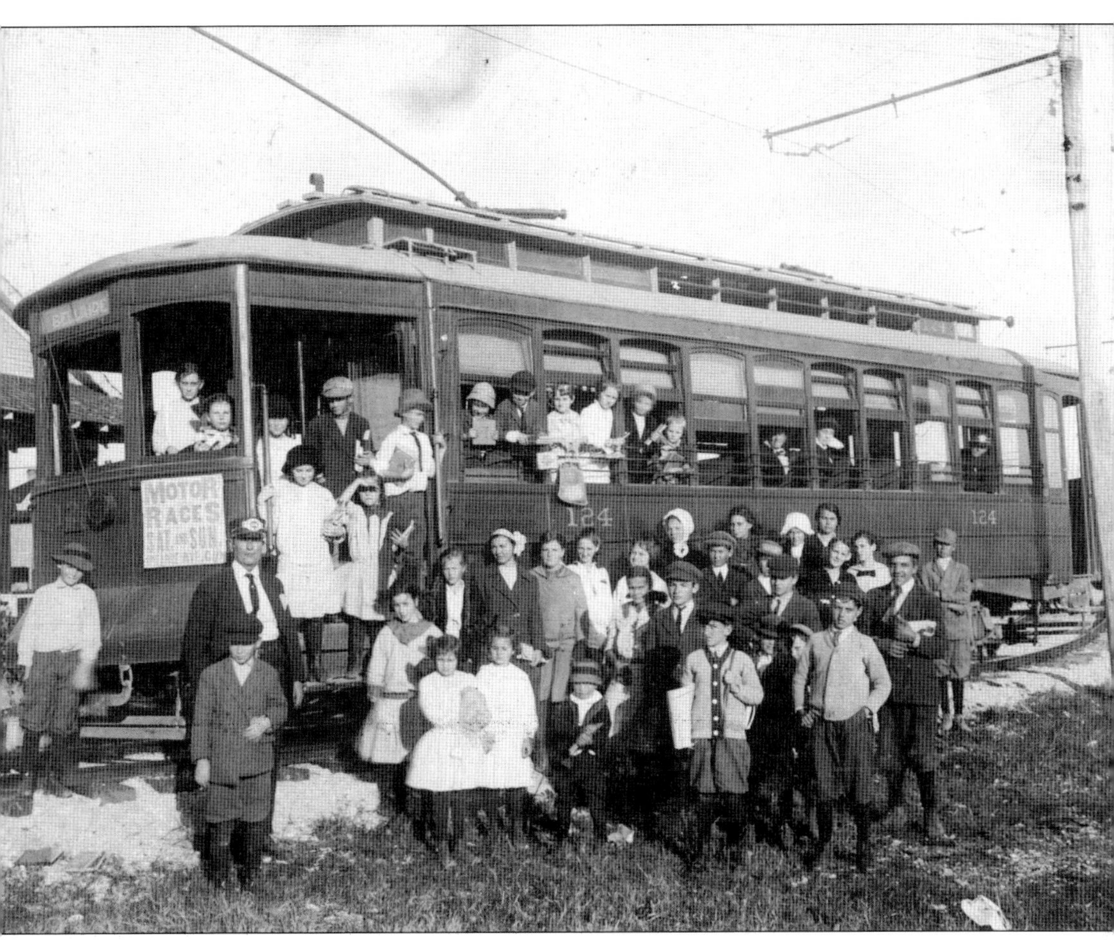

The Bellaire line ran from the southern part of downtown Houston approximately four miles west to South Rice Avenue in Bellaire, Texas. The tracks formed a turnaround loop there, and a pavilion for waiting passengers (visible behind the trolley in this early photograph) was constructed. The Bellaire line began service on December 29, 1910, and passed through what would become West University Place and Southside Place. Although passengers could transfer between trolley lines in Houston for no additional fare, the Bellaire line was outside city limits and required an additional 5¢ fare. For a time, developers offered free tickets on the Bellaire line to encourage passenger traffic and real estate sales. (Courtesy of the Teas family and Rice.)

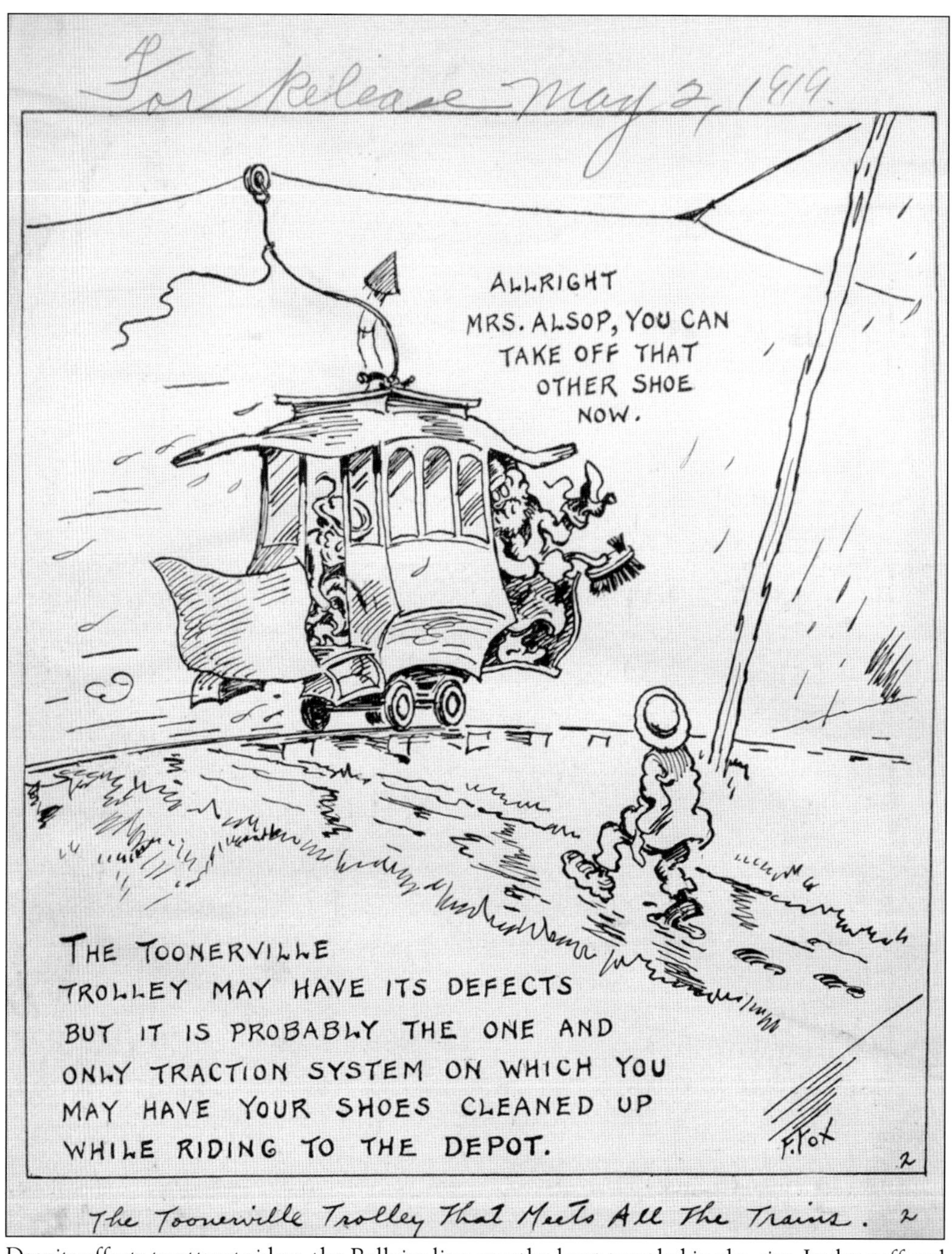

Despite efforts to attract riders, the Bellaire line was the least traveled in the city. It also suffered from poor construction and a lack of maintenance that caused frequent derailments. Its maladies earned it the nickname the "Toonerville Trolley." The popular syndicated comic drawn by Fontaine Fox, *The Toonerville Trolley That Meets All the Trains*, portrayed a mythical suburb's eclectic residents who rode on a rickety trolley to catch the commuter trains into the city. The popularity of the comic was so widespread that many claimed the nickname "Toonerville Trolley" for any antiquated street railway. (Courtesy of Lilly Library, Indiana University.)

Two

Creating a Community

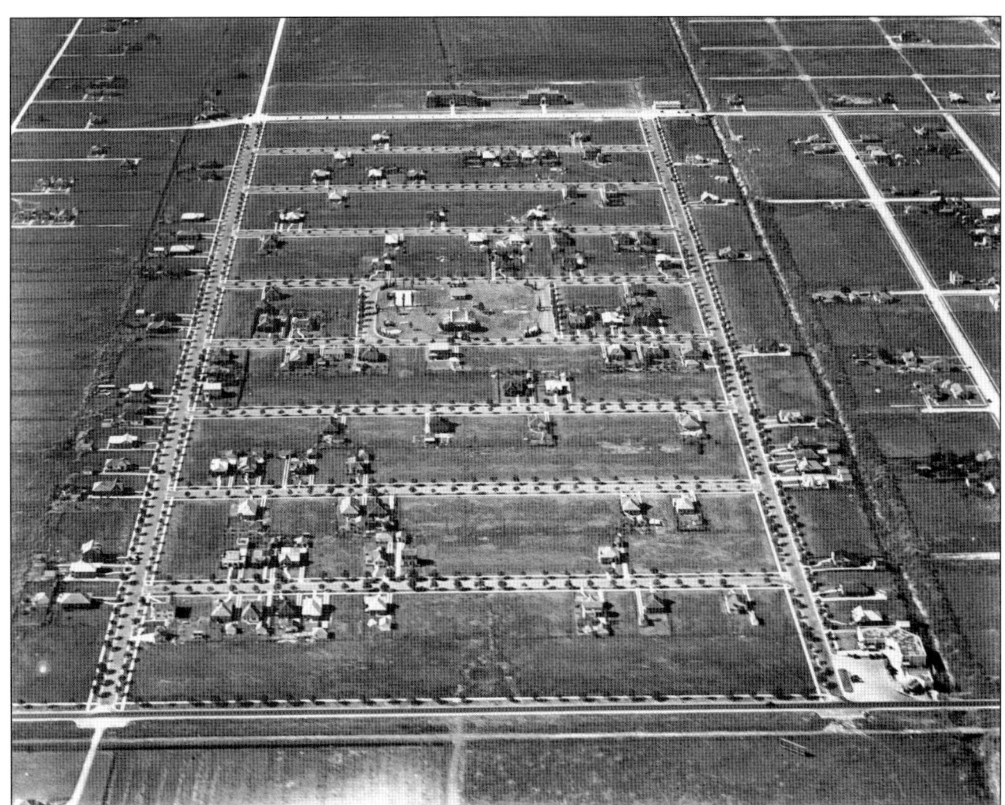

E.L. Crain filed the original plat and map of the Southside Place subdivision on October 3, 1924. Comprised of 13 sections, it was bordered by University Boulevard on the north, Bellaire Boulevard on the south, Edloe Street on the east, and Haden Street (later renamed Auden Street) on the west. Beginning with Bellaire Boulevard, the nine east-west streets were named alphabetically from south to north. Although initially Crain sold many lots, home construction was slowed by the Depression, as shown in this glass plate negative from the late 1920s. (Courtesy of HMRC.)

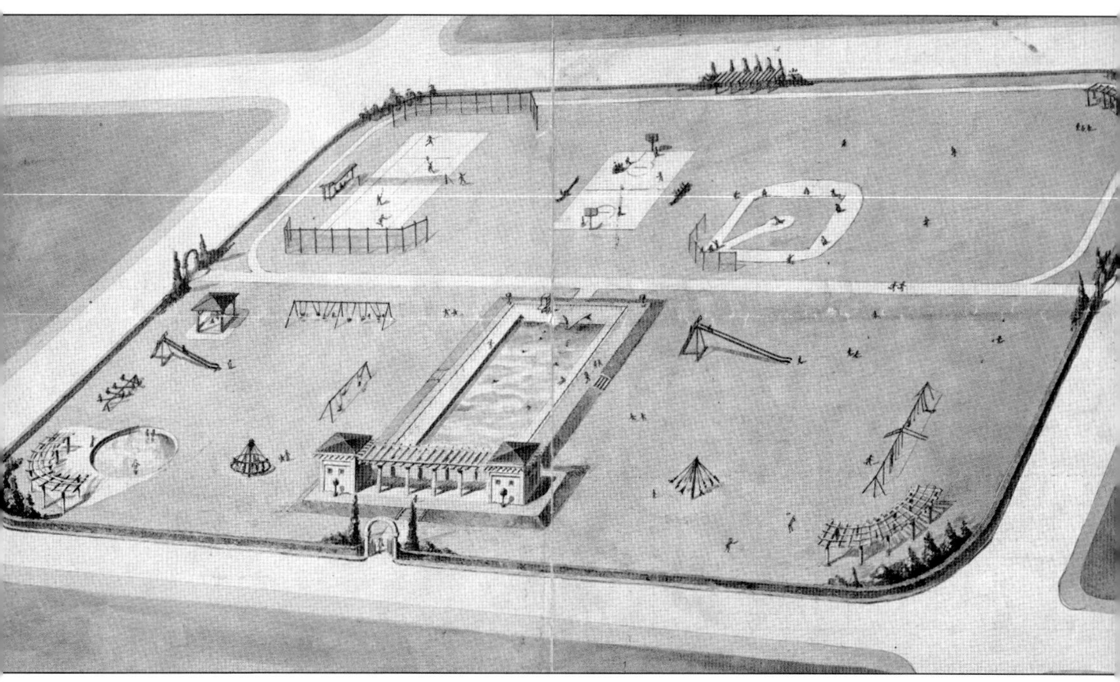

After installing modern improvements, such as concrete curbs and sidewalks, gutters, gravel streets, and sewers, E.L. Crain's first order of business was to plan the park at the center of Southside Place. A community space the size of eight lots in the heart of the subdivision was a natural by-product of Crain's efforts to combine the roles of investor, developer, and builder, as well as an early attempt at city planning. According to the promotional literature, Crain spent $50,000 to create and improve the park with such amenities as a swimming pool and a tennis court, making Southside Place likely the first Houston subdivision to provide such facilities for the use of its property owners. (Courtesy of HMRC.)

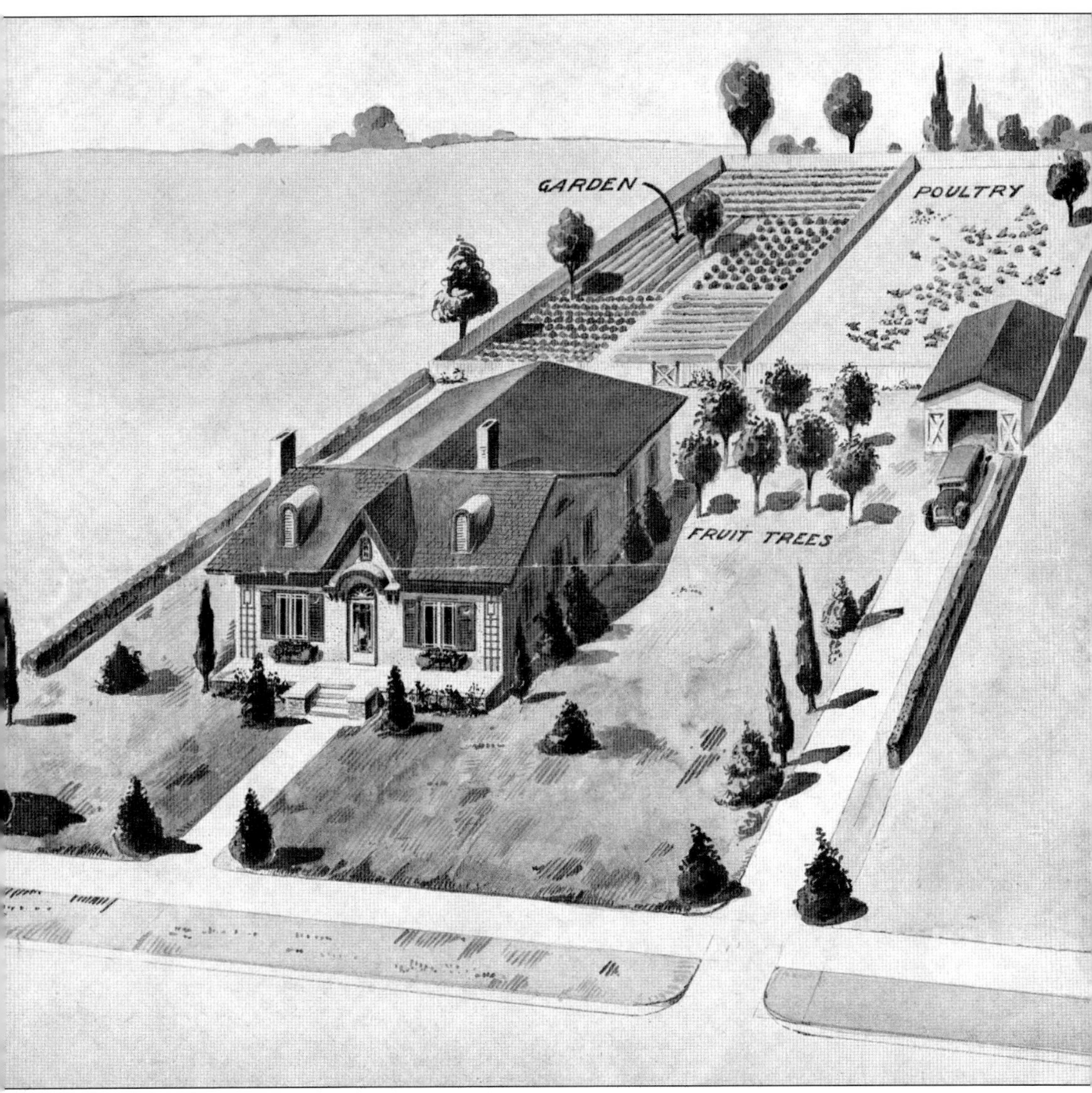

Because of its proximity to Bellaire Boulevard and the streetcar line, the initial development of Southside Place began south of the park. The subdivision was advertised as a quiet community out on the prairie away from the noise of the city. Early brochures touted the lots as "much larger than the average city lot . . . [with] plenty of room for a garden or chickens in the back yard." Although the area south of Bellaire Boulevard abounded with orange and pecan trees, Southside Place was nearly devoid of trees. E.L. Crain hired Teas Nursery to plant fast-growing Chinese tallow trees and radiant red rose bushes on the easement in front of each lot and fig trees in the backyards of some of the larger lots. (Courtesy of HMRC and SSP.)

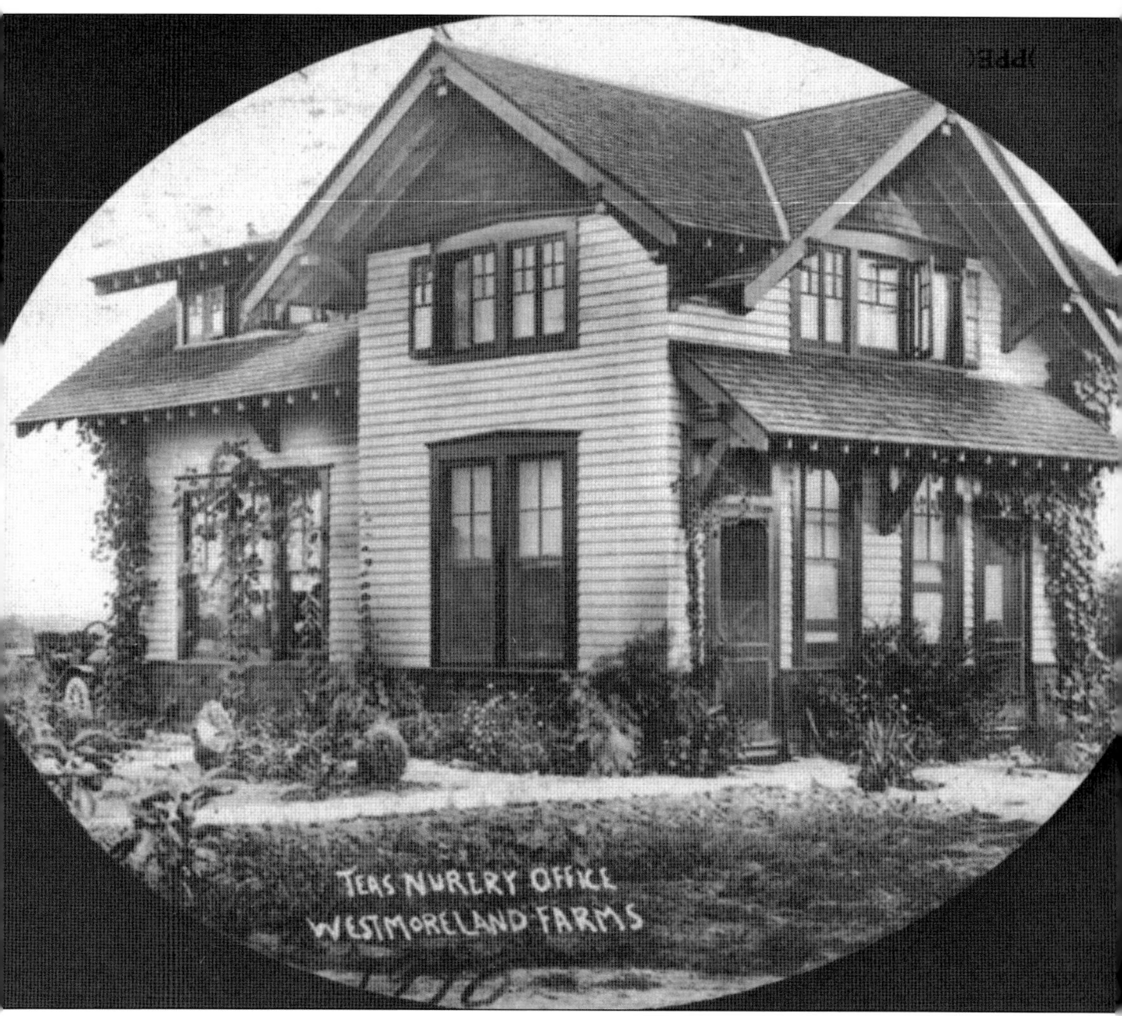

W.W. Baldwin, the developer of Westmoreland Farms, hired Missouri horticulturalist Edward Teas Sr. to execute the planting designs for Bellaire Boulevard and neighborhood streets. Teas began working in Bellaire in 1909, and by 1910, he had moved his family from Missouri and opened Teas Nursery Company at 4400 Bellaire Boulevard. In addition to Bellaire and Southside Place, Teas Nursery also landscaped Rice University and River Oaks. By 1951, it was estimated that Teas Nursery had planted over one million trees in the Houston area. When Teas Nursery closed in 2009, it was the oldest nursery in Houston. (Courtesy of the Teas family and Rice.)

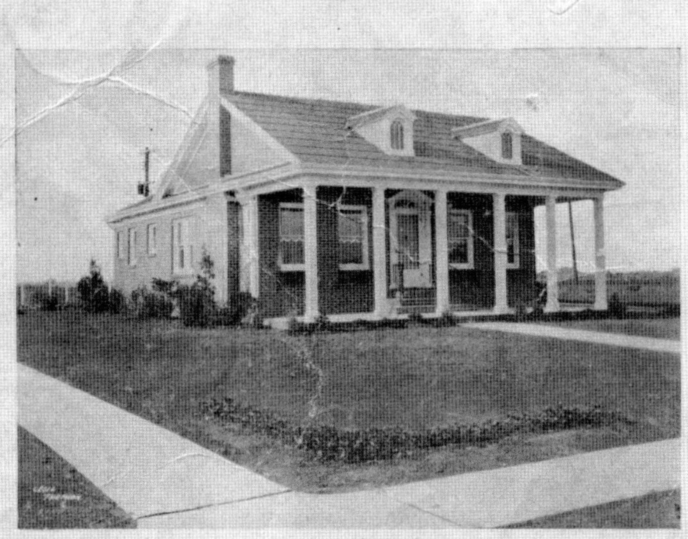

This well constructed, admirably planned six-room, brick veneer

Colonial Bungalow

with fire-place, mantle, built-in features; tile bath, built-in tub, shower; electric hot water heater, electric stove; hardwood floors in living room and dining room; on this 75x150 foot corner lot, with garage, chicken lot, and shrubbery.

Price $9000

DESIRABLE TERMS

Crain Ready-Cut House Company

Phone Preston 3448 • Corner Polk and Milby Streets

The Southside Place subdivision officially opened on Easter Sunday, April 12, 1925, with four cases of colored eggs hidden in the neighborhood from the park to Bellaire Boulevard. Reportedly, 500 people attended the opening to enjoy the park and tour the three speculative homes E.L. Crain had built in six months. The first home Crain constructed was the two-story Colonial Bungalow, with six white Greek Revival pillars across the front, at 3722 Farbar Street. The most expensive of the three speculative homes, it was located on a corner lot directly east of the park. It sold for $9,000 on June 17, 1925, and was purchased by Margie and Edward F. Frier. Edward was a superintendent at the Bemis Brothers Bag Company. (Courtesy of SSP.)

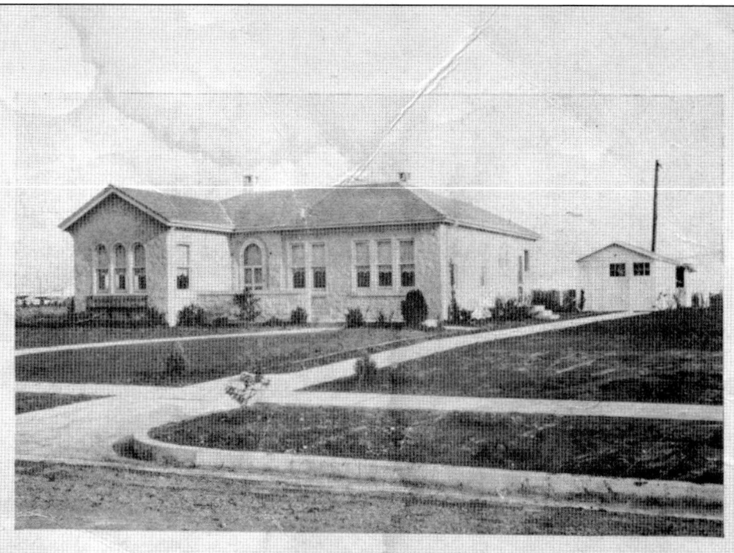

This unusual beautiful seven-room stucco

Spanish Bungalow

Special design of fire-place and mantle; tile bath, shower, built-in tubs; electric water heater; electric stove; hardwood floors in living and dining room; many attractive built-in features; composition shingle roof; lot 75x150 foot; garage, shrubbery, etc.

Price

$7750

ATTRACTIVE TERMS

Crain Ready-Cut House Company

Phone Preston 3448 Corner Milby and Polk Avenue

The Spanish Bungalow, a seven-room stucco home at 3709 Farbar Street, was the second dwelling E.L. Crain built but the first one to be sold in Southside Place. It was located down the street from the park, closer to Edloe Street. Haddie and Albert Bevans purchased the home for $7,750 on June 8, 1925, nearly two months after the neighborhood's opening. Albert was employed as a clerk for a local insurance company, Houstoun and Tyler. (Courtesy of SSP.)

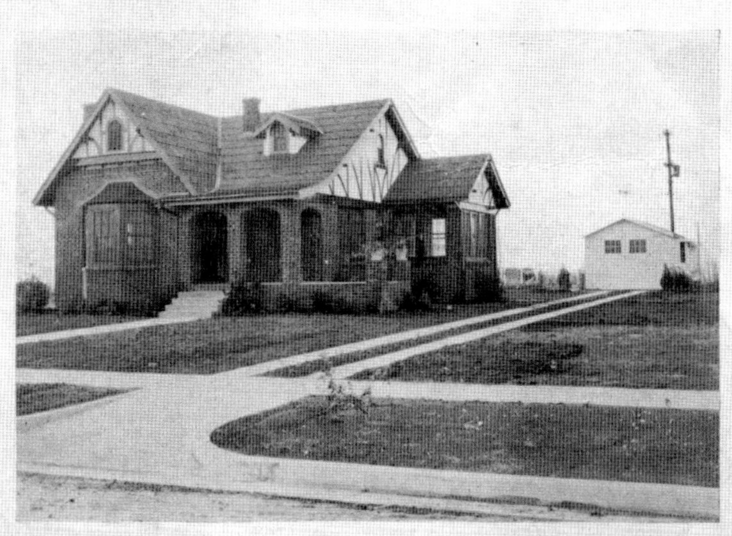

This typical design, six-room, brick veneer

English Bungalow

Special fire-place and mantle, built-in cabinets and other features; electric hot water heater and electric stove; unusual lighting fixtures; hardwood floors in living room and dining room; flower garden, porch, garage, chicken lot, flowers, shrubbery and fruit trees all on 75x150 foot lot.

Price

$8200

CONVENIENT TERMS

CRAIN READY-CUT HOUSE CO.

Phone Preston 3448 *Corner Polk and Milby Streets*

The English Bungalow, built at 3734 Elmora Street, boasted an 11,000-square-foot lot, unusual lighting fixtures, a flower garden, and fruit trees. The last of the three homes to be sold, it was purchased for $8,200 by John Grant Murphy on July 31, 1925. It was also the last surviving speculative home in the city until it was torn down in 2012. (Courtesy of SSP.)

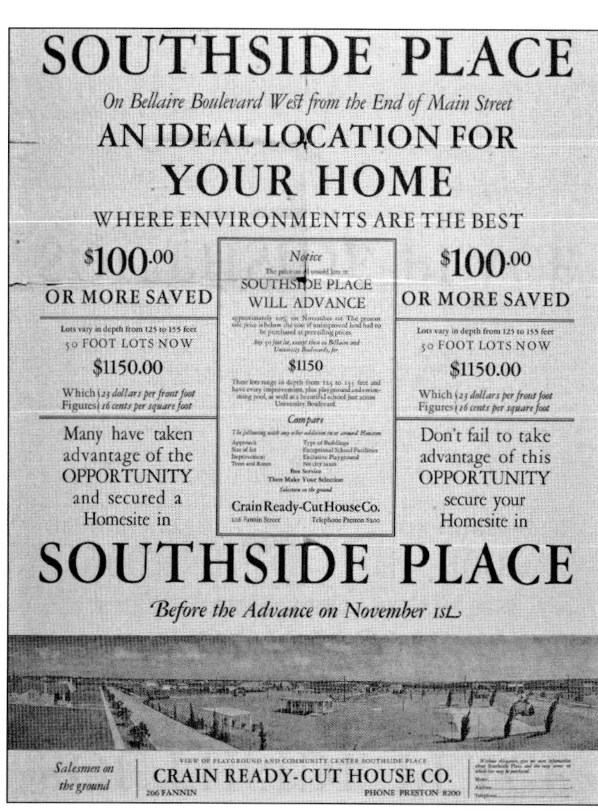

E.L. Crain marketed the neighborhood's amenities and proximity to downtown to both potential homeowners and investors. The abrupt abandonment of the Bellaire line on September 26, 1927, due to its poor condition and light use, did not deter his efforts. Bus service replaced the trolley the next day, and Crain modified his marketing materials accordingly. (Courtesy of HMRC.)

Although development of the second section of Southside Place north of the park, from Harper Street to University Boulevard, began in 1926, the neighborhood remained thinly settled and isolated. This photograph from the 1930 National Balloon Race at the Houston Speedway (in what is Braes Heights today) shows Southside Place in the distance. (Courtesy of Story Sloane's Gallery.)

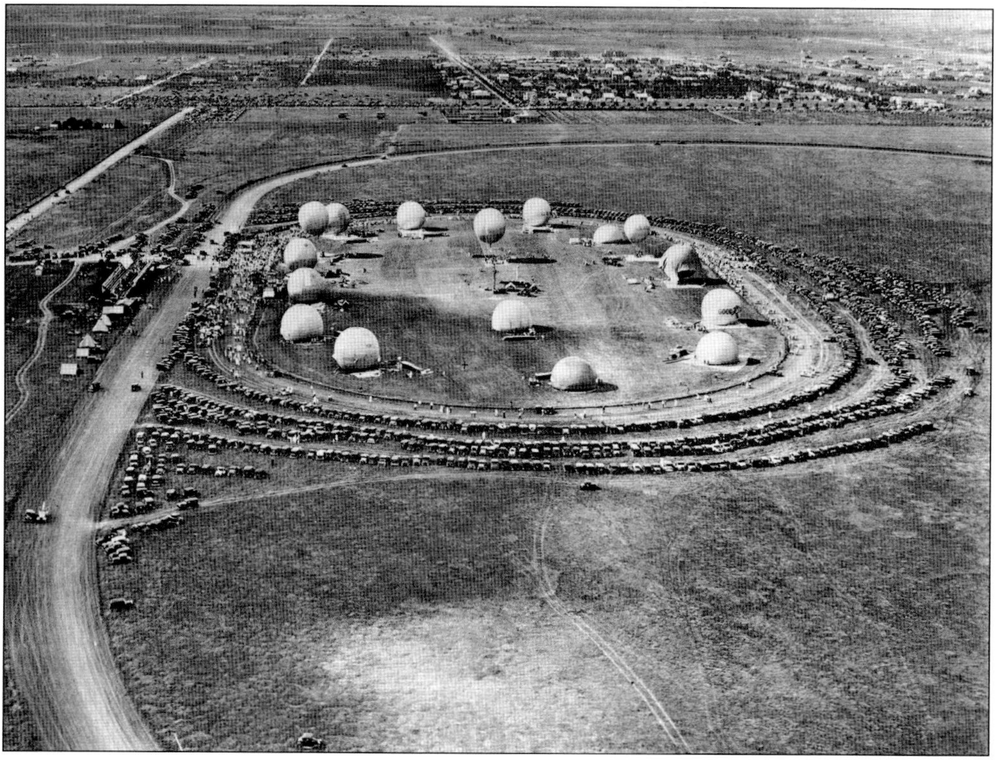

The Depression stalled E.L. Crain's plan of a tidy neighborhood filled with uniformly built Ready-Cut Houses. Undeterred, Crain diversified into prefabricated commercial buildings and the construction of portable restaurants. Prefabricated, or "sectional," buildings were intended to house workers in the railroad, oil, and mining industries. Since the mid-1920s, Crain had been promoting this commercial application in separate catalogues and advertising campaigns. (Courtesy of Kate McCormick.)

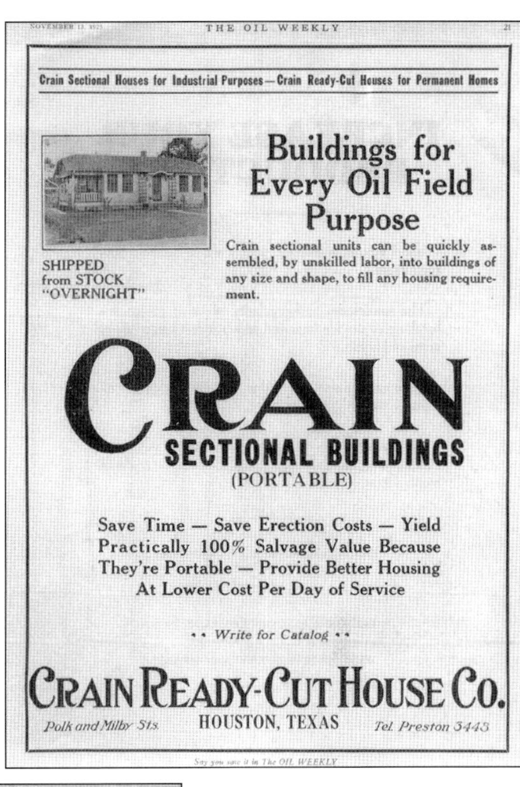

During the Depression, E.L. Crain's company also designed and built Toddle House diners for Houston lumberman J.C. Stedman. Stedman reportedly began the popular restaurant chain as a way to utilize leftover building supplies. For Crain, the Ready-Cut manufacturing methods were easily adapted to create Toddle House diners, which were notable for their standard design and uniform appearance both inside and out. Toddle House locations in Houston included 2802 South Shepherd Drive, which later became a Chinese restaurant, Chicken 'N Egg Roll, until it was raised in 2009. (Courtesy of Kate McCormick.)

DROP THIS ENTIRE COUPON IN BOX
Your name and street address MUST be written BELOW

Name ....

Address ....

For further details read "THE HOUSTON POST" or call Preston 0438. No Attention given Mail Communications.

Good for one chance on Two 1932 "Silver Anniversary Model" WILLYS - OVERLAND Cars to be given FREE, April 21 and July 4, 1932 and "THE HOME THAT ADVERTISING BUILT" to be given FREE Sept. 5, 1932.

All Drawings will be held at 4:00 P. M. at SOUTHSIDE PLACE. (It is NOT necessary to attend drawings in person)

G 196975 | SEE OTHER SIDE

WELDON, WILLIAMS & LICK, FT. SMITH, ARK.

By 1931, E.L. Crain was building again in Southside Place. In an effort to jump-start home construction and lot sales, Crain devised an ingenious marketing scheme: he gave away a completely furnished home in Southside Place in a raffle in 1931 (3768 Jardin Street) and again in 1932 (3768 Harper Street). These tickets are from the 1932 raffle of the home on Harper Street. (Courtesy of SSP.)

"The Home That Advertising Built"

CONTEST RULES

1—The contest is now running and will end at the close of business hours on Thursday, September 3, 1931.

2—Anyone except employes of The Houston Post-Dispatch or members of their families may compete. This home can only be deeded to the winner subject to the restrictions prevailing in Southside Place.

3—Employes of the participating institutions may compete but will not be permitted to enter tickets distributed through the firm for which they work.

4—The tickets will be given by the participating firms on purchases or paid on accounts, gratis. In no case shall these tickets be sold by either the firms participating or by individuals.

5—The basis upon which the tickets will be given is announced in the various advertisements in this section . . . Read every announcement carefully.

6—"The Home That Advertising Built" will be given away to the holder of the stub of the ticket which will be drawn from among those entered at 3 p. m. Monday, September 7, 1931 (Labor Day.)

7—If you cannot be present at the drawing, your name and address should be written on the stub before being deposited in the boxes.

8—Regardless of where you get your free chances you may deposit them in any of the "stub boxes" in the various stores participating. Also for your convenience there is a deposit box located in the "Home That Advertising Built" office, 416 Kirby Bldg.

ASK AT ANY OF THE PARTICIPATING FIRMS OR CALL CAPITOL 1442

Dubbed "The Home that Advertising Built," nearly 100 businesses participated in the 1931 raffle by giving away raffle tickets each time a consumer shopped at a participating business or purchased a designated product. Each ticket entered the holder in a raffle to win a professionally decorated and completely furnished and landscaped home. The rules (pictured right) required the holder to be present at the drawing to win or to write their name and address on the ticket stub before depositing it. Rule 7 would later become the subject of a lawsuit concerning who was the rightful owner of the first raffled home in 1931. (Courtesy of SSP.)

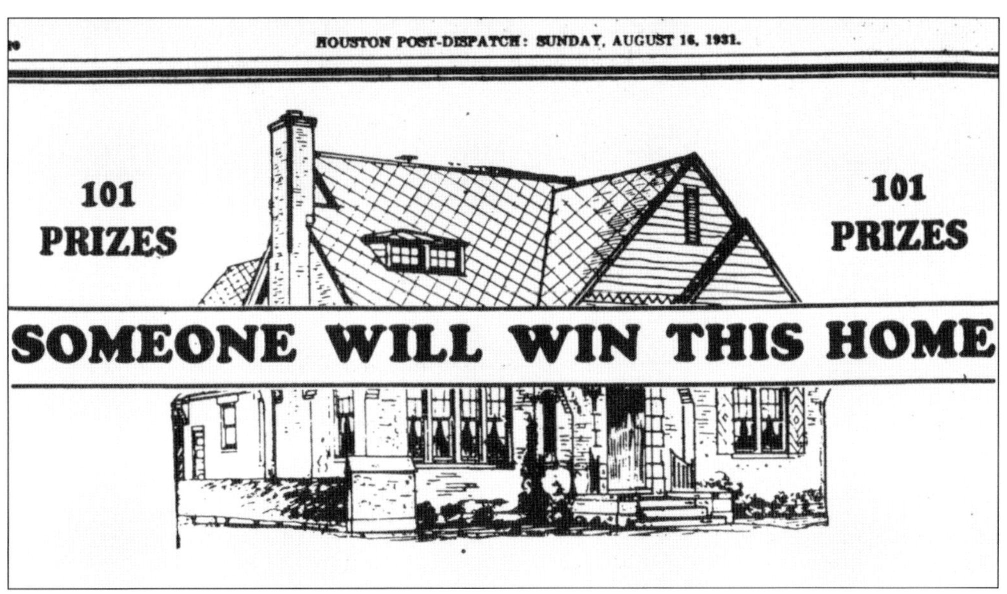

HOUSTON POST-DISPATCH: SUNDAY, AUGUST 16, 1931.

101 PRIZES

101 PRIZES

SOMEONE WILL WIN THIS HOME

In the months leading up to the 1931 raffle, the *Houston Post-Dispatch* devoted an entire section of the Sunday paper (above) to the house at 3768 Jardin Street (pictured today, below). It included detailed progress on the home, as well as "articles" (thinly veiled advertisements) featuring those companies providing materials and labor for the home. The home's front facade today (pictured below) is virtually unchanged from 1931 and a testament to the timeless design and quality of construction materials used. (Above, courtesy of SSP; below, Robert Gray.)

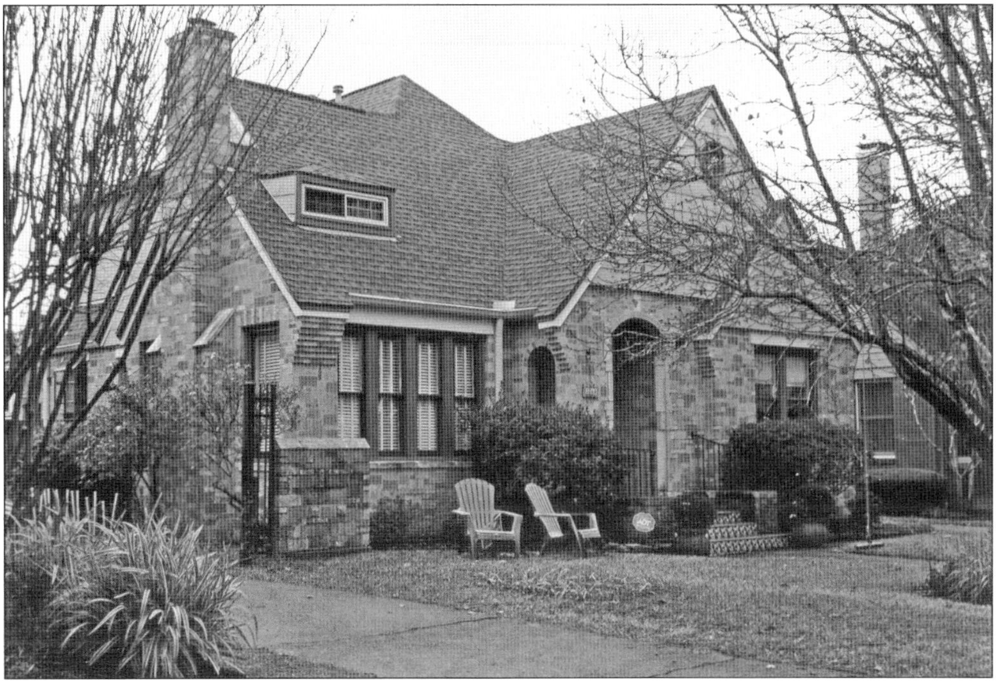

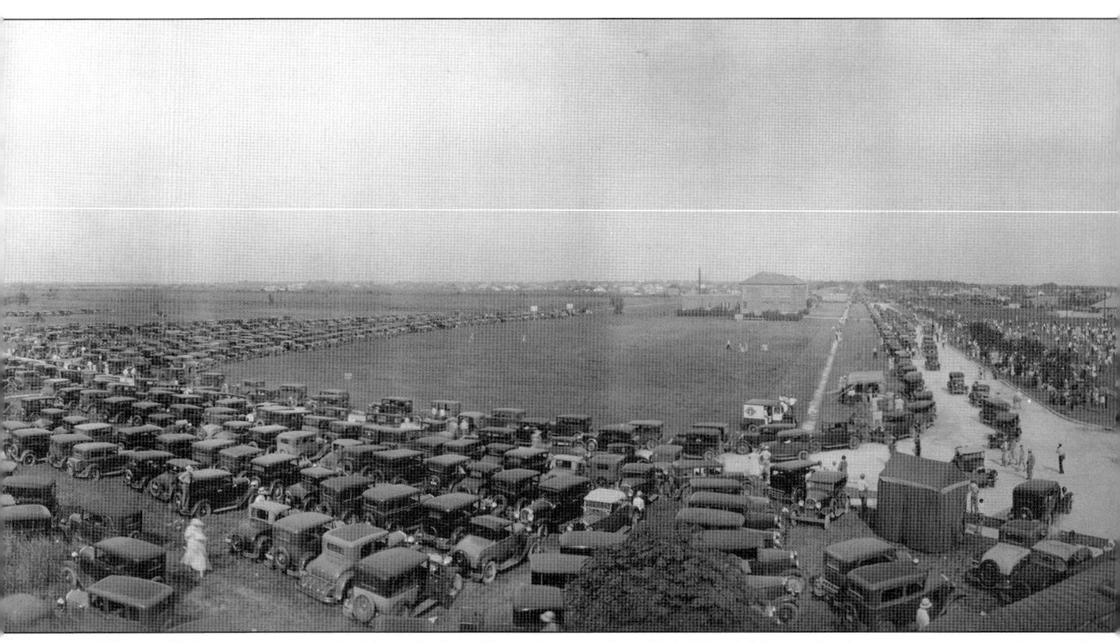

The raffle drawing was held on Labor Day, September 7, 1931. Although the newspaper estimated the crowd at 40,000, this photograph suggests a robust but significantly smaller crowd. The first raffle ticket drawn had only the initials "MS" written on it and a partial address. When no one came forward at the drawing within an hour to produce the stub corresponding to the ticket drawn, the judges drew another ticket. The second ticket belonged to Thelma Brown, age 21, who was present at the drawing. Max Sternenberg, a beekeeper from New Ulm, Texas, who sold

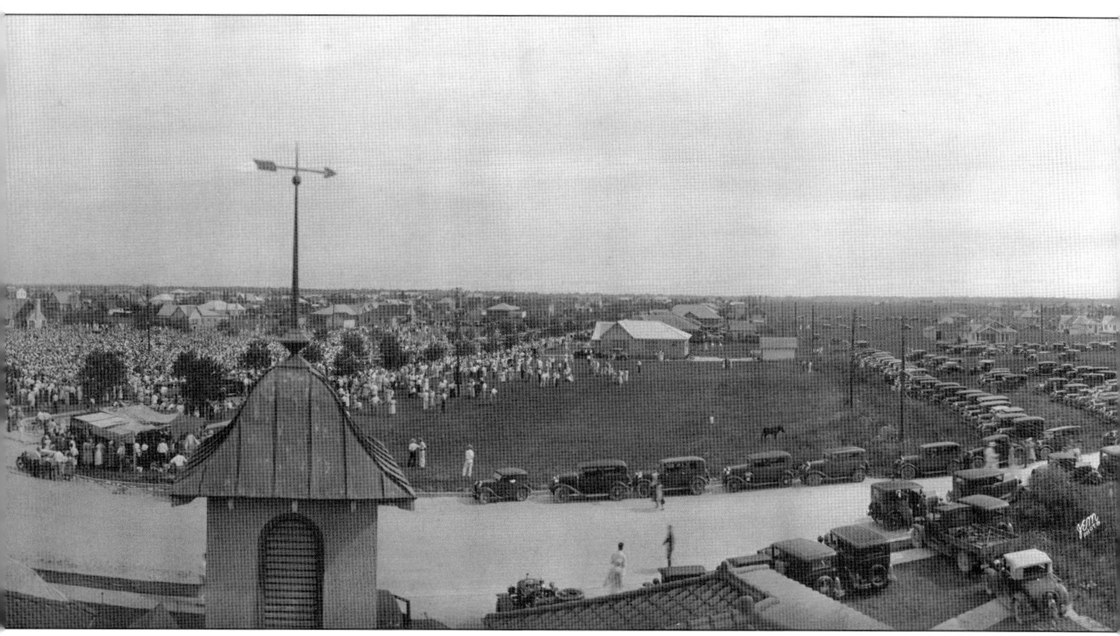

honey at Houston farmers' markets, later filed suit claiming that he was the rightful winner of the house. Reportedly, Sternenberg had tried to charter a plane to Houston when he learned from his sister that his ticket had been pulled. Although Sternenberg was able to obtain an injunction to prevent the Browns from taking possession of the home, District Judge Roy Campbell ultimately rejected his claim, and Thelma and Rex Brown were deemed to be the winners. The Browns and their two-and-a-half-year-old son moved into the Jardin Street home. (Courtesy of SSP.)

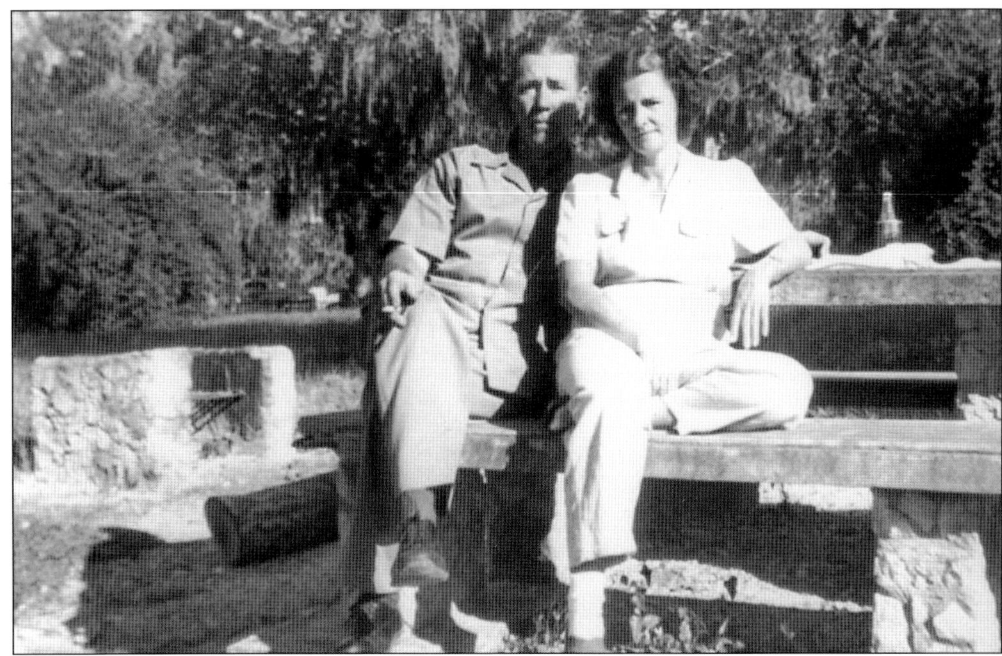

At the time they won the home, Rex Brown was employed as a day maintenance man by Kier-Nickles Automobile Hotel on Texas Avenue, Houston's first full-service public parking garage (pictured below). In addition to the home and its furnishings, taxes and insurance were paid for one year. The Browns also enjoyed a year's worth of groceries, dry cleaning, pharmacy, and millinery services, among other perks. The Browns' time enjoying the home was short-lived. Five years later, their second son tragically died of pneumonia. The financial burden of the home also became a concern, and the Browns sold the home in 1936 for $3,500 and moved to Spring, Texas. Thereafter, the home has transferred privately within the same extended family for nearly 80 years. The "home that advertising built" at 3768 Jardin Street remains standing today. (Both courtesy of Dena Wagner.)

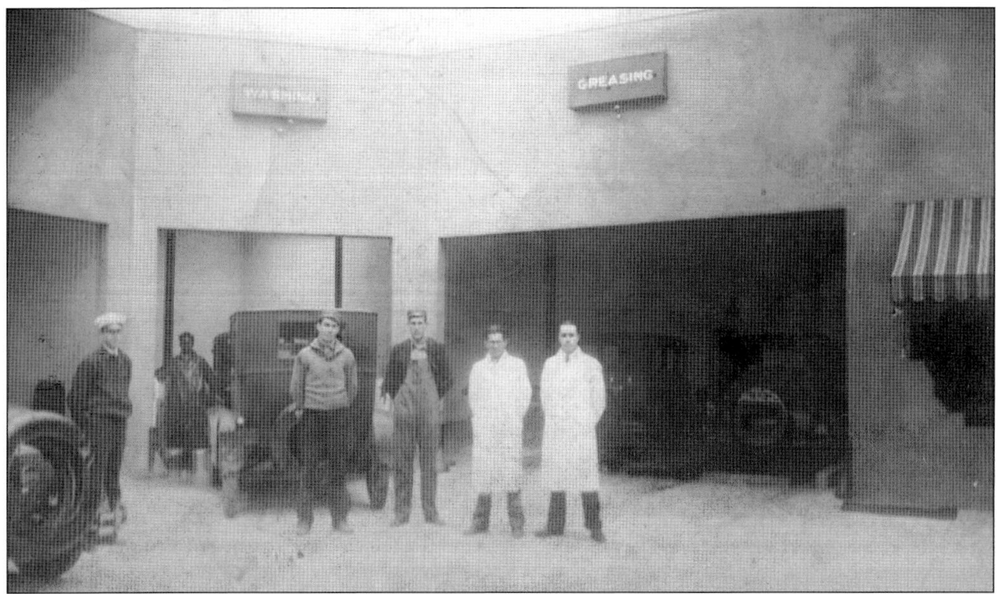

Three

A Subdivision Becomes a City

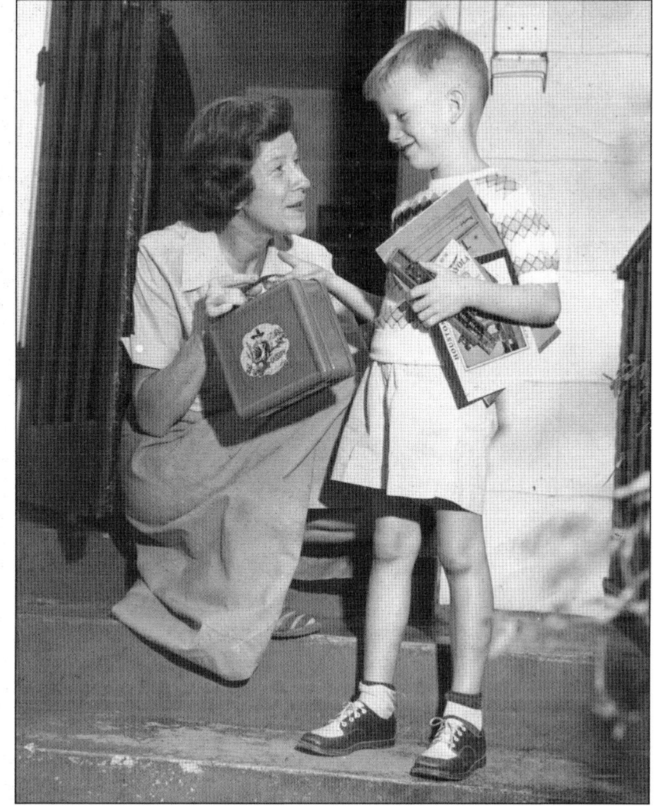

In 1924, the West University Place Independent School District was organized to serve the growing population of West University, as well as the new Southside Place subdivision. Although the district was only in existence for four years, an elementary and a middle school were constructed during that time. Expanded and modified over the years, the buildings remain integral to both communities nearly 90 years later. In this timeless photograph, Elmora Street resident Paul Brewer is seen with his mother, Elda, leaving for his first day of school at West University Elementary School. (Courtesy of Paul Brewer.)

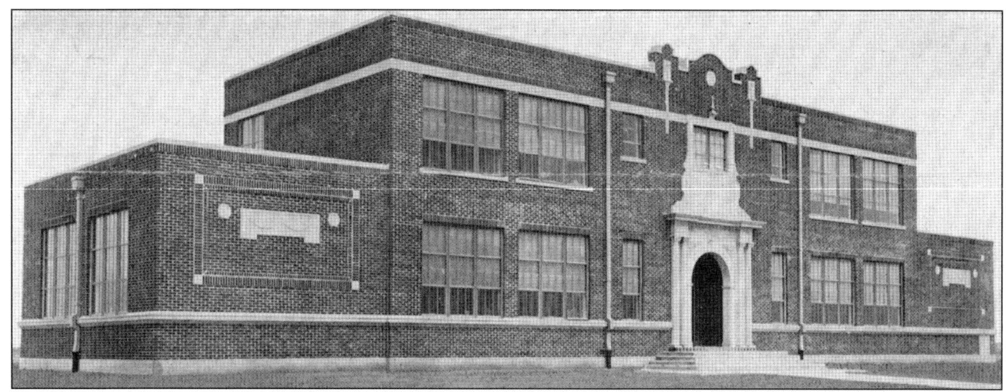

Real estate investors/developers D.T. Austin and W.D. Haden, for whom Auden Street was named, donated most of the land on the 3700 block of University Boulevard for the new school. In 1925, citizens passed a $55,000 bond to construct West University Elementary School, the building located closest to the corner of Edloe Street and University Boulevard. Architect Lamar Q. Cato designed the redbrick, flat-roofed building with Spanish Renaissance detailing. When the building was not completed by the start of the 1925 school year, kindergarten students attended classes in the Southside Place sales office, located on Bellaire Boulevard. Older students met at the Platte School, east of Kirby Drive on what is now Bissonnet Street. (Courtesy of SSP.)

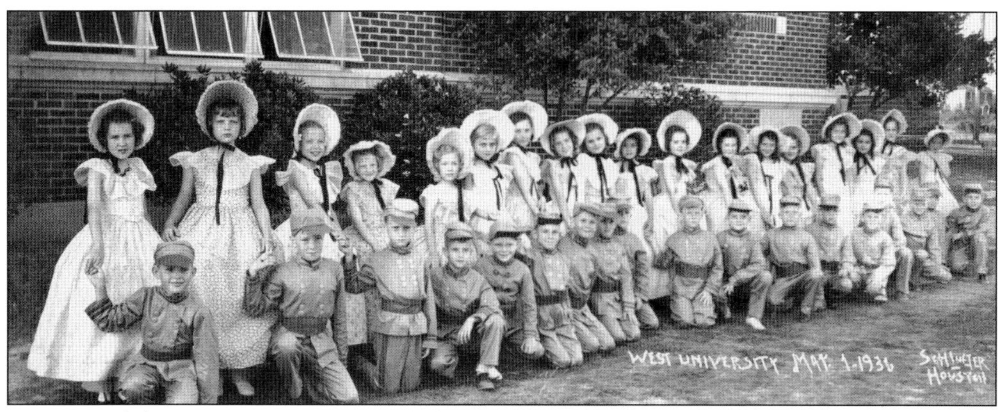

May Day celebrations at West University Elementary School included costumed children dancing around maypoles. In this photograph of the May Day celebration in 1936, children wear Southern belle and Confederate soldier costumes sewn by their mothers. (Courtesy of Roger Judson.)

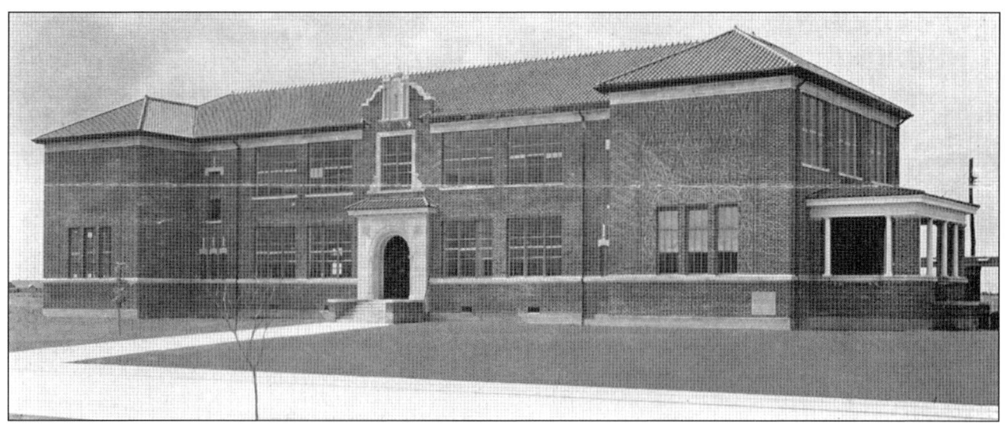

By 1928, the original 50-student enrollment at West University Place Elementary School had swelled to 250 students. Lamar Q. Cato was again commissioned by the school district to design a new building to house a junior high school. Located adjacent to the elementary school on University Boulevard, Pershing Junior High School (pictured above) was completed at a cost of $80,000. Cato's design of Pershing, as well as the West University Place City Hall and Fire Station, also completed in 1928, reflected the Spanish influences found in the elementary school. Middle school students attended this school until 1949, when a new Pershing Middle School campus was built south of the city. The 1945 graduating class from Pershing Junior High School is pictured below. (Above, courtesy of SSP; below, Roger Judson.)

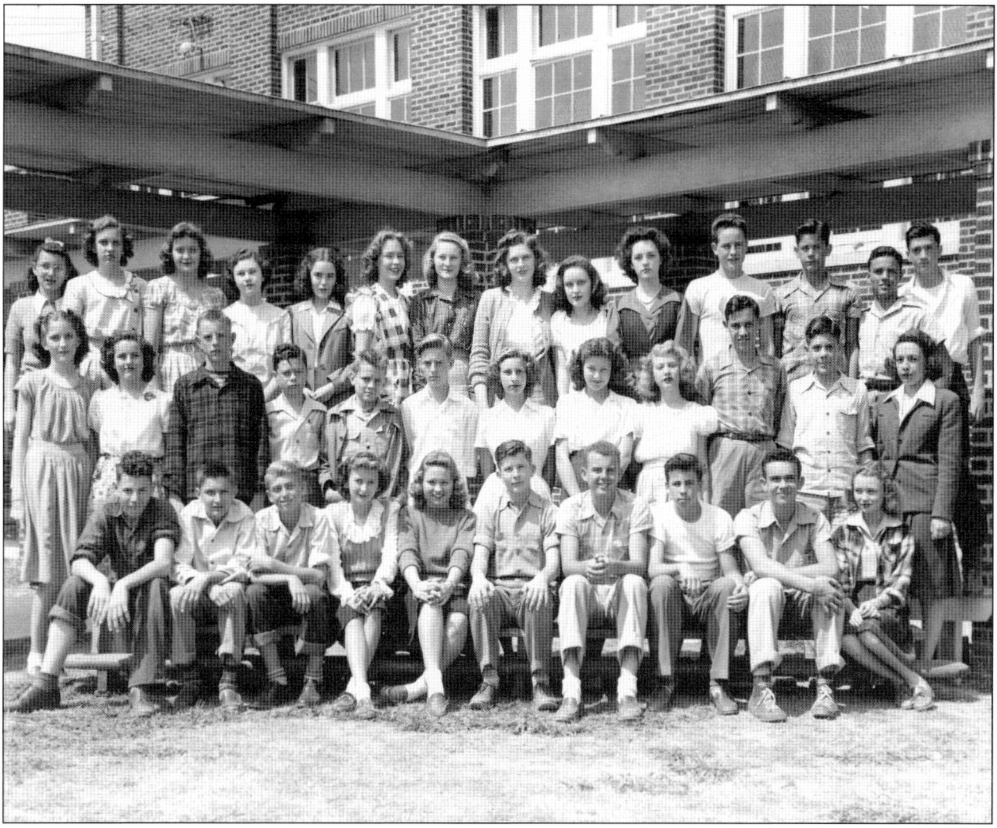

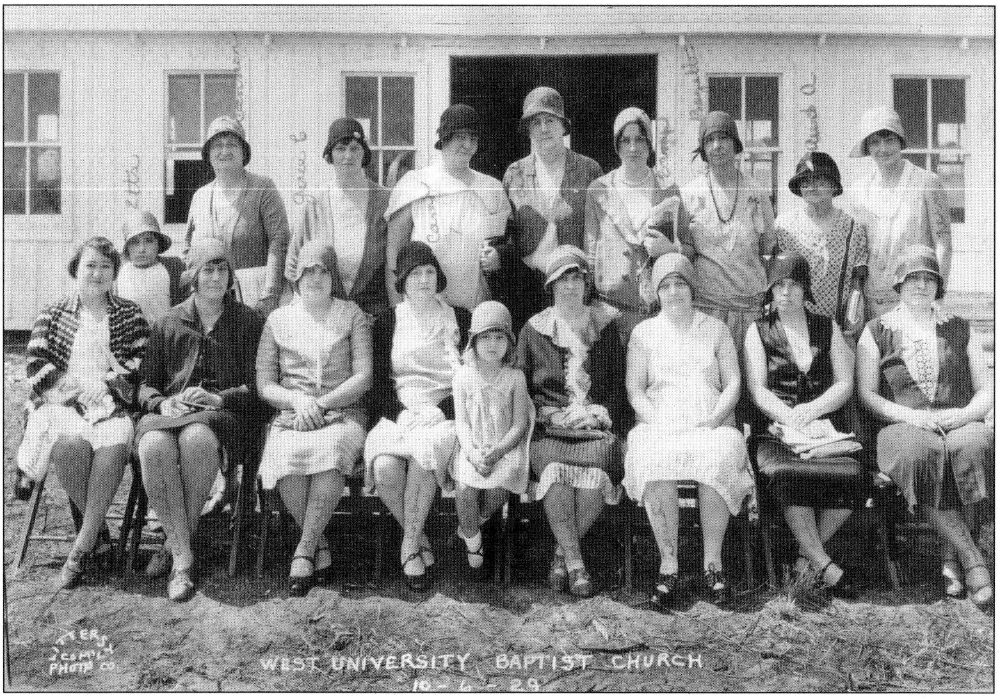

As the area grew, so did the community's social and spiritual needs. Religious institutions soon staked claim to the four corners of the subdivision. West University Baptist Church began as a bible study group on the front porch and lawn of Nannie B. David's home on Buffalo Speedway. In 1928, seventeen charter members (pictured above in 1929) met at West University Elementary School and founded the church. The next year, the congregation purchased land near University Boulevard and Auden Street for $650 from the City of West University Place and built an auditorium (pictured below) with church labor. A portion of the land was later sold back to West University Place to create Amherst Street. (Both courtesy of West University Baptist Church.)

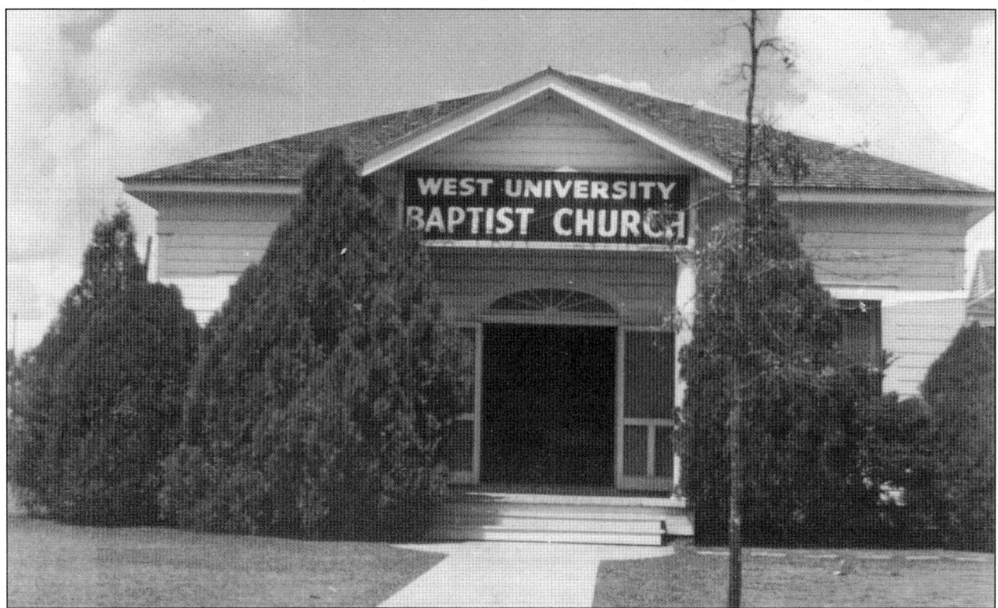

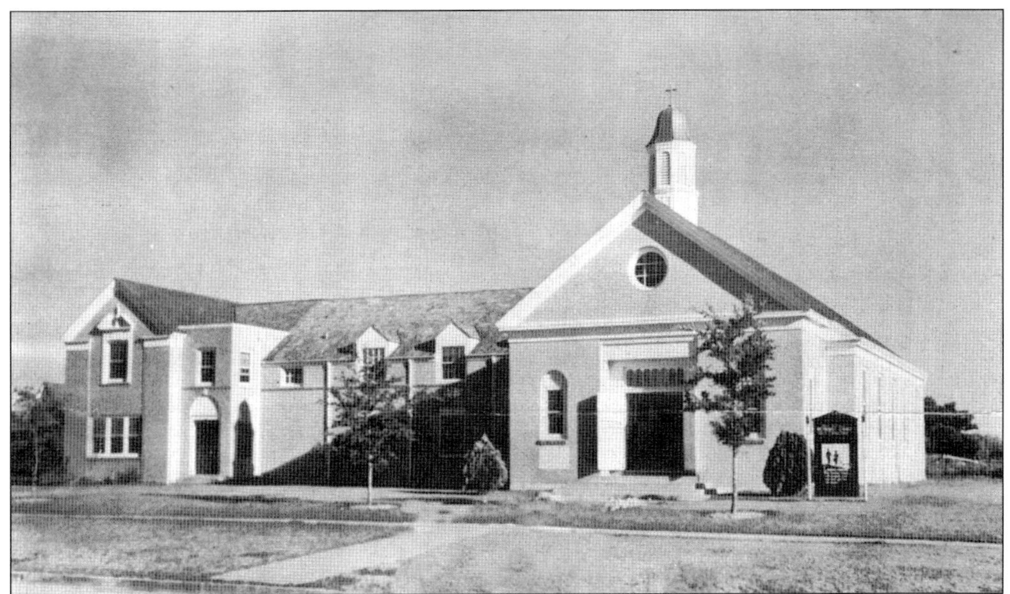

In 1936, one hundred committed charter members from a Sunday school at St. Paul's Methodist Church formed the West University Place Methodist Church. Four members signed an $800 promissory note to purchase land at 3611 University Boulevard near the Poor Farm Ditch. The cornerstone for the sanctuary was laid in August 1939. Since then, the church has acquired adjoining lots and built a larger sanctuary and a preschool. The original sanctuary is now a chapel that seats 60 worshippers. (Courtesy of West University United Methodist Church.)

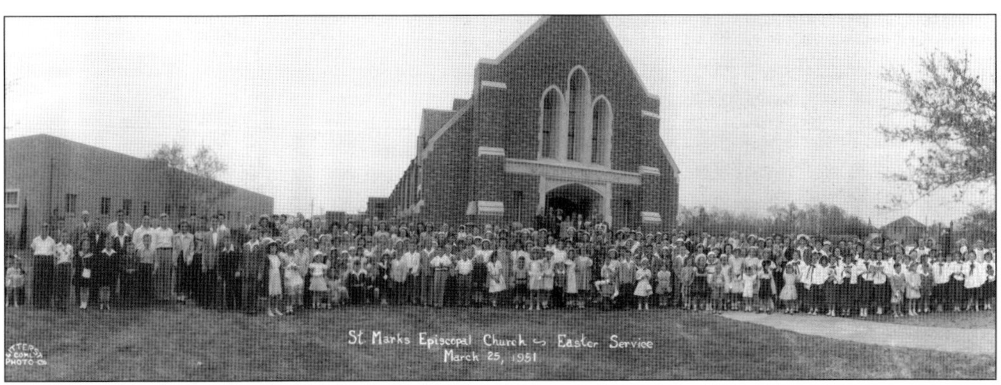

St. Mark's Episcopal Church held its first service in the University Theatre in the 3600 block of University Boulevard in October 1939 and vowed to have its own building within a year. Several failed attempts to find suitable property followed because of opposition by residents concerned about commercial development in residential areas. By 1941, the parish had completed construction of the church at 3816 Bellaire Boulevard at a cost of $45,000. The growing congregation is shown here at its Easter service in 1951. (Courtesy of St. Mark's Episcopal Church.)

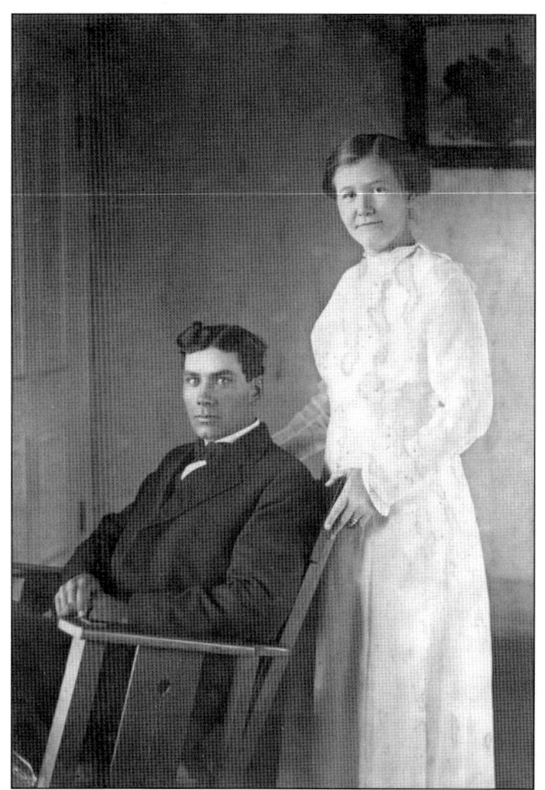

As more families moved into the neighborhood, the desire for self-governance grew. Glenn Miller, known as "Mr. Southside," and Tim Evans, Southside's first mayor, were instrumental in this transition. Miller (pictured with wife Amy on their wedding day in 1915) was originally hired to be the developer's construction superintendent. Miller wore many hats over the years, and citizens relied heavily on his in-depth knowledge of the city. (Courtesy of Arthur Hirdler.)

In 1925, Tim Evans and his wife, Grace, moved to their home in Southside Place, where they lived with their nine children on Farbar Street. Evans was head of the Houston Chamber of Commerce Foreign Trade Department. When Southside Place became incorporated and held its first city council meeting in 1931, Evans was named its first mayor and served three terms. The family called Southside Place home for more than 60 years. (Courtesy of Kelly Mears.)

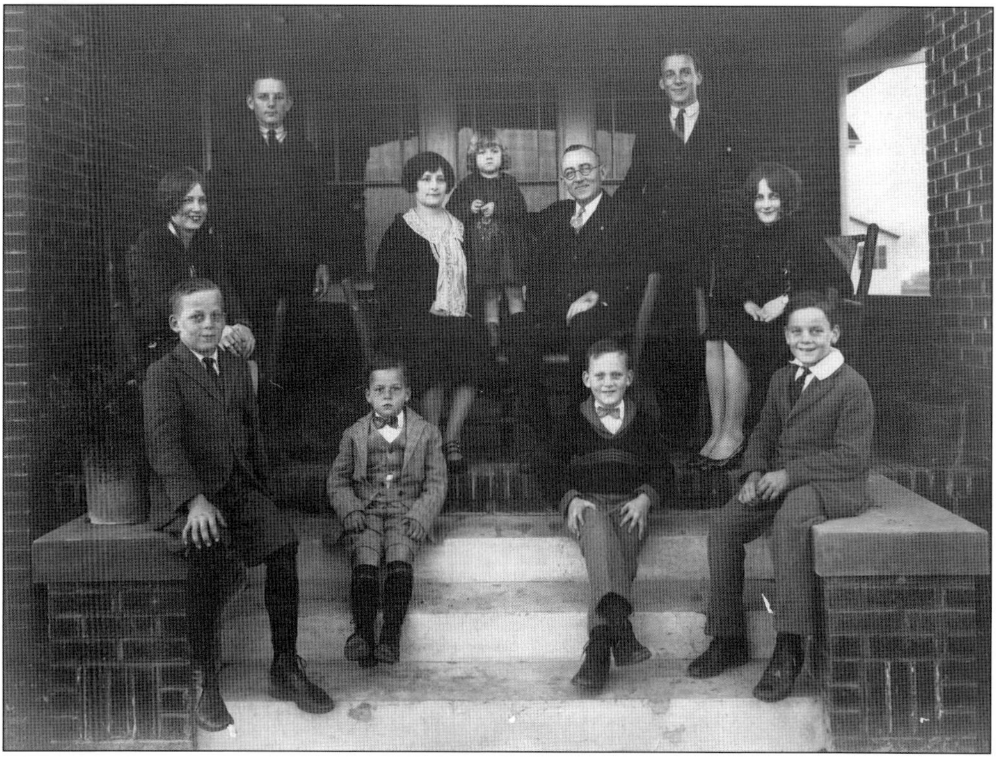

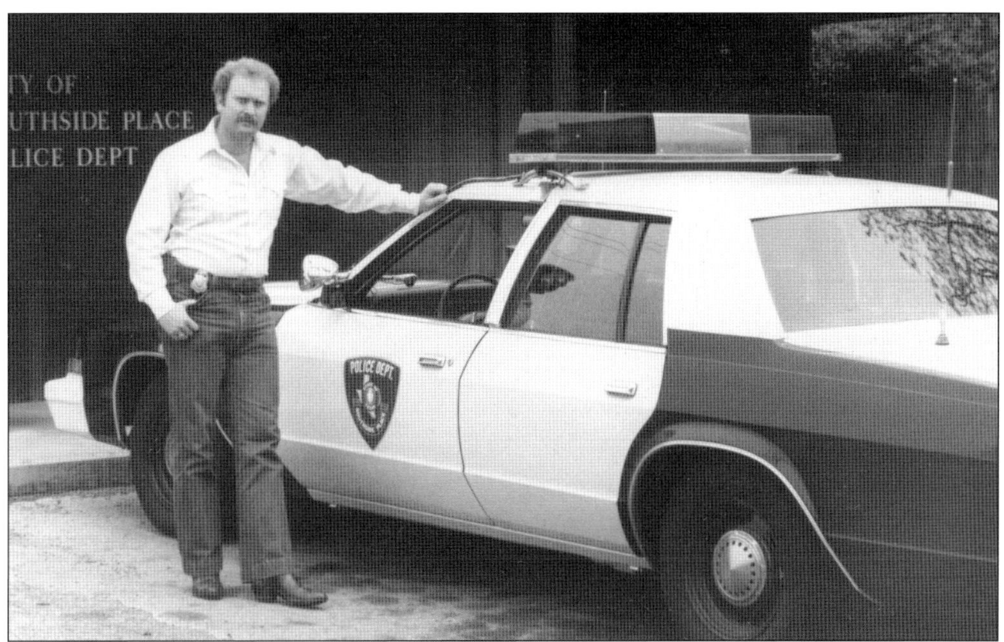

The first order of business for the new city council and mayor was to appoint R.F. Kachtick as city marshal. For many years thereafter, the police department consisted of a single officer who patrolled the neighborhood in an unmarked car. City superintendent Glenn Miller took citizen calls and dispatched the police or fire department as needed. In 1979, J.M. "Mike" Staggs (pictured above) was hired as the city's first full-time police chief, and he served for 24 years. The department grew to include a team of professional police officers and full-time dispatchers to provide 24-hour protection. To date, the city has had five police chiefs, including Lonnie Bernhardt (pictured below on the first row at far right as a patrol officer in the 1980s), who served as chief from 2003 to 2013. (Both courtesy of SSP.)

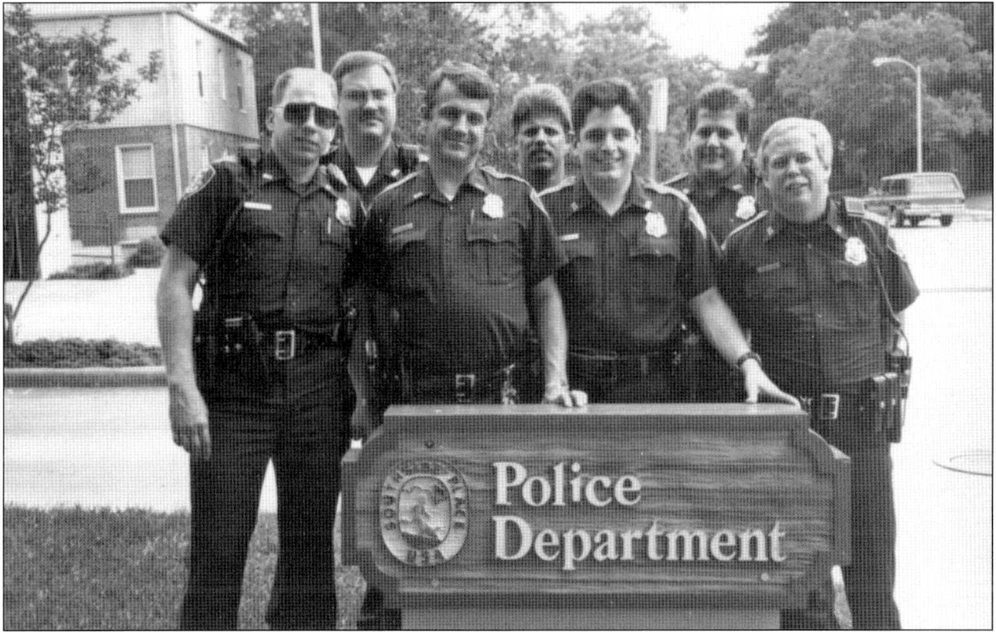

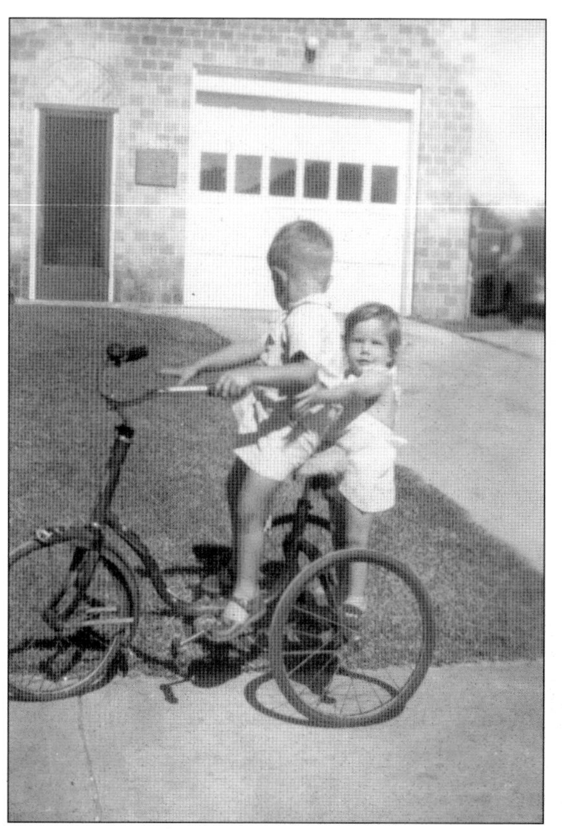

On August 3, 1934, Southside Place became a sovereign city, and under Mayor J.P. Lindsey, plans were made to build a city hall to house the growing city offices. Constructed of buff brick and designed to look like a home, the building was dedicated and hosted its first city council meeting in November 1935. The new city hall at 6709 Edloe Street included a second-floor apartment, where city superintendent Glenn Miller and his family lived for a time, as well as a garage to house the city's new fire truck and provide a meeting place for the newly created volunteer fire department. The Millers' granddaughter, Ann Louise Hirdler, and a friend are pictured at left in front of the original city hall building. (Courtesy of Arthur Hirdler.)

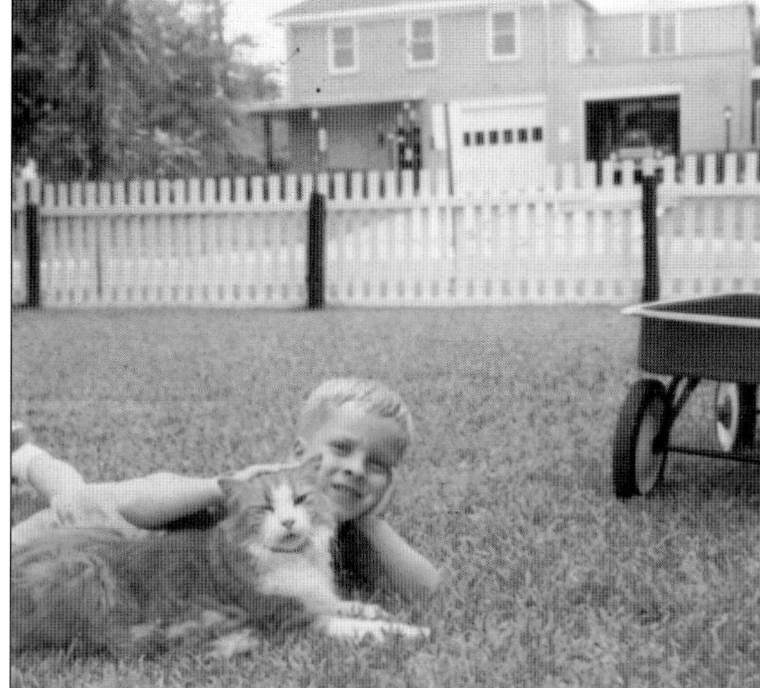

This 1969 photograph of Jamie Wood taken from the side yard of his home at 3702 Jardin Street shows the expansion and modification of the original city hall over time. (Courtesy of Liz White.)

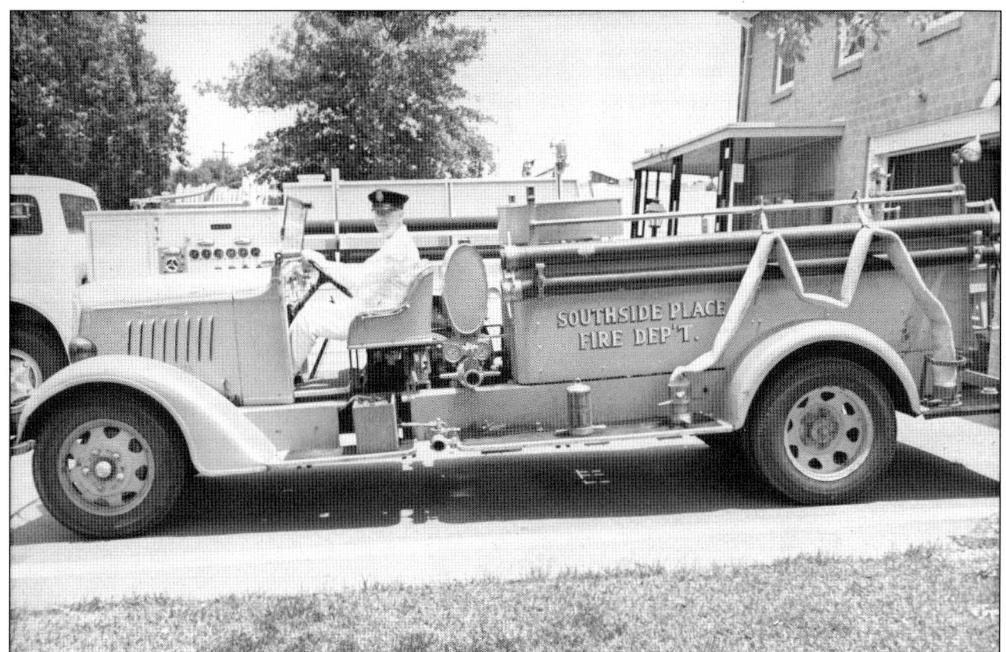

The Southside Place Volunteer Fire Department was organized in response to the loss of two homes to fire. In 1931, B.J. Clark was awakened in the middle of the night by the sound of a dog barking and discovered his neighbor's home ablaze. The dog who alerted him to the fire, nicknamed "Happy," was a stray taken in by the Clark family just a week earlier. Because the community had no fire hydrants and no fire department, neighboring cities responded to the blaze. When the fire trucks ran out of water, firefighters laid hose through the yards to draft water from the neighborhood swimming pool. Despite this, the homes at 3755 and 3759 Darcus Street were lost. (Courtesy of SSP.)

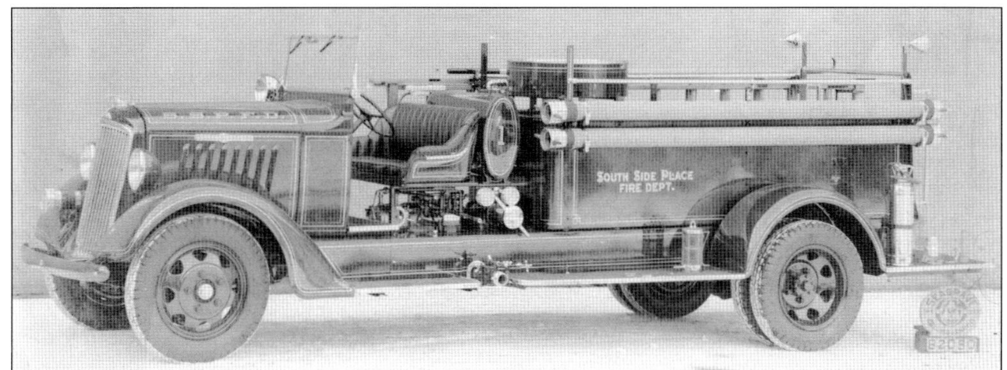

In November 1935, the fire department held its first meeting and elected A.P. Kinghorn as its first chief. A month later, the city took delivery of a Seagrave fire truck (pictured here in a photograph from the manufacturer) at a cost of $6,000. By February 1936, the first siren was placed in the park to call volunteers for duty. The siren was disabled in 2005 due to the increased number of alarms. (Courtesy of SSP.)

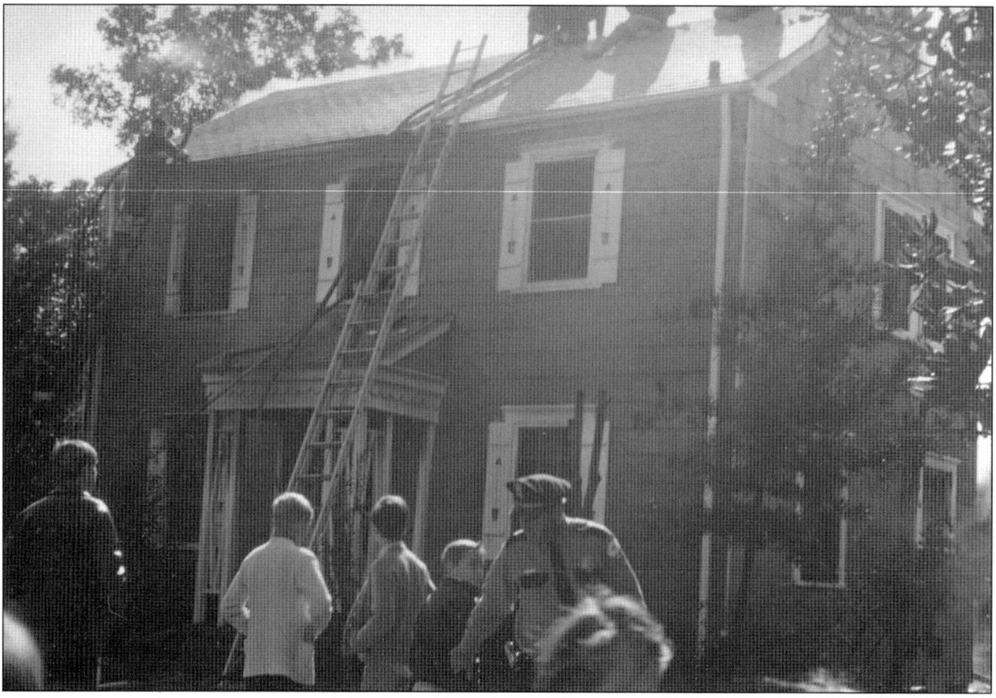

Today, the fire department answers 90 alarms a year, such as this house fire at 3723 Carlon Street in the 1970s. While the department was initially comprised of civic-minded adult male citizens, in more recent years, aspiring professional firefighters seeking experience and the occasional neighborhood teenager also fill its ranks. It remains one of the last all-volunteer fire departments in a major urban area. (Courtesy of Ann Young.)

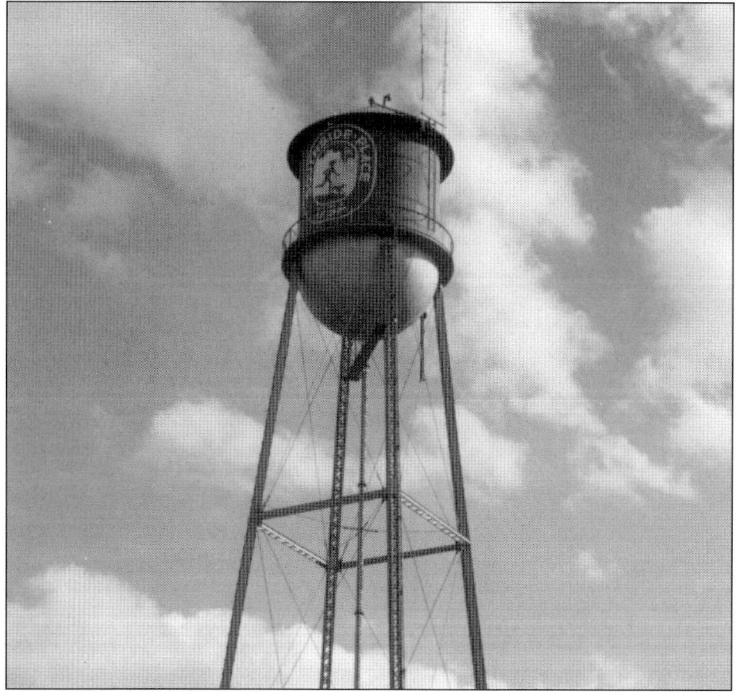

After the Darcus Street home fires in 1931, citizens also voted to issue a $45,000 bond to purchase the well water system from E.L. Crain and build the city waterworks. For many years, the most visible part of the well waterworks was the elevated water tower, located behind city hall near Poor Farm Ditch. Built in 1936 by Chicago Bridge and Iron, the 50,000-gallon water tower stood watch over the city until 2005. (Courtesy of SSP.)

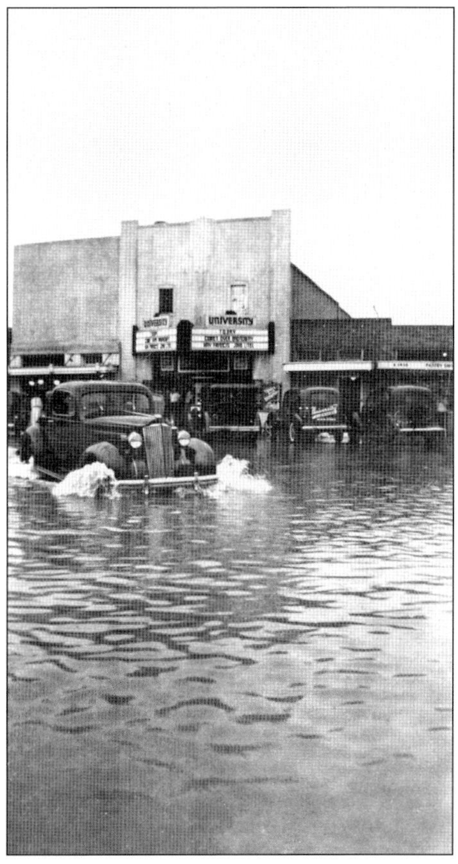

In 1947, bonds were issued to finance much-needed infrastructure improvements to address street flooding. Since inception, controlling overflow water has been Southside Place's greatest challenge. The city lies 50 feet above sea level, 50 miles from the Gulf of Mexico. The land is flat and lies in the 100-year flood plain in the Poor Farm Ditch Watershed. The city relies on an underground storm sewer system that drains into the larger Braes Bayou Watershed. For nearly 80 years, the city has worked in tandem with neighboring city governments and county flood control entities to develop a drainage infrastructure that could one day keep rainwater at bay. The history of flooding is well documented in these University Boulevard (1947) and Edloe Street (2004) photographs. Despite these concerted efforts, however, the flooding that plagued the shell streets of yesteryear continues to plague the same streets today. (Right, courtesy of HMRC; below, Annalea Flam.)

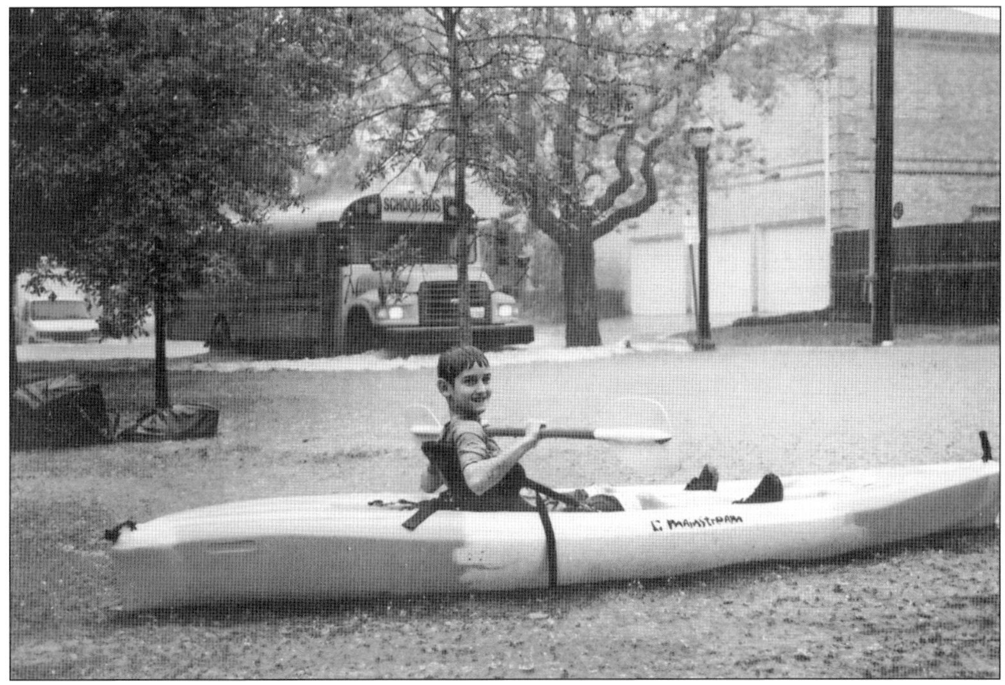

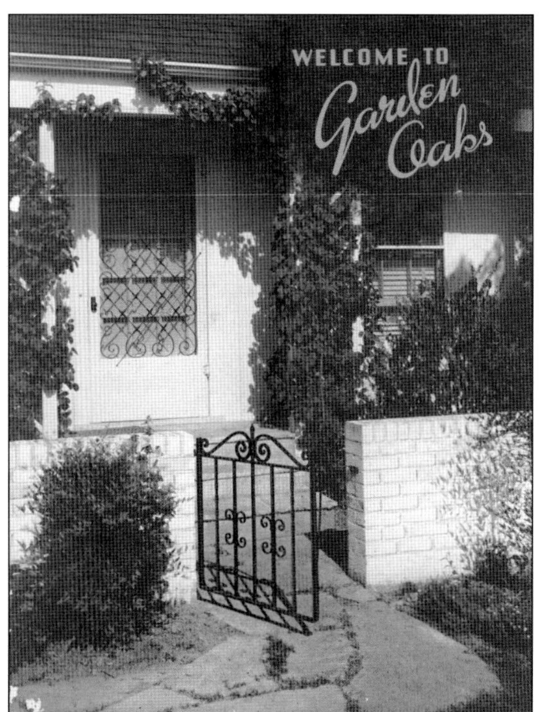

Although E.L. Crain still owned many undeveloped lots, his involvement in the city waned after he sold the water system. In 1937, Crain began work on what would be his final project, Garden Oaks. Located on 750 acres northwest of the Houston Heights, Garden Oaks capitalized on national mortgage programs following the Depression and World War II that made home ownership possible for the middle class and returning GIs. When completed, its five sections held approximately 1,400 homes. (Courtesy of HCA.)

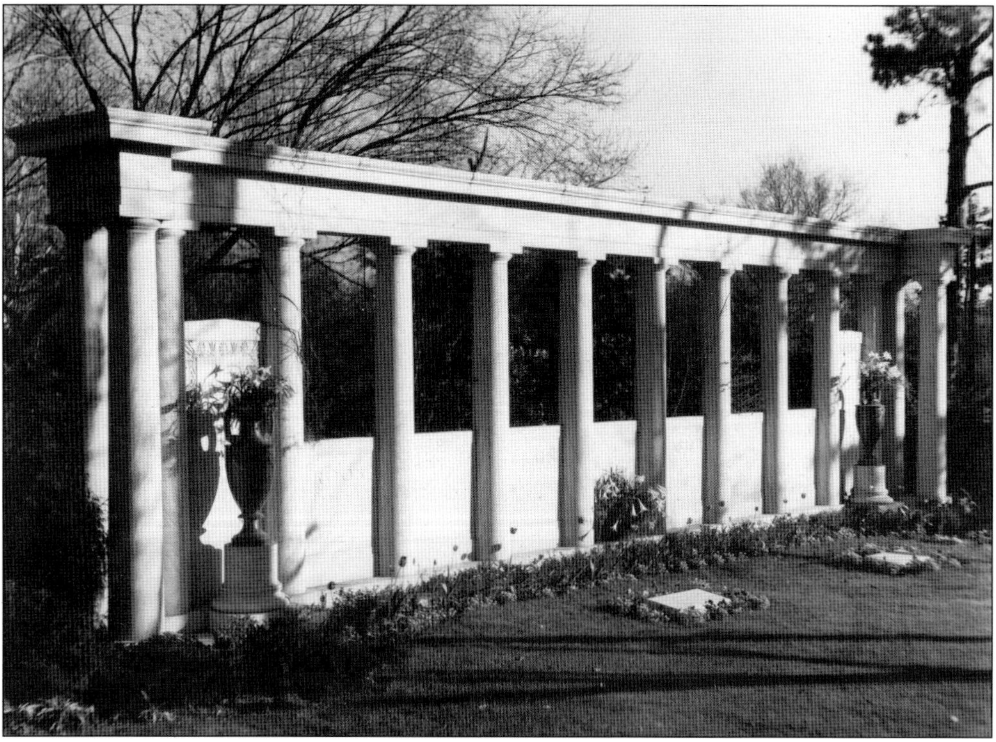

When Crain died in 1950 at the age of 65, he was buried at historic Glenwood Cemetery alongside his wife, Annie, and his three-year old son, Richard John. Rice Institute architect William Ward Watkin designed the family monument in 1928. (Courtesy of Rice.)

Four

The 1930s

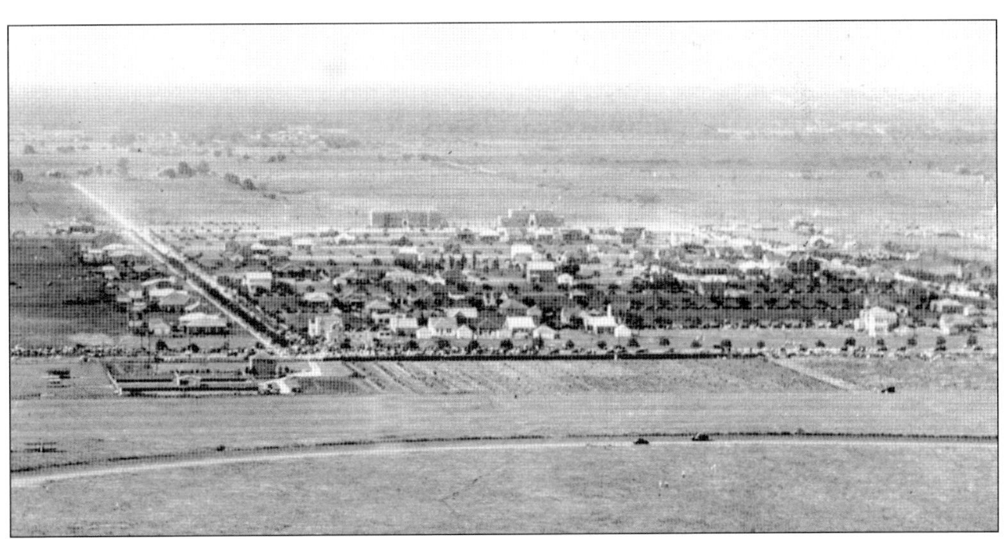

With the brick and mortar of city government solidified, a sense of neighborhood began to take shape. Notwithstanding its urban aspirations, the texture of life in Southside Place remained in many ways rural during the 1930s as a result of the Depression and the city's isolated location. This 1930 aerial photograph of Southside Place (taken from what is now Braes Heights) shows a commercial poultry farm and a citrus orchard just south of the city. (Courtesy of Story Sloane's Gallery.)

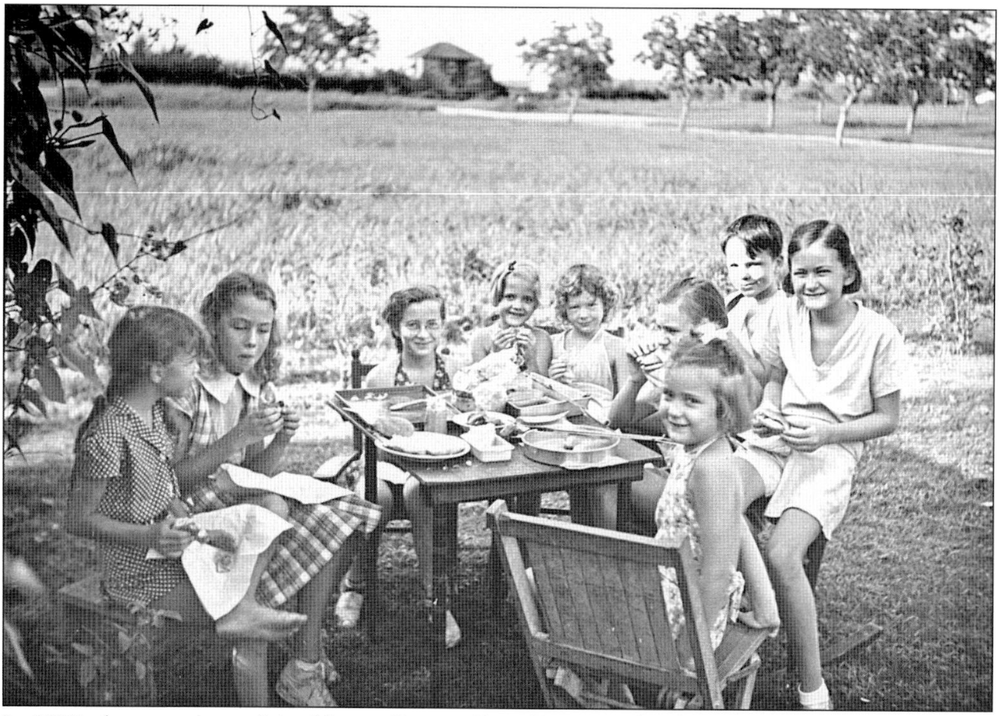

In 1930, the remnants of the Harris County Poor Farm north of University Boulevard sat idle awaiting development, and West University Place had made only modest inroads developing the land that bordered Southside Place. The view beyond the Carlon Street picnic (seen above in this 1936 photograph) is the 3700 block of Bellaire Boulevard prior to any notable commercial development. With few homes built during the Depression, streets in Southside Place remained sparsely settled. (Both courtesy of Roger Judson.)

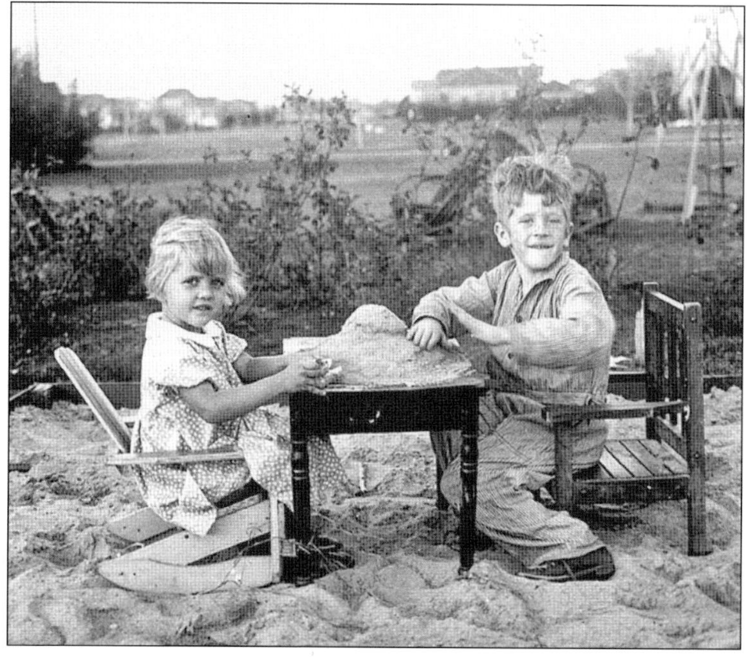

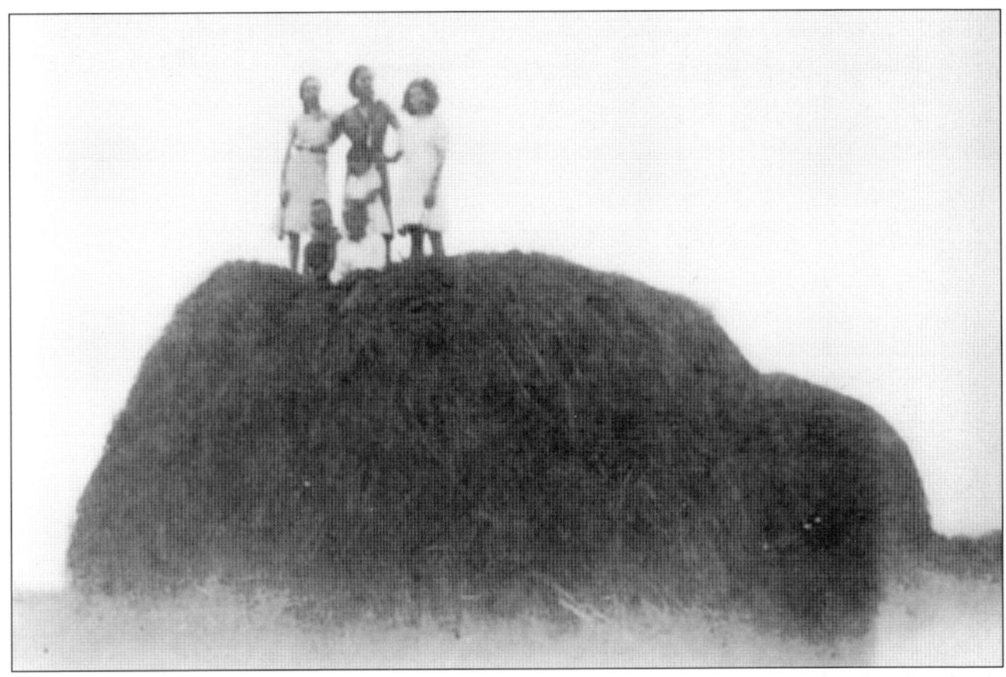

When E.L. Crain purchased part of the former Harris County Poor Farm to develop Southside Place, the remaining tract north of University Boulevard remained wide open and undeveloped. During this time, the Skelton family of Garnet Street leased a portion of the property for farming. They hired two families to maintain their livestock and actively farm the lease, including harvesting hay into bales for animal feed as seen in this early photograph. The Skeltons and their neighbors enjoyed fresh eggs, milk, and butter daily. (Courtesy of Kelly Mears.)

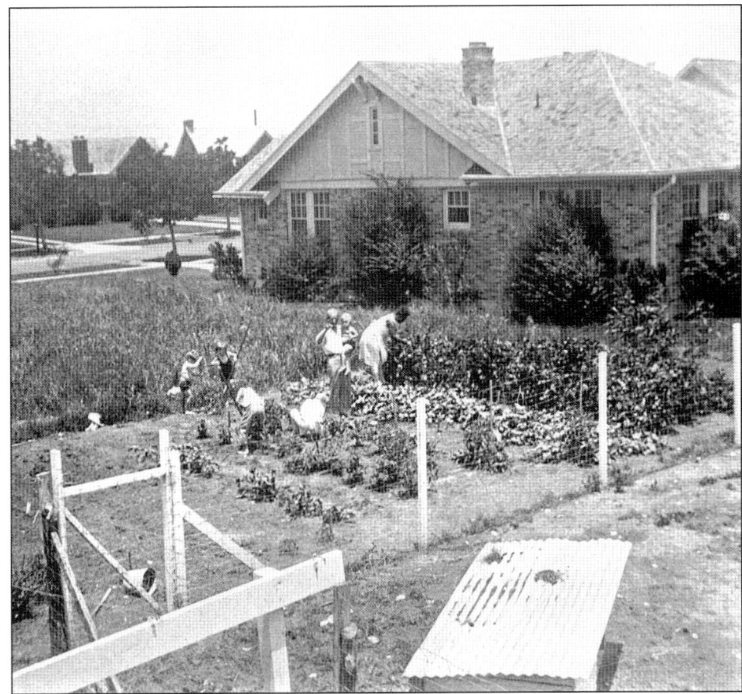

Other residents embraced the promise of the subdivision marketing materials that their lots were large enough to accommodate a garden or chicken coop in the backyard. The Judson family planted a garden in the empty lot they owned next to their home on the corner of Carlon and Auden Streets. Cows were staked on side lots, and horses were used for milk delivery. (Courtesy of Roger Judson.)

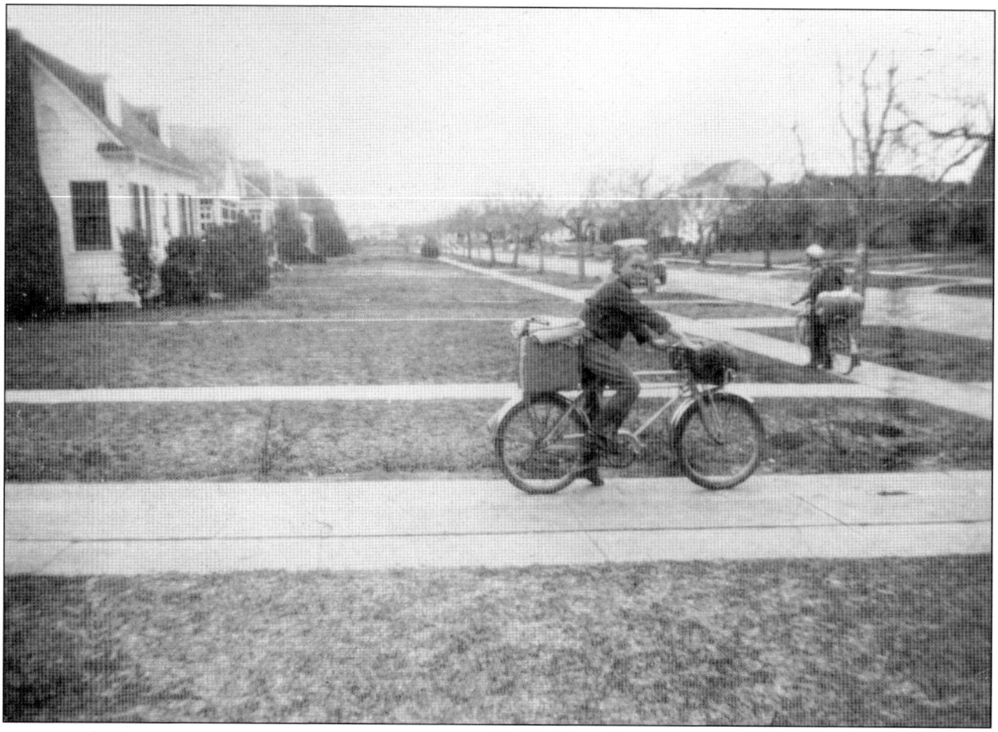

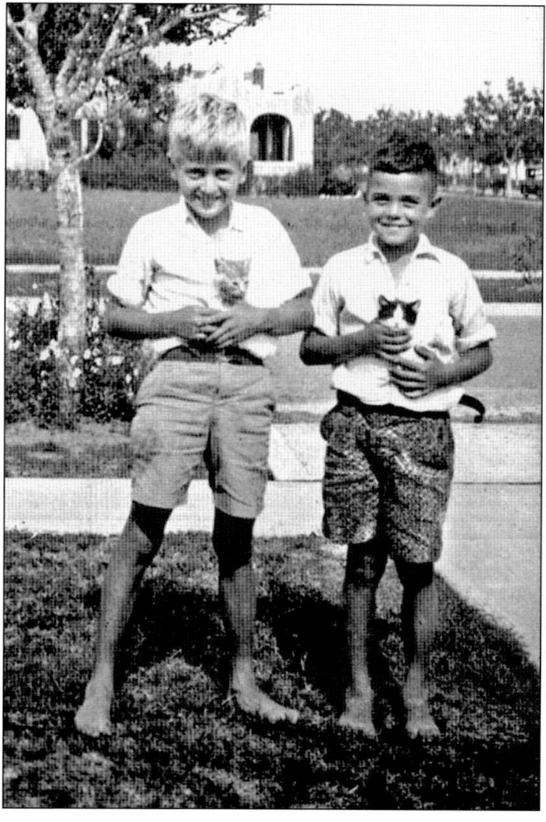

Empty subdivision lots as far as the eye could see were fair game for outdoor play. Boys with adventurous spirits (such as Edward Rose Jr., seen in the photograph above leaving his home on Harper Street) packed their bikes with sleeping rolls for camping on a remnant of the Harris County Poor Farm property. With no fencing, and properties seemingly undivided, children roamed freely with few boundaries—so did their most trusted companions. (Above, courtesy of Edward Rose; left, Roger Judson.)

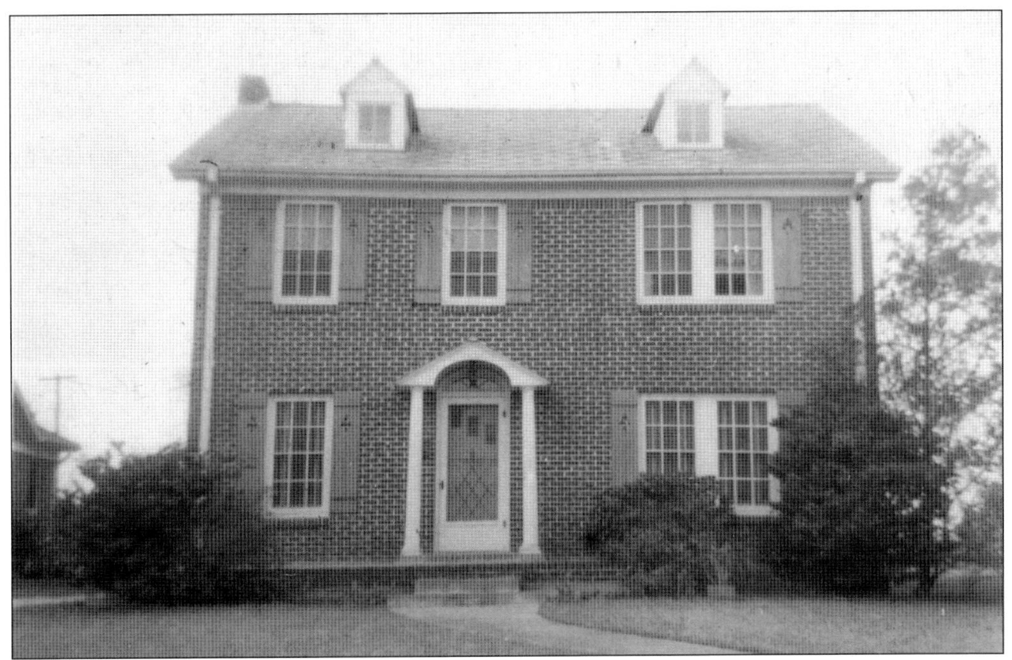

While many Southside Place children were sheltered from the harshness of the Depression, most families were impacted on some level. Bank failures and the loss of employment caused many residents to move away, leaving homes idle or available for tenancy. The resourceful family who owned the home above at 6642 Auden Street leased it as a source of additional income when they moved to a more economical home in West University Place. Other families took in boarders by renting single rooms or garage apartments. A room behind city hall was home to a municipal worker and his dog, pictured below. (Above, courtesy of Henri Gadbois; below, Kelly Mears.)

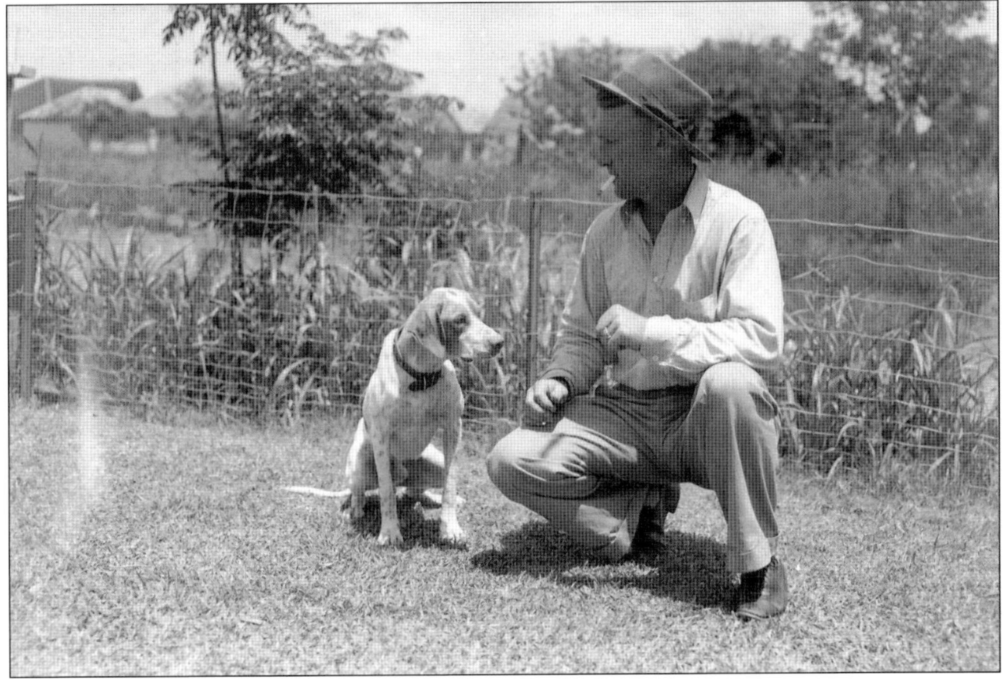

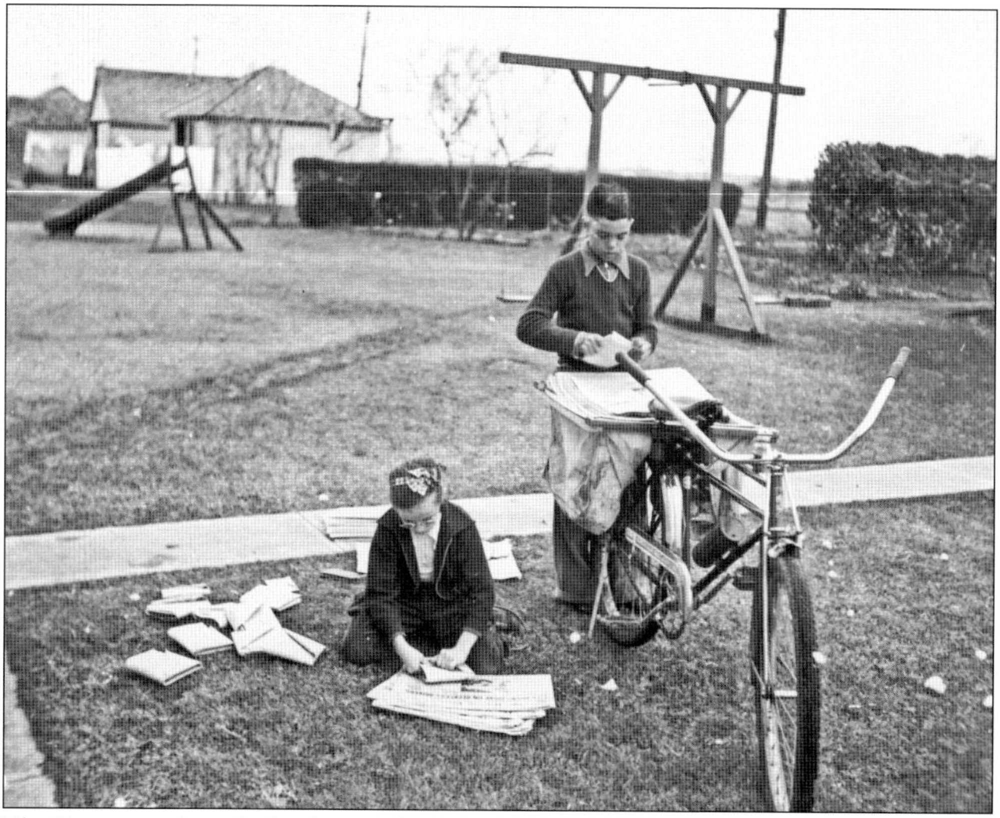

The Depression brought hard times for newspapers, whose revenue suffered from the loss of advertising. As a result, the industry shifted from using newsboys, or "newsies," to hawk individual newspapers on street corners to neighborhood paperboys selling newspaper subscriptions via cheap home delivery by bicycle or horse (above). Even after the economy recovered, however, paper routes remained a common first job for neighborhood children, as seen in this 1952 photograph (below). (Above, courtesy of Roger Judson; below, Kelly Mears.)

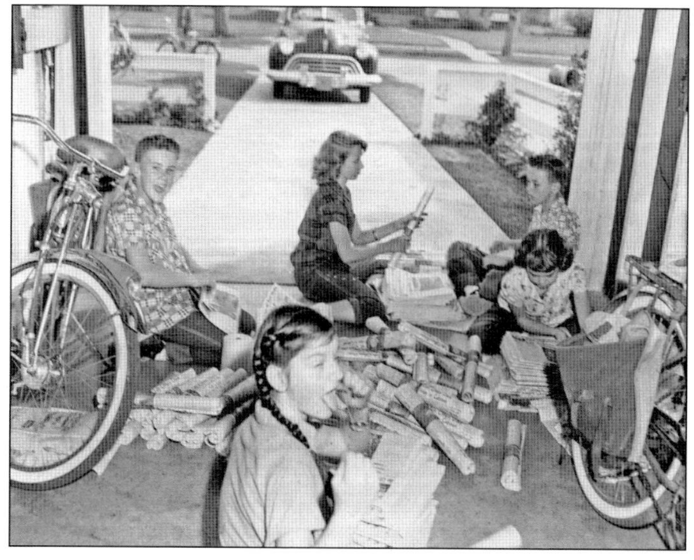

There were three main newspapers in Houston in the 1930s: the *Houston Post*, the *Houston Press*, and the *Houston Chronicle*. Southside Place resident Larry Evans (right), seen here working in downtown Houston in 1937, began as a copyboy for the *Houston Chronicle* and later became a staff photographer. Neighbor and Darcus Street resident John Hodge was a wire correspondent for the Houston division of the Associated Press. (Right, courtesy of Kelly Mears; below, Roger Judson.)

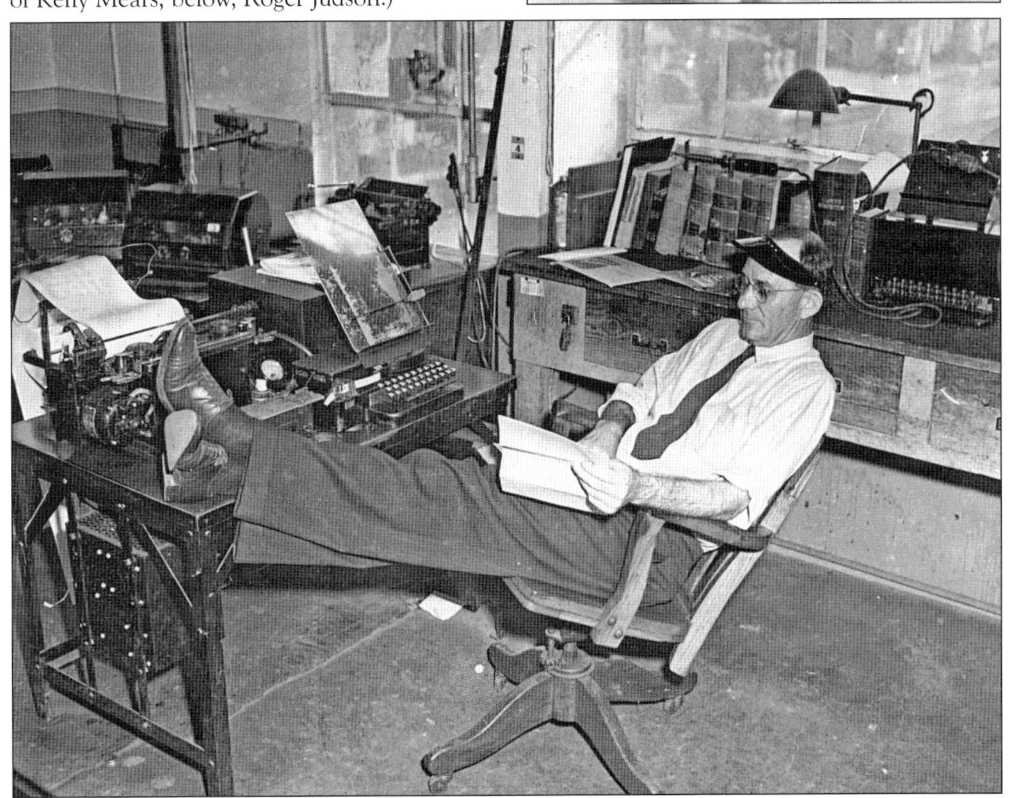

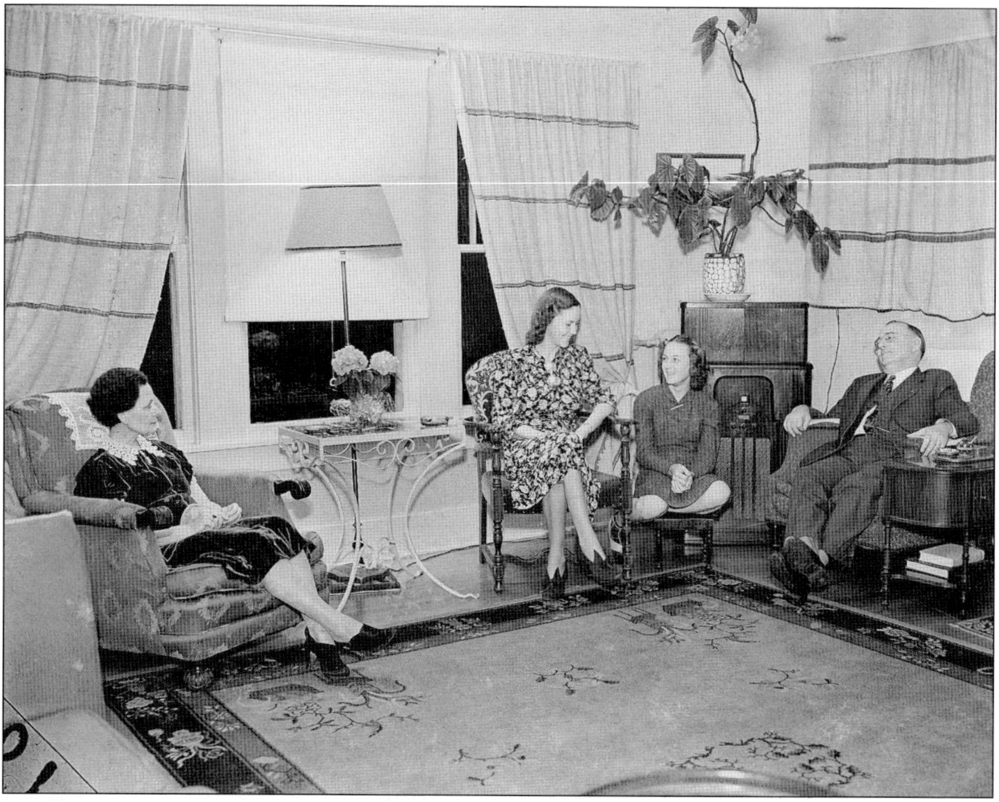

In addition to newspapers, the radio played an important role in disseminating information to communities. In 1930, there were four radio stations in Houston and two in Galveston. Families would sit in their living room by crackling radios and listen to news, baseball, and an array of lively and entertaining variety shows. The Evans family (pictured here) were like many Southside families who enjoyed listening to the radio. National magazines such as *Life*, the *Saturday Evening Post*, and *Reader's Digest* were also popular at the time. (Both courtesy of Kelly Mears.)

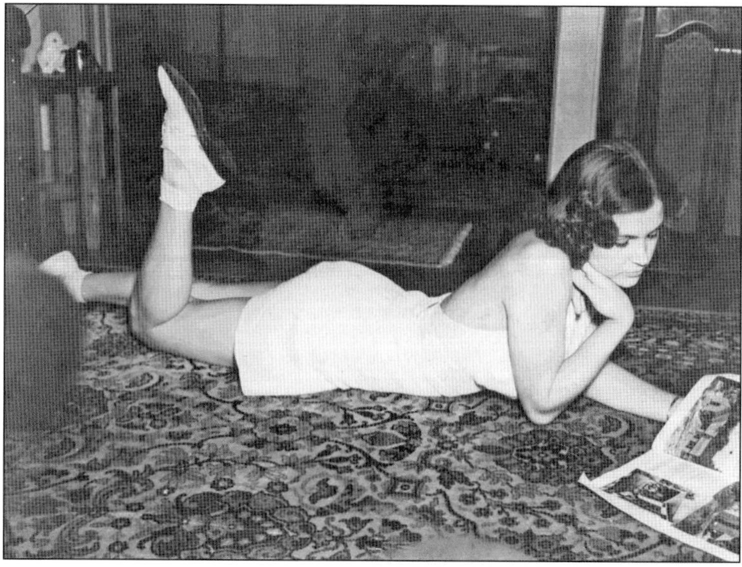

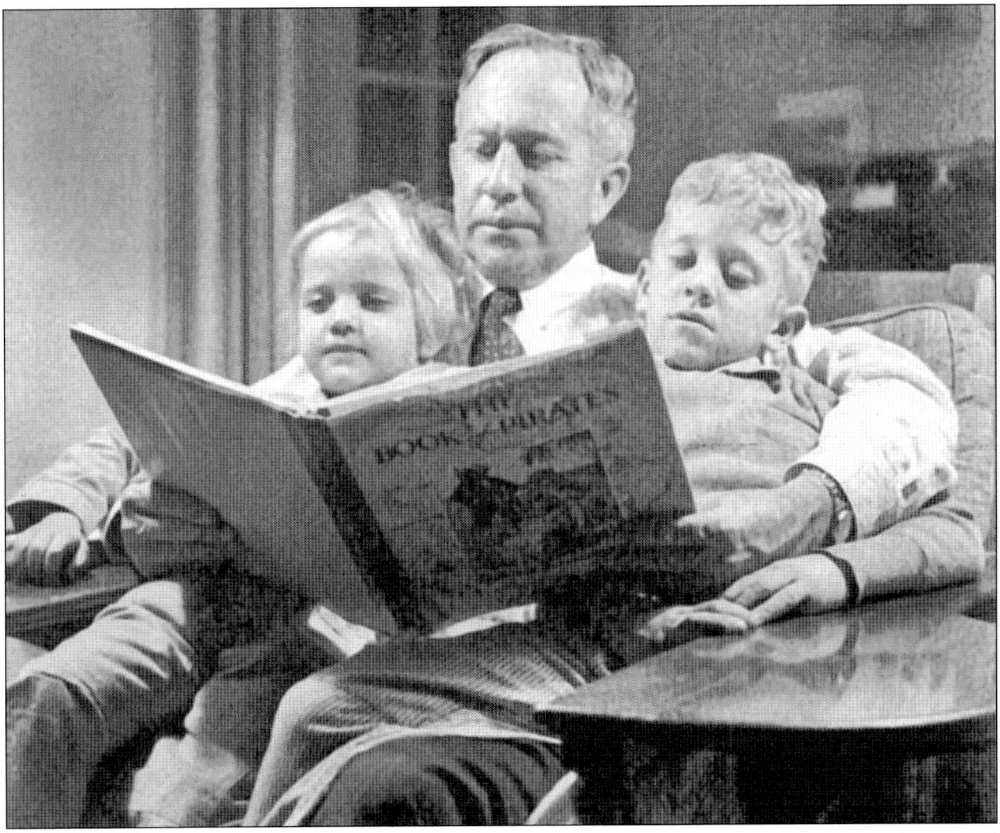

With listening to the radio and reading as common pastimes, many popular radio shows and storybook characters came to life in ordinary childhood play. Picture books and comics fueled a child's imagination. (Above, courtesy of Roger Judson; below, Edward Rose.)

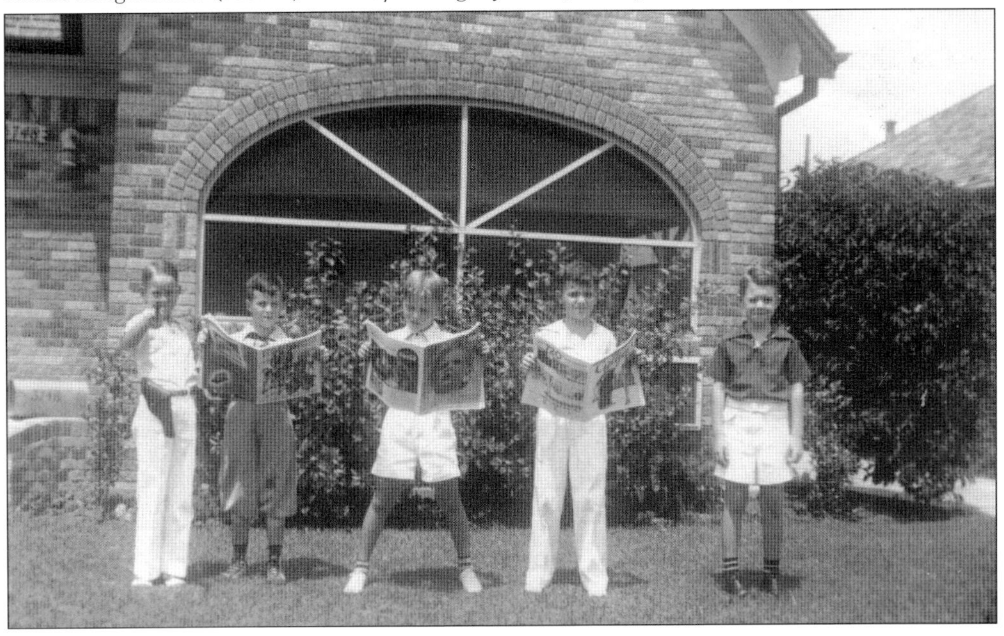

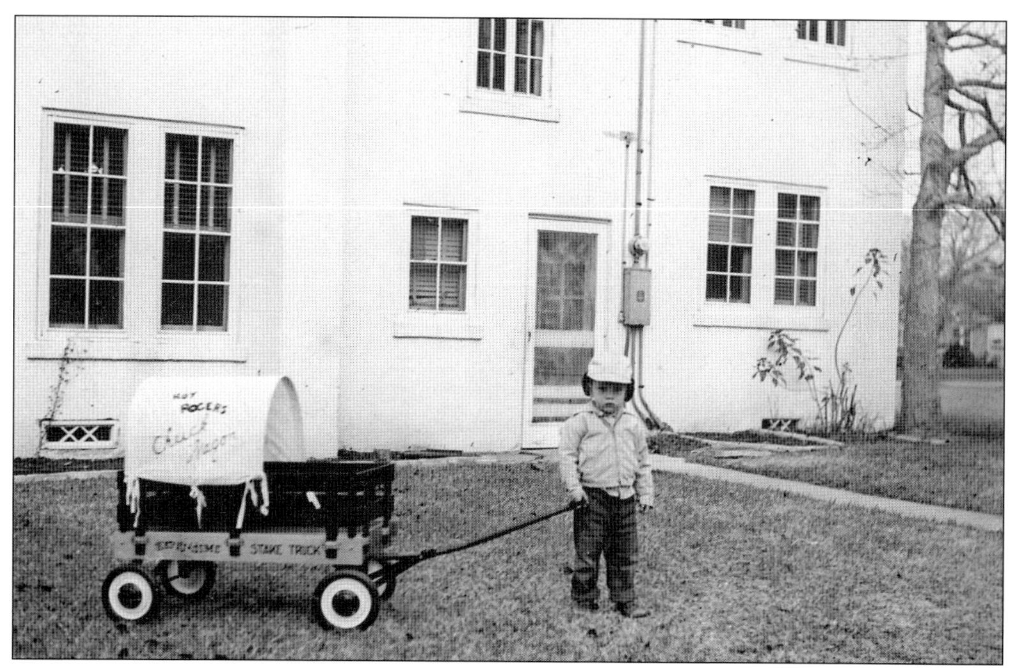

To grow up in Texas was undoubtedly to idolize the cowboy. Roy Rogers was an idol to many children through his film and radio shows. For a time, he was second only to Walt Disney in the volume of merchandise marketed with his name or likeness. With a dog named Bullet and a horse named Trigger, neighborhood boys of all ages wanted to be "King of the Cowboys." (Above, courtesy of Roger Judson; below, Edward Rose.)

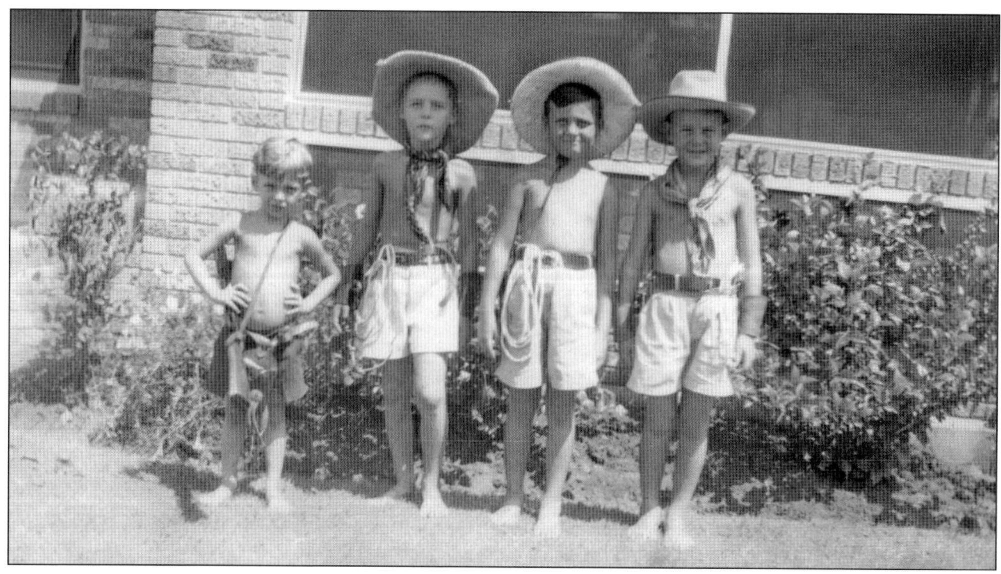

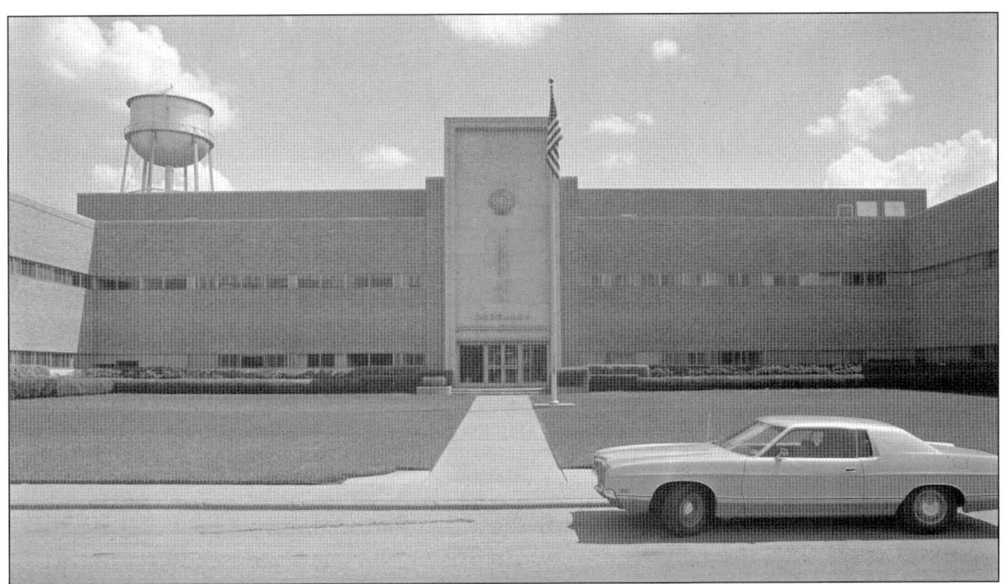

Life in Southside Place was not destined to remain quiet and rural. In the early 1930s, the commercial sector of Southside Place was comprised of a handful of grocery stores, service stations, and small businesses on University Boulevard and Bellaire Boulevard. All that changed in 1936, when Shell Oil Company entered the city and built a technology center at 3737 Bellaire Boulevard. Over the years, Shell expanded the facility to include 10 acres and a research laboratory. A major player in the oil and gas industry, Shell's presence inadvertently jump-started the city's yet-to-be-realized commercial tax base and drew employees to the area to purchase homes and raise their families. Thereafter, Southside Place systematically benefited from the many businesses, both large and small, that invested along its 0.7-mile southern corridor. (Both courtesy of HMRC.)

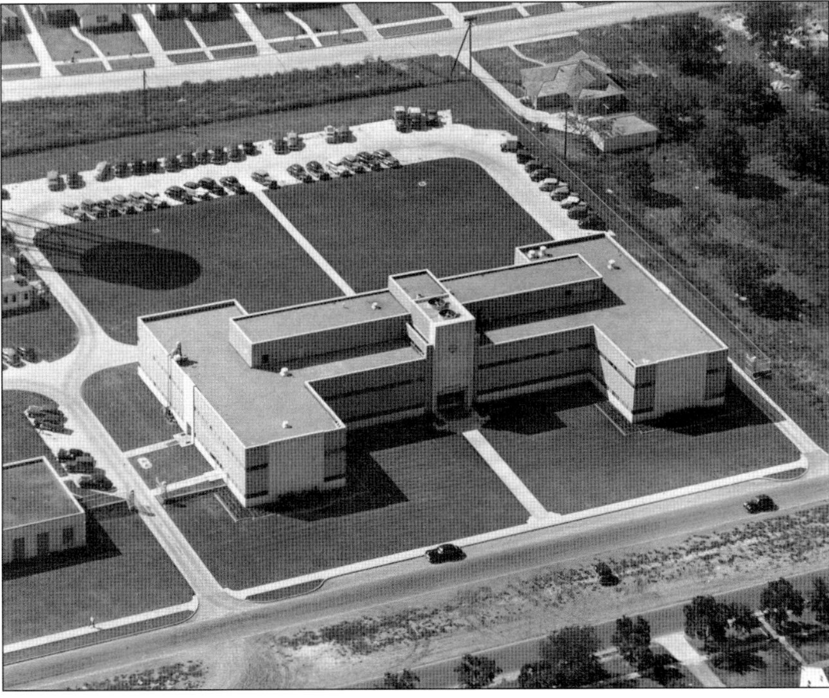

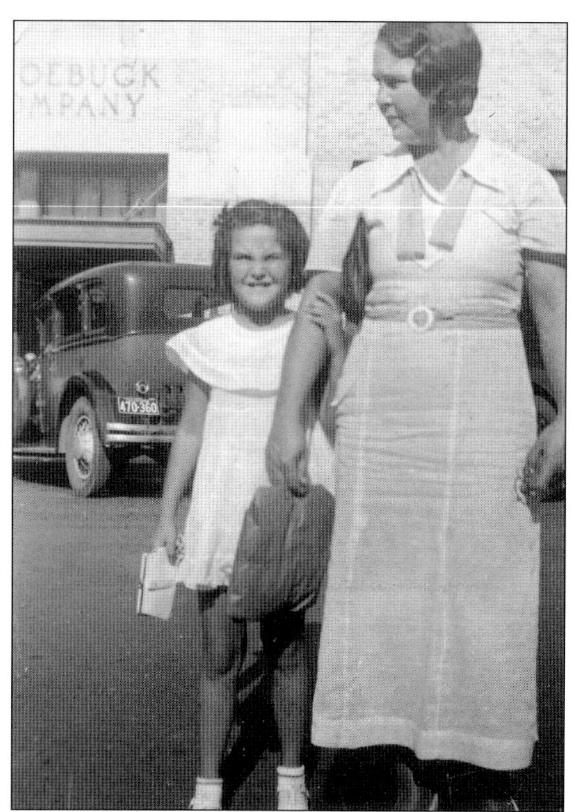

By the close of the decade, Houston was the largest city in Texas, and Harris County was the most populous county in the state. The economy rebounded. In 1939, Sears, Roebuck & Company opened a flagship store at 4201 Main Street in Houston that was unprecedented at the time for both its cost (reportedly $1 million) and because it provided shoppers the luxury of an escalator and central air-conditioning. Sears's smaller Allen Parkway store, seen here behind five-year-old Rosemary Skelton and her mother, eventually transitioned from a retail store to a warehouse. (Courtesy of Kelly Mears.)

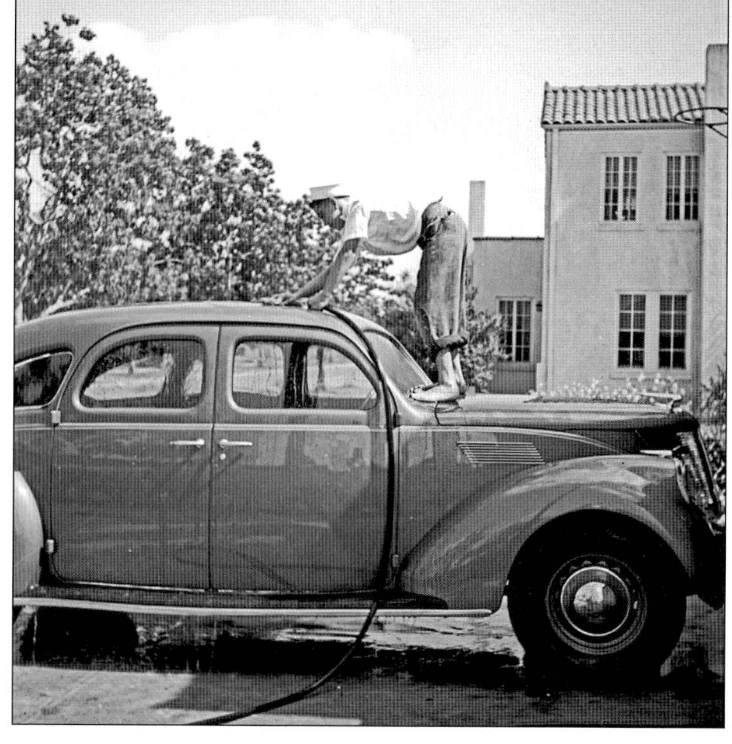

The economic hardships of the 1930s gradually dissipated as well. This image of Bob Judson in 1939 eagerly washing the family automobile at 3783 Carlon Street symbolically illustrates the air of optimism that prevailed as the decade came to a close. As tensions mounted overseas, however, much would change with the start of World War II. (Courtesy of Roger Judson.)

Five

WORLD WAR II, EVERYONE'S SACRIFICE

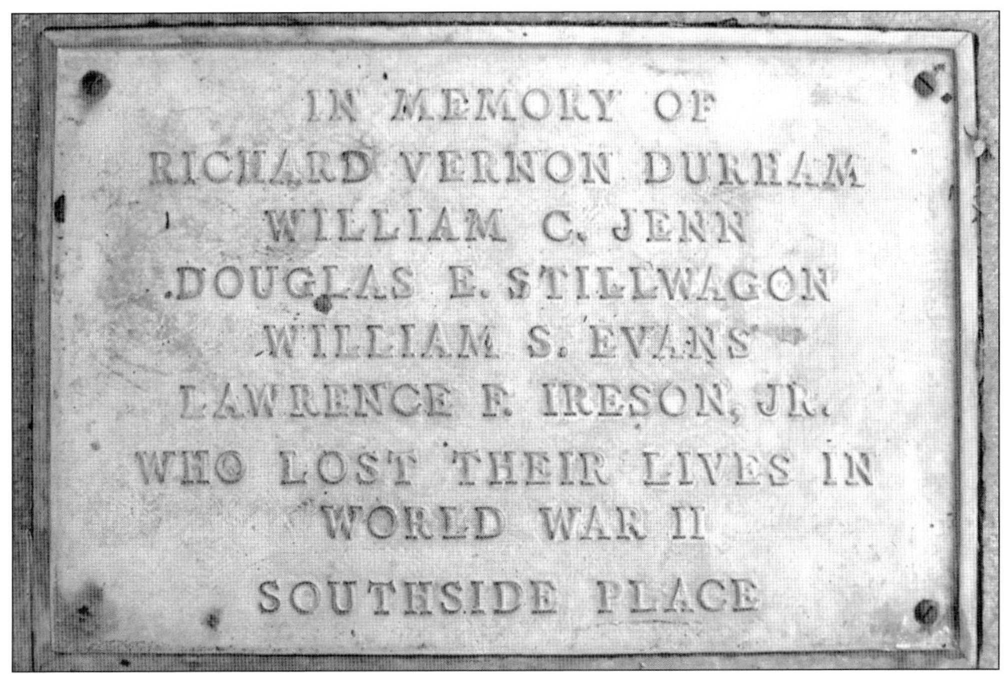

A war plaque rests in the garden of the Southside Place Clubhouse honoring five men who lost their lives in World War II. The plaque serves as a reminder of the sacrifices a community and a country made to defend a nation, its sovereignty, and its freedom. The neighborhood endured the loss of these five men within one year's time. Three of the men resided on Auden Street. (Courtesy of Kris Holt.)

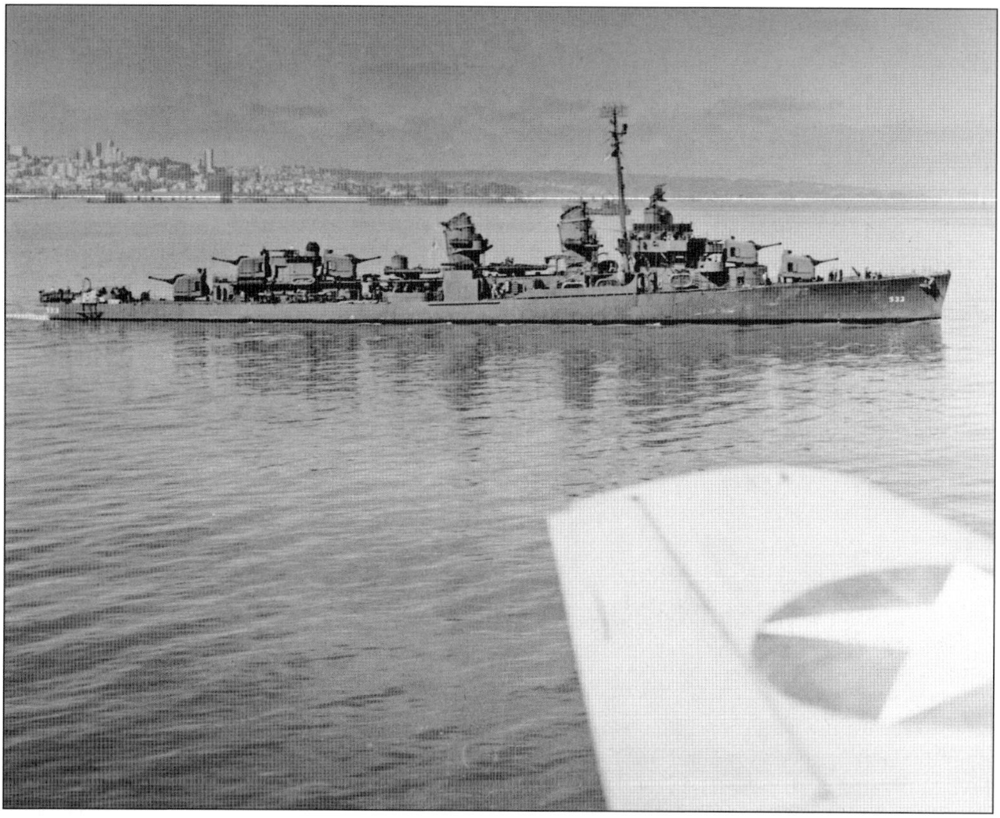

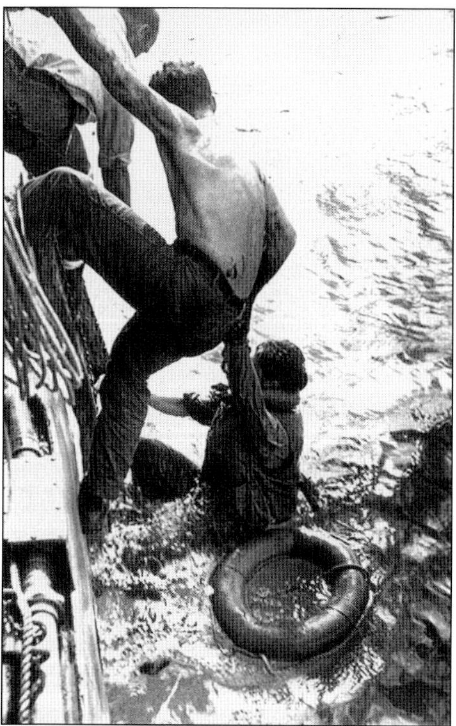

Douglas E. Stillwagon, age 18, was a neighborhood paperboy who became a Navy seaman assigned to the destroyer USS *Hoel* (pictured above). With his parents' permission, Doug left the Agricultural and Mechanical College of Texas (now Texas A&M University) and enlisted. In 1944, the *Hoel* sank in the night after enduring more than 40 strikes from a large Japanese armada off Samar Island in the Philippines. Stillwagon was plucked from the Pacific Ocean alive but died in a life raft while awaiting rescue. The photograph at left shows survivors being rescued off Samar Island on October 25, 1944. (Both courtesy of Naval Historical Foundation.)

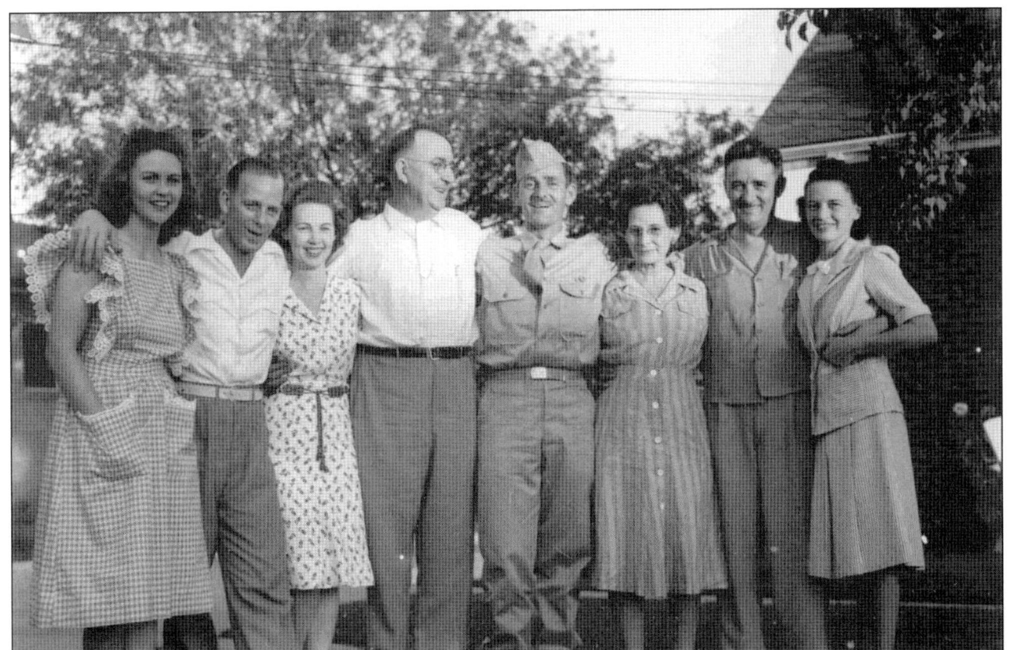

William S. Evans, known by his family as "Stanton," was a first sergeant in the 101st Airborne and a member of the infamous E Company (or "Easy Company"), 2nd Battalion of the 506th Parachute Infantry Regiment. A 34-year-old accountant who became a paratrooper, Evans and his group were immortalized in the Stephen Ambrose book and popular HBO miniseries *Band of Brothers*. Evans's plane was shot down by the Germans en route to a drop location over Normandy, France, on D-Day in 1944. Stanton is pictured above surrounded by family while on leave and below during a training exercise in 1942. Evans, platoon leader Dick Winters, and 2nd Lt. James Diel are pictured from left to right. (Above, courtesy of Kelly Mears; below, Susan Smith Finn.)

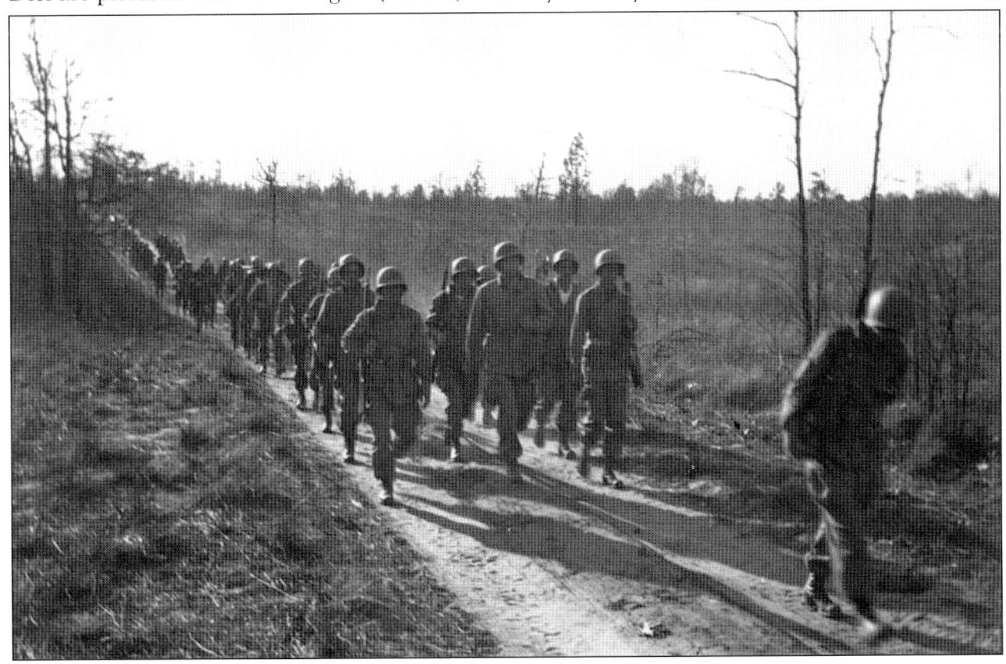

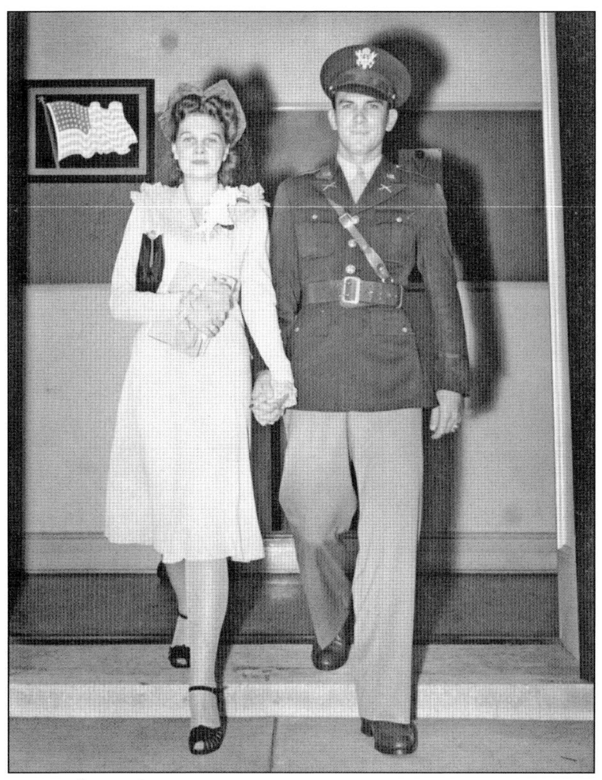

Lt. William C. Jenn was a 24-year-old Army Air Corps pilot stationed in England. On June 25, 1944, Jenn took off for a retrieval mission in Normandy when he encountered low clouds and light rain, which impacted visibility. Jenn was killed when his C-47 aircraft crashed into a range of low-lying cliffs along England's southern coastline. A neighborhood boy, "Billy" was a proud and highly distinguished Texas Aggie. He left behind a wife, Bernice, and an infant son, William Jr. (Both courtesy of J'Lynn Proctor.)

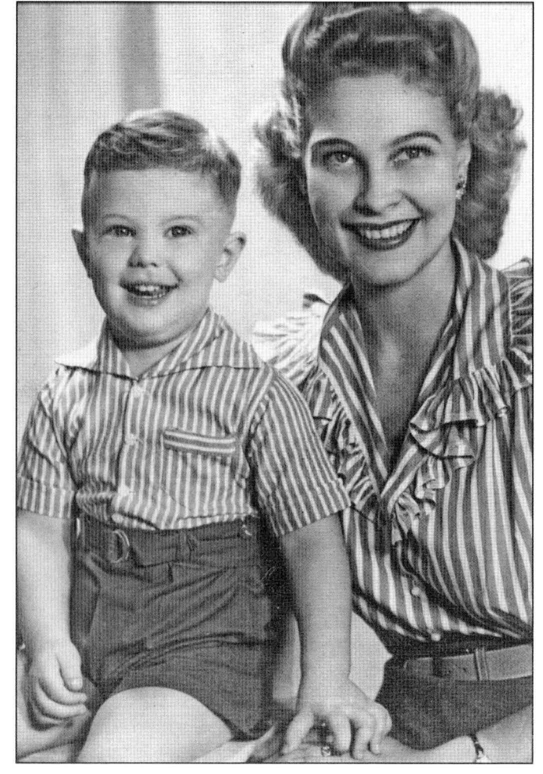

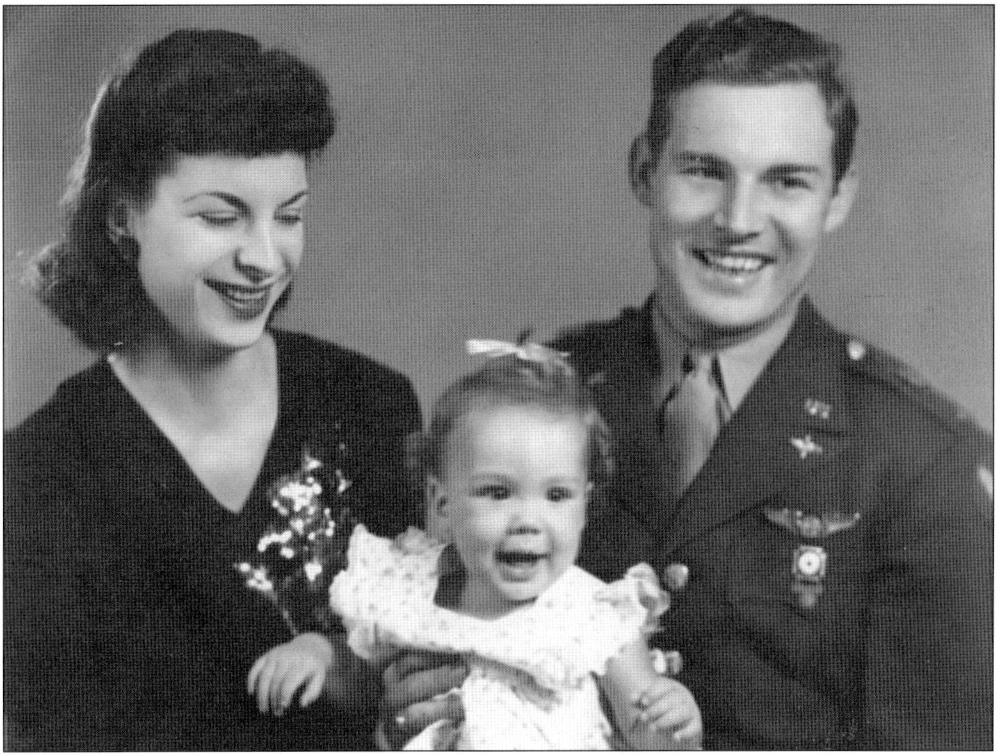

Lawrence F. Ireson Jr. was a 27-year-old first lieutenant who grew up in Colorado and moved with his family to Southside Place after high school. A talented artist, he was an architecture student at Rice University. He married a Southside Place girl, the former Jean Hendricks, whose family resided at 3722 Farbar Street, and had a daughter, Ann. As an Army Air Force flight navigator, his aircraft flew unarmed, unescorted supply missions over a treacherous section of the Himalayas known as "The Hump." In 1945, his plane nose-dived during takeoff, killing all on board but the copilot. The accident was reportedly caused by a mechanical service oversight with the landing gear. Ireson's remains were ceremoniously buried at the National Memorial of the Pacific, Punch Bowl Crater, in Honolulu, Hawaii. (Both courtesy of Mary Ethel Ireson.)

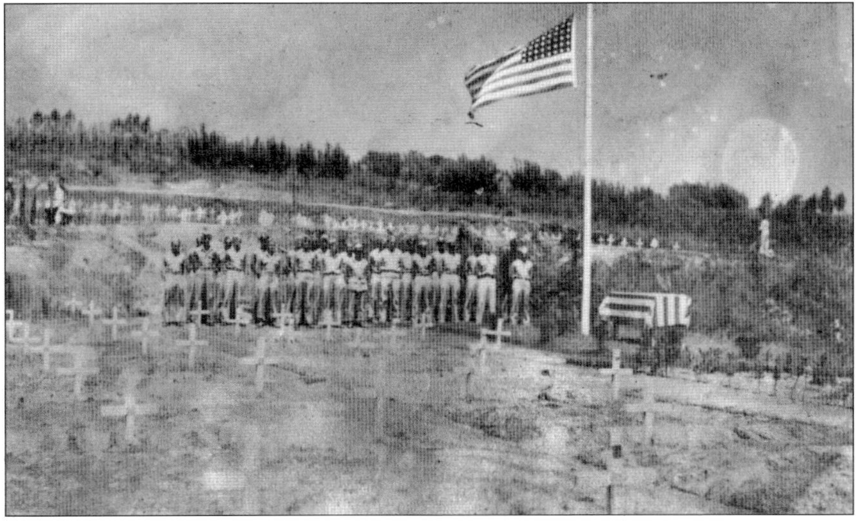

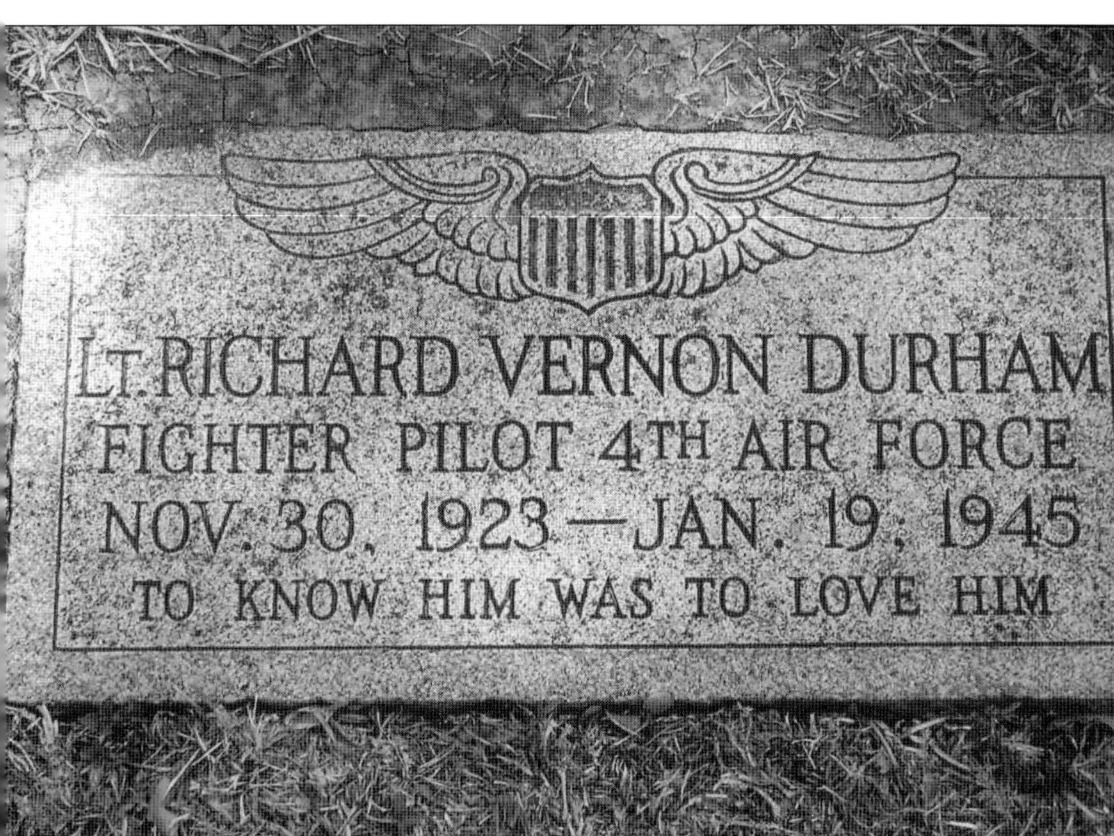

Lt. Richard V. Durham was training as a fighter pilot in the Fourth Air Force when his plane accidentally crashed in Santa Barbara, California, in 1945. During four years of the war, the US Army Air Force suffered approximately 50,000 aircraft accidents, with more than 6,000 fatalities, in the continental United States while preparing men for overseas service. Durham, who was only 21 years old at the time of his death, was being groomed to support naval operations in the Pacific theater, where his older brother was also serving. His remains were returned to Houston, and he is buried at Forest Park Lawndale Cemetery. (Courtesy of Kris Holt.)

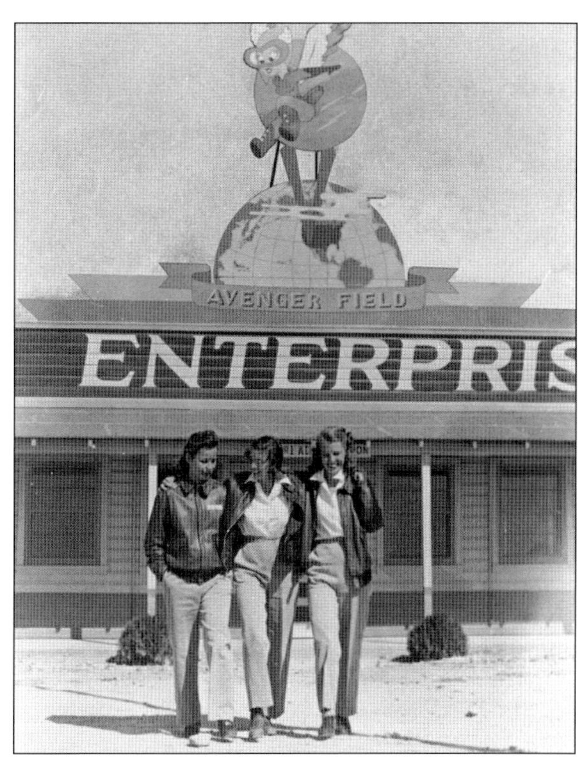

The demand for pilots during World War II was so great that civilian women were recruited to fly noncombat missions. This paramilitary aviation organization became known as the Women Airforce Service Pilots (WASP). A precursor to the WASP program trained at the Houston Municipal Airport (now Hobby Airport) for a brief period in 1942. The women's group relocated to Avenger Field (right) in Sweetwater, Texas, in 1943. Southside Place resident Edward Rose (below) served as the general manager of Avenger Field and moved his family to Sweetwater that same year. When the war ended, the WASP program was deactivated, and the Rose family returned to Southside Place, where descendants still reside. (Left, courtesy of the WASP Archive, The Woman's Collection, Texas Woman's University; below, Edward Rose.)

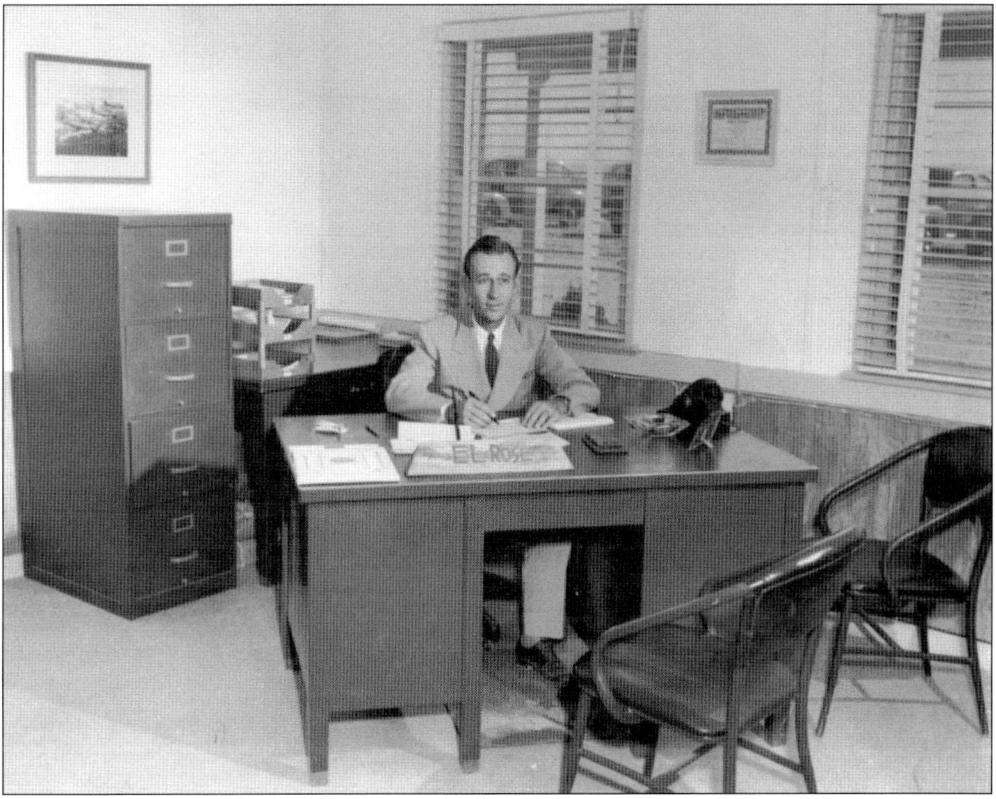

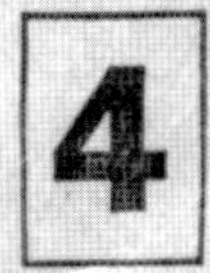

414248 AF

UNITED STATES OF AMERICA
OFFICE OF PRICE ADMINISTRATION

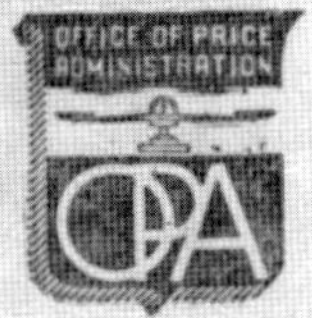

WAR RATION BOOK FOUR

Issued to Eunice Herzog
(Print first, middle, and last names)

Complete address 3735 Darcus st.
Houston - Texas.

READ BEFORE SIGNING

In accepting this book, I recognize that it remains the property of the United States Government. I will use it only in the manner and for the purposes authorized by the Office of Price Administration.

Void if Altered ____________________
(Signature)

It is a criminal offense to violate rationing regulations.

OPA Form R-145 16—35570-1

The civilian population played an important role during World War II by putting forth a unified and steadfast defensive effort on the home front. The Southside Place Garden Club sold war bonds and assembled relief packages for servicemen. Families saved metal cans, leather, rubber, silk, and other scarcities. Government ration books that restricted the purchase of gasoline, dairy, meats, sugar, and other goods were issued to each household. (Both courtesy of Kathy Kokas.)

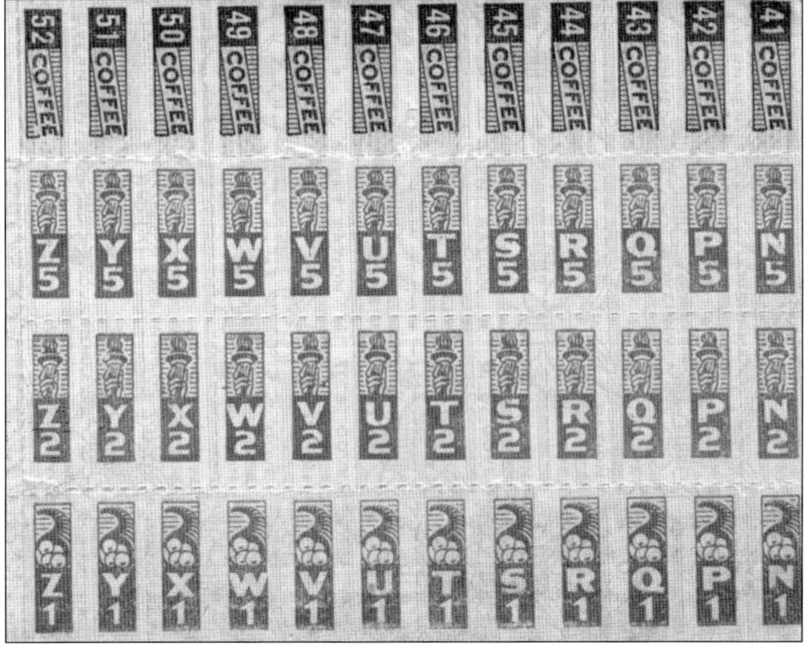

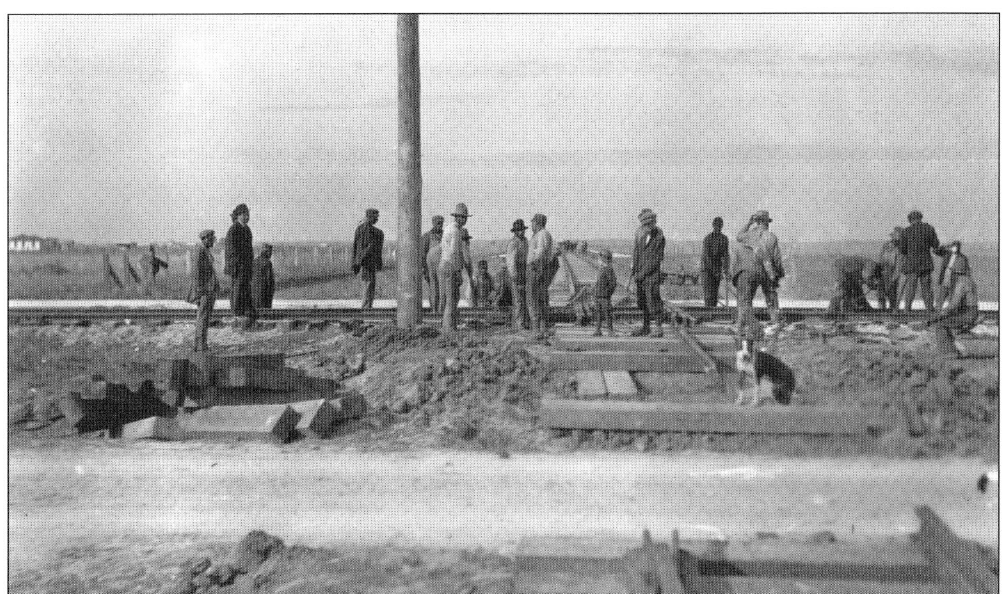

Families adhered to mandatory blackouts after sundown. Children attending West University Elementary and Pershing Junior High Schools carried out air-raid drills by sheltering in the Poor Farm Ditch on Edloe Street. Timber casing and steel tracks from the defunct Bellaire trolley line (seen here during construction in 1910 where Bellaire Boulevard crosses the Southern Pacific railroad tracks) were removed and reused as part of the war effort. (Courtesy of the Teas family and Rice.)

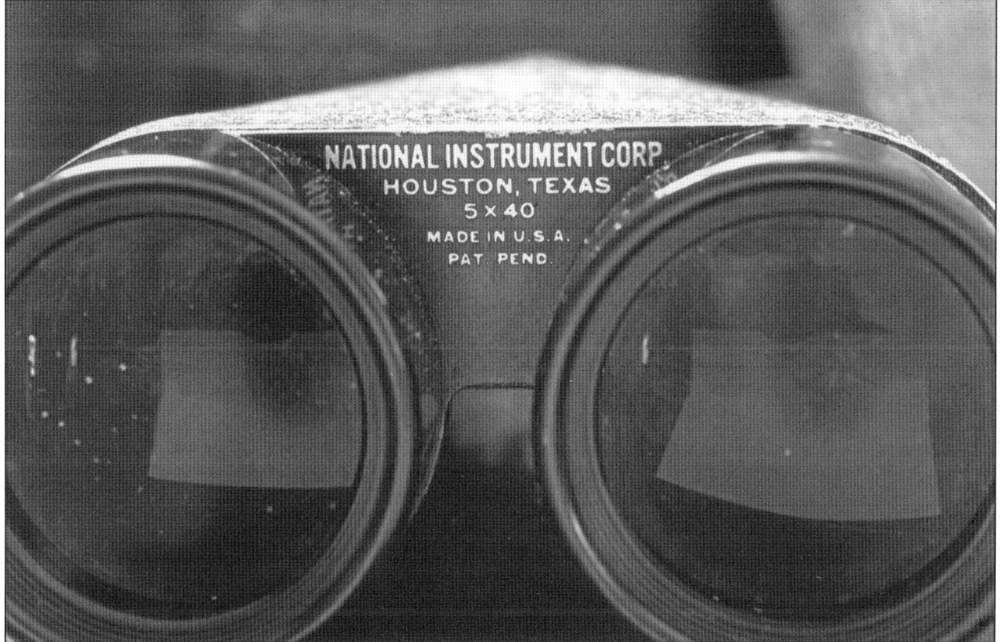

The US War Administration owned property at 4001 Bellaire Boulevard from 1943 to 1946 for the National Instrument Corporation to operate a binocular manufacturing plant. Workers were primarily women and teens who hand-polished lenses for war reconnaissance. Military binoculars produced at the Southside Place facility are considered military collectibles and are actively sold in the resale market. (Courtesy of Joe Gayle.)

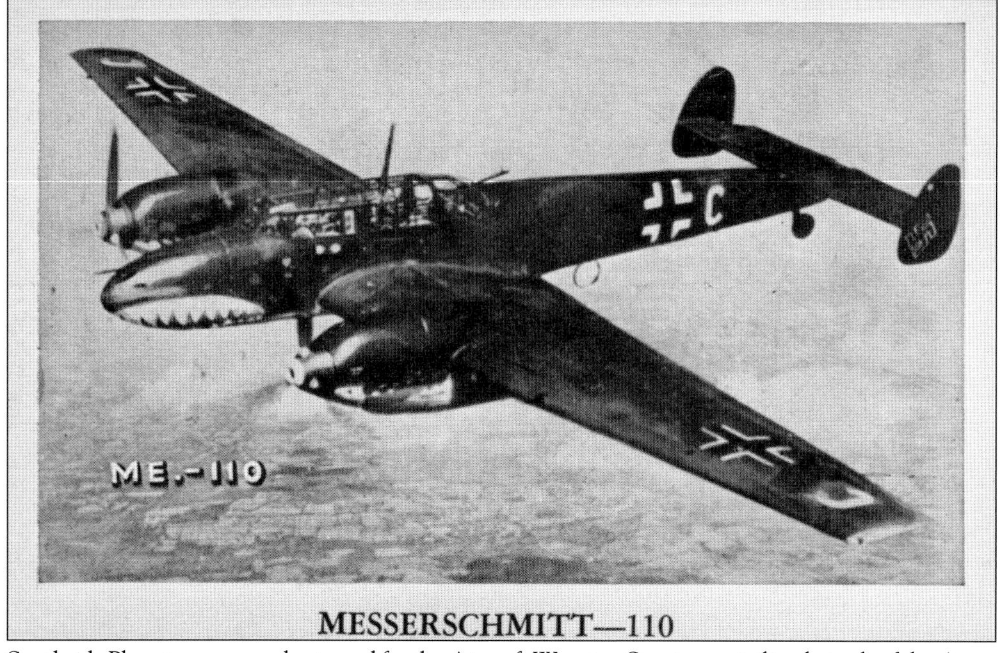

Southside Place teenagers volunteered for the Aircraft Warning Service, a civilian branch of the Army Air Force Ground Observation Corps. Civilians were trained as aircraft spotters and stood watch in a tower adjacent to the West University Fire Station on Auden Street. Government-issued spotter cards were used to identify and report aircraft flying overhead. (Courtesy of Kate McCormick.)

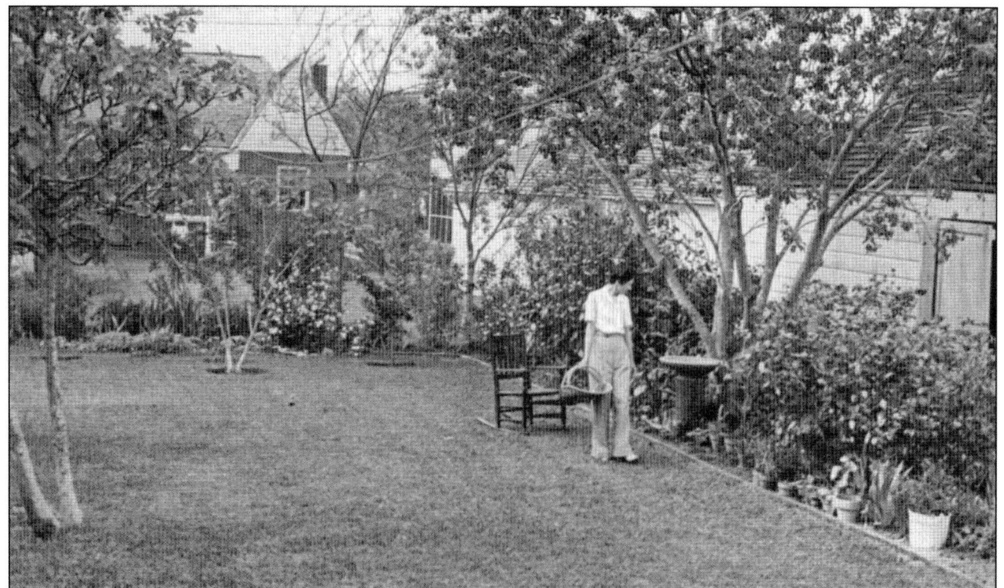

Backyards and empty lots in the subdivision were converted to Victory Gardens to provide fruits and vegetables for personal consumption. By 1944, reportedly half of America's fresh vegetables were harvested from Victory Gardens. The Southside Place Garden Club gave canning demonstrations, held meetings, and offered tips on soil maintenance, seasonal planting, and how best to have a productive yield. Eunice Herzog was photographed in her backyard garden at 3735 Darcus Street in 1942 for a Shell Oil publication. (Courtesy of Kathy Kokas.)

By the end of World War II, more than 10 million men had been inducted into the armed services, either by the draft or by enlistment, upending the families they left behind. With communities struggling at home, a new breed of patriotism was born, particularly with the youngest residents. Whether engaged in imaginative war games on empty subdivision lots or through quiet play at home, the war added a new spin on how children played and whom they admired. (Right, courtesy of Jackie Duffie; below, Kelly Mears.)

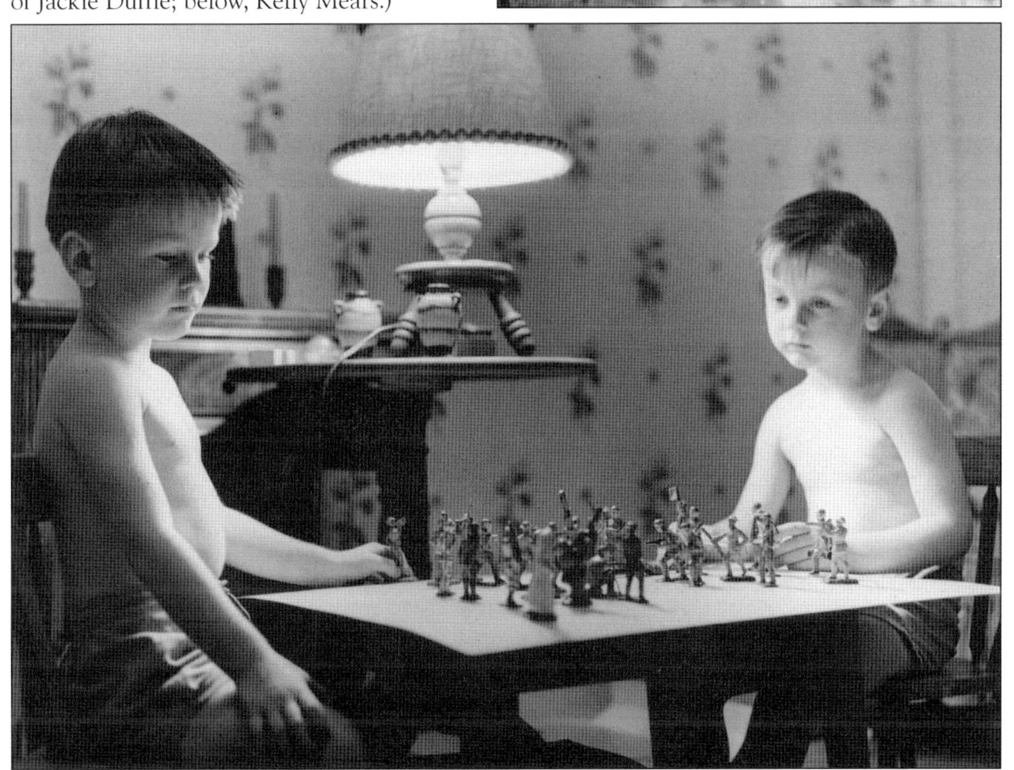

PROUDLY WE PAY TRIBUTE TO THESE, OUR MEN AND WOMEN IN THE ARMED FORCES OF THE UNITED STATES IN WORLD WAR II

*—Denotes those who have given their lives for their country:

AUDEN STREET

BURKE, Kenneth A.
BURKE, William L.
WARK, R. K., Jr.
CHENAULT, Claude
CLARK, W. Cullen
DURHAM, Ardis H.
*DURHAM, Richard
ELAM, Robert E. Jr.
GREGORY, Merle Jr.
GREER, Hubbard
JENN, E. T. Jr.
*JENN, William C.
JOHNSON, Preston E.
JOHNSON, William D.

BELLAIRE BLVD.

ISBELL, Jack D.
JORDAN, Gerald E.
WIDEL, William M.

CARLON STREET

CASH, Joseph
COX, Alex S.
GRAY, Robert
JORGENSEN, Roy
JUDSON, Ed.
JUDSON, Robt. Sidney
McDONALD, Fred B. Jr
MORECROFT, Ralph A.
ONSTAD, William J.
PARKS, Charles C. Sr.
PARKS, Charles C., Jr.
PASENHOFER, Arlo H.
ROBINSON, W. A.
SHAW, William E.
TILLEY, E. B.

DARCUS STREET

BOWDEN, George W. Jr
DAWDY, J. E. Jr.
ESTESS, Dr. Berthal H.
HOWARD, Willis M.
HUGHES, Jack
KACHTICK, Robt. F. Jr
KINLOCH, Wallie
MIIA, Jimmie
PRINCE, Dalton B.
SCHROCK, Lawrence
SEARS, Nelson B.
TENNISON, J. W.

EDLOE STREET

ALEXANDER, K. E.
CAMP, Richard
CAMP, Herbert
FECTEAU, Edw. T. Jr.
HARRISON, Olin
HENDRICKS, D. N., Jr.
JORGENSEN, H. F.
MATHEWS, H. M.
McREYNOLDS, Stephen
ROYALL, C. M.
VONHEEDER, Byron C.

ELMORA STREET

BEST, D. M.
BRENNER, Robert C.
BRENNER, Milton L.
CAPPS, Forest D.
CAPPS, Lee W.
HEWITT, Clarke N.
HEWITT, Thurman H.
HEWITT, Warren S.
LACY, Olin M.

MERONEY Geraldine M.
SCHAPPER, S. O.
SCHEID, Theo G.
*STILLWAGON Douglas E.
STILLWAGON, Geo. C.

FARBAR STREET

COOK, Clem
COOK, Donald
EVANS, Charles P.
EVANS, R. E.
*EVANS, William S.
*IRESON, Lawrence F. Jr.
JOSEY, W. E.
SCHUHMANN, Robt. E.
WOMACK, N. T. Jr.

GARNET STREET

EGAN, Glen A. Jr.
KELLEY, Howard Clay
MARRS, James H.
McFARLAND, Gerald M.
MOSSOTTI, Armand V.
ORMAN, Forest C.
ORMAN, W. Kenneth
PATRICK, William L.
POPE, Arthur N.
POPE, George W. Jr.
POPE, John G.
SKELTON, James A.
SKELTON, Thomas W.

HARPER STREET

COOKE, Bernard F.
FORSON, Billie F.
JACKSON, James C.
JETT, Jesse A.
PIERCE, Hazel

INGOLD STREET

BAYLESS, Chas. Robt.
CHRISTIANSEN, R. E.
COLEMAN, T. V., Sr.
COLEMAN, T. V. Jr.

GEARING, Herman S.
KIRK, Robert Dyrel
LOVE, Lee M.
LOVE, Shelton
LOVE, T. S.
McGEE, S. F.
RAGSDALE, Frank
ROBERTSON, Glenn Jr.
ROBERTSON, Don L.
SCHOELMAN, W. W. Jr.
SIMMS, Ned
WILSON, Robert
YOUNG, James N.
YOUNG, Milton F.

JARDIN STREET

BELL, Exter Frank
BELL, Willa Mae
BRADLEY, Robert
BUIE, C. M.
BUSTER, Alan A.
BUSTER, Winston Sr.
BUSTER, Winston Jr.
CARNES, J. Dorian
CARNES, J. W.
CARNES, Marion
CHILDS, J. Marvin, Jr.
GOLDING, Thomas, R.
GOODMAN, John F.
HUDSON, R. C.
HUDSON, Robert D.
LAWS, Cecil E.
MARSTON, Tovell
MARTIN, W. H. Sr.
MARTIN, W. H. Jr.
MARTIN, Don
PACKARD, Vernon L
RAINEY, Walter M.
ROBBINS, David
WATSON, Morris

UNIVERSITY BLVD.

GILBERT, John
WESTBROOK, W. L.

The 1945–1946 Yearbook of Southside Place, a directory assembled by the Southside Place Garden Club, recognized the 140 men and women who served in the four branches of the US armed forces during World War II. Larry and Jerry Evans (below) from Darcus Street had five cherished uncles, all Southside Place residents, serving in the armed forces at one time. (Above, courtesy of SSP; below, Kelly Mears.)

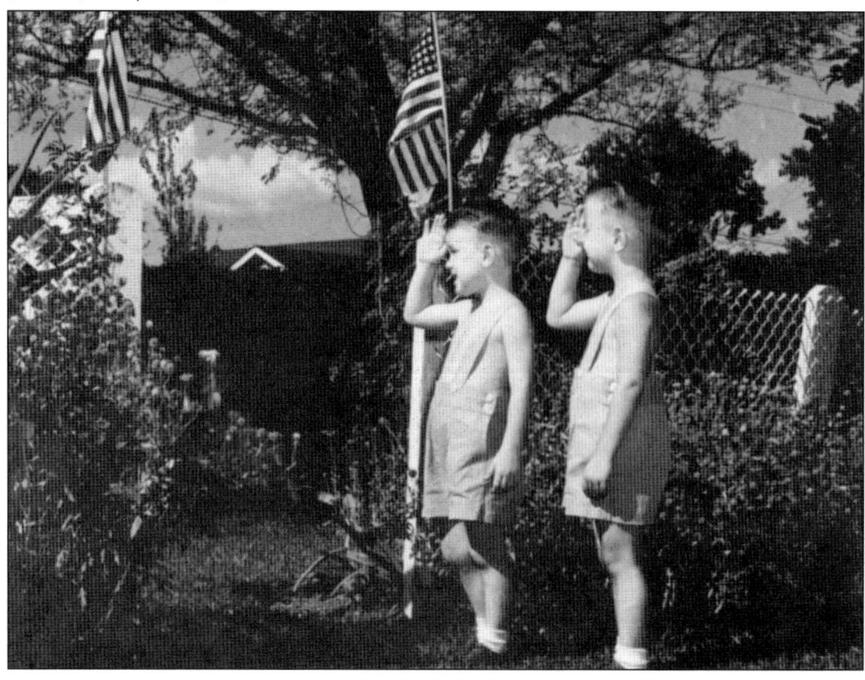

Six

Postwar Growth and Prosperity

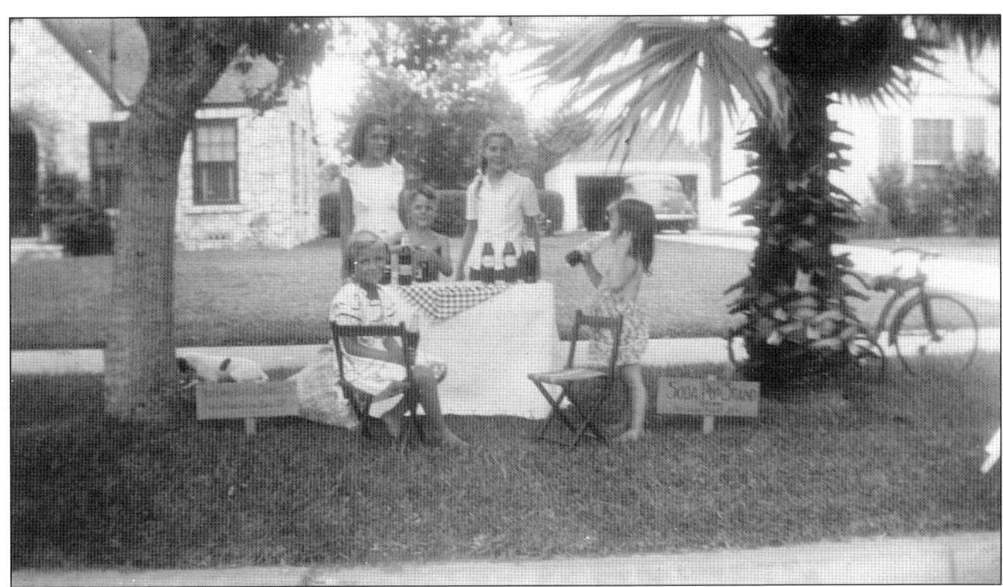

The country experienced a surge of growth after World War II. The GI Bill of 1944 allowed for low-cost mortgages, loans for businesses, and educational assistance for veterans. Southside Place, along with neighboring communities, made considerable strides in population, housing, and commerce. Southside Place's population more than doubled to 1,500 residents from 1930 to 1950. E.L. Crain's housing model of the 1920s afforded the influx of young families renewed opportunity and a chance for the American Dream. (Courtesy of Gayle Bowyer.)

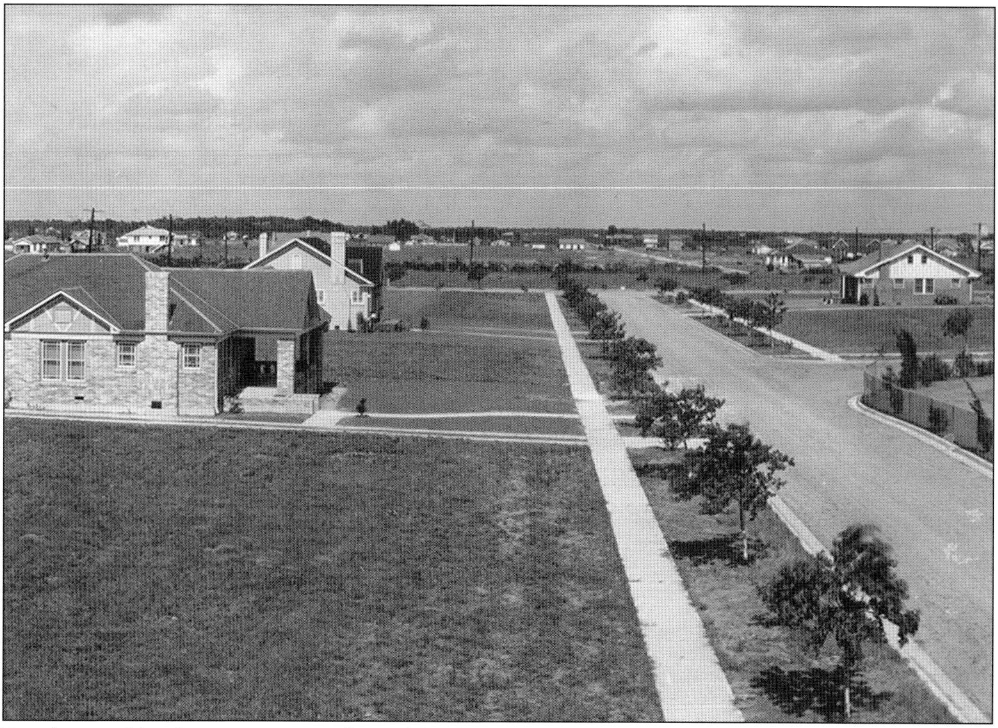

Bonds issued by the city in 1947 allowed for the paving of Southside Place's shell streets, and soon shiny new automobiles began to dot the city's residential landscape. These opposing photographs (taken in 1926 and 1953, respectively) in front of the same home at 3734 Garnet Street depict a dramatic streetscape change from the 1930s to the 1950s. (Above, courtesy of SSP; below, Kelly Mears.)

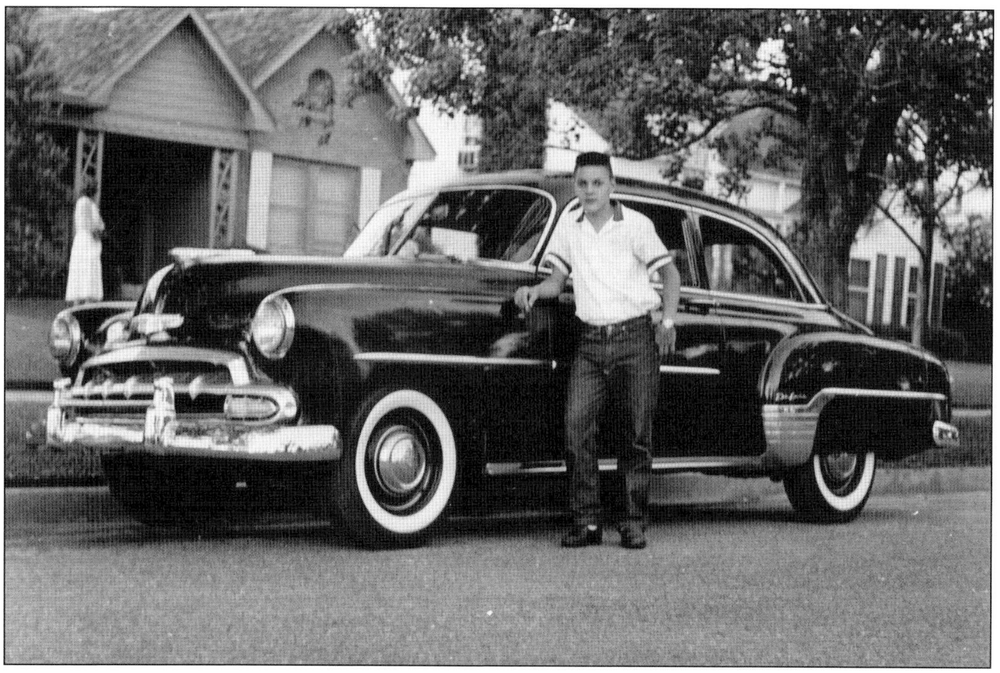

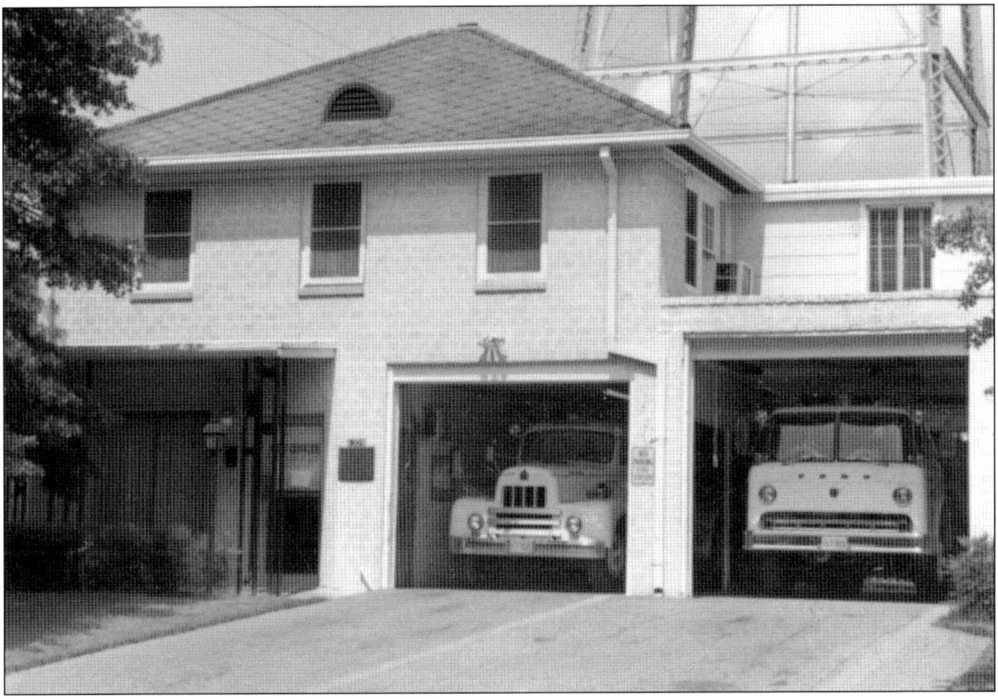

A developing tax base allowed for the expansion of the original Southside Place City Hall at 6309 Edloe Street. In 1952, city labor built a new bay for the fire truck and the original garage was converted into offices for the growing city administration. When the city purchased an additional fire truck in 1970, a second truck bay was added as seen above. (Courtesy of SSP.)

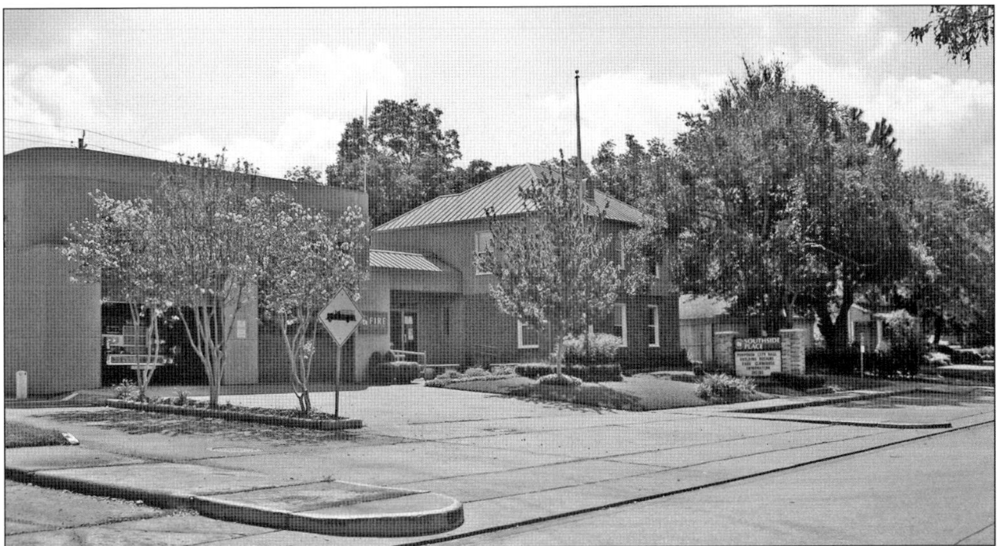

Continued growth required further expansion. In the early 1980s, the city acquired a house two lots south of the original city hall for $100,000. The police and fire station remained in the original city hall building, while the city administrative offices were relocated to the house. In 1986, a court room/city council chambers were added. The construction of a fire hall and larger fire truck bays linked the original city hall and the house as seen above. All these buildings would be replaced in 2010 with the construction of a modern city hall complex. (Courtesy of Kris Holt.)

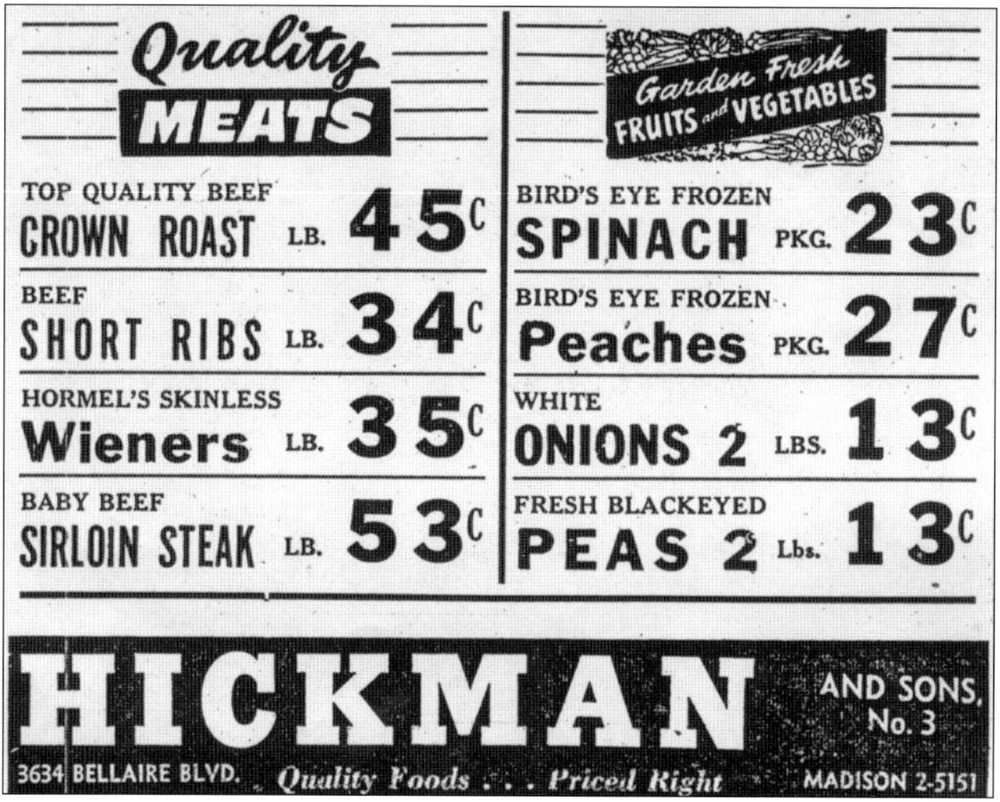

Quality MEATS			*Garden Fresh* FRUITS *and* VEGETABLES		
TOP QUALITY BEEF CROWN ROAST	LB.	45¢	BIRD'S EYE FROZEN SPINACH	PKG.	23¢
BEEF SHORT RIBS	LB.	34¢	BIRD'S EYE FROZEN Peaches	PKG.	27¢
HORMEL'S SKINLESS Wieners	LB.	35¢	WHITE ONIONS 2	LBS.	13¢
BABY BEEF SIRLOIN STEAK	LB.	53¢	FRESH BLACKEYED PEAS 2	Lbs.	13¢

HICKMAN AND SONS, No. 3

3634 BELLAIRE BLVD. *Quality Foods . . . Priced Right* MADISON 2-5151

After the war, homes began to occupy the remaining lots that once sat idle. A swelling population, improved roads, and expanded city services benefited existing small businesses that grew during the 1950s. The influx of new families supported several local grocery stores. Hickman and Sons opened its third grocery store in Houston in 1943 on the corner of Bellaire Boulevard and Edloe Street in Southside Place. In 1950, the store was expanded to twice its original size and reconfigured to face Edloe Street. The JMH Supermarket at 6204 College Street in West University Place (now Huffington Park) operated from 1938 to 2007. (Above, courtesy of Kate McCormick; below, Celestine and Rudy Darelik.)

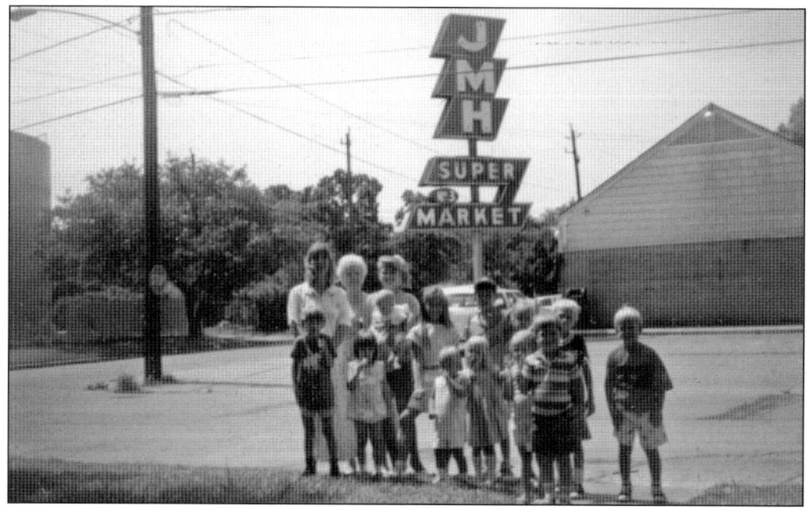

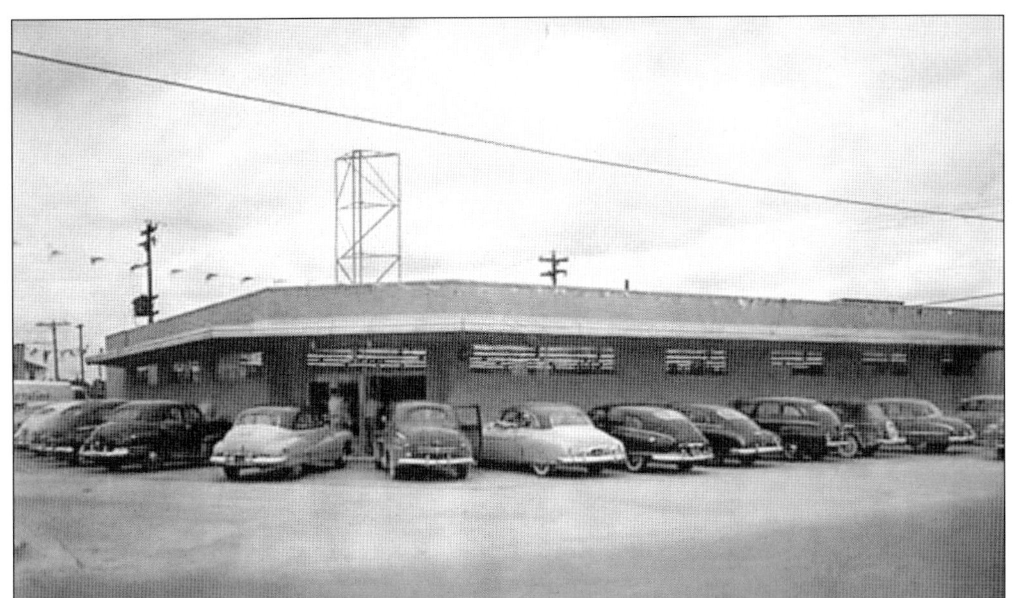

In 1950, JMH Grocery Stores expanded from one to two area locations with the opening of JMH No. 5 at Rice Boulevard and Edloe Street (pictured above on opening day). The second store was larger and had a courtesy booth (pictured below) and larger aisles. Regular customers enjoyed the convenience of house charge accounts. The original owners sold the store in 2001, and the small, friendly store maintained a loyal customer base until it closed permanently in 2007. The building was redeveloped into commercial space and a restaurant in 2010. (Both courtesy of Celestine and Rudy Darelik.)

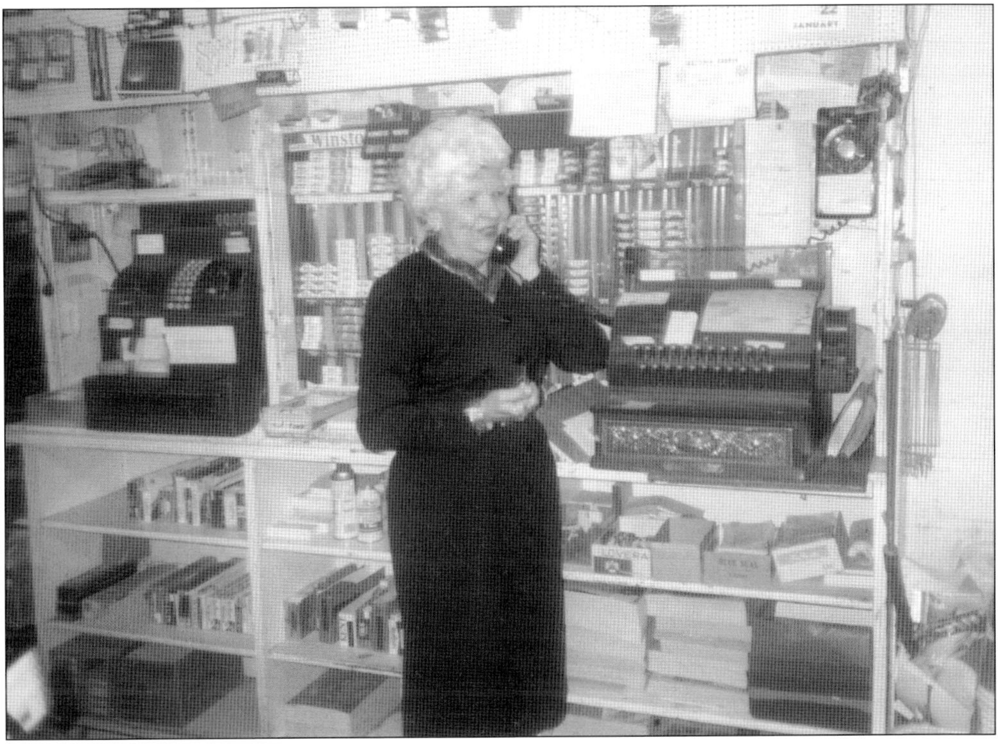

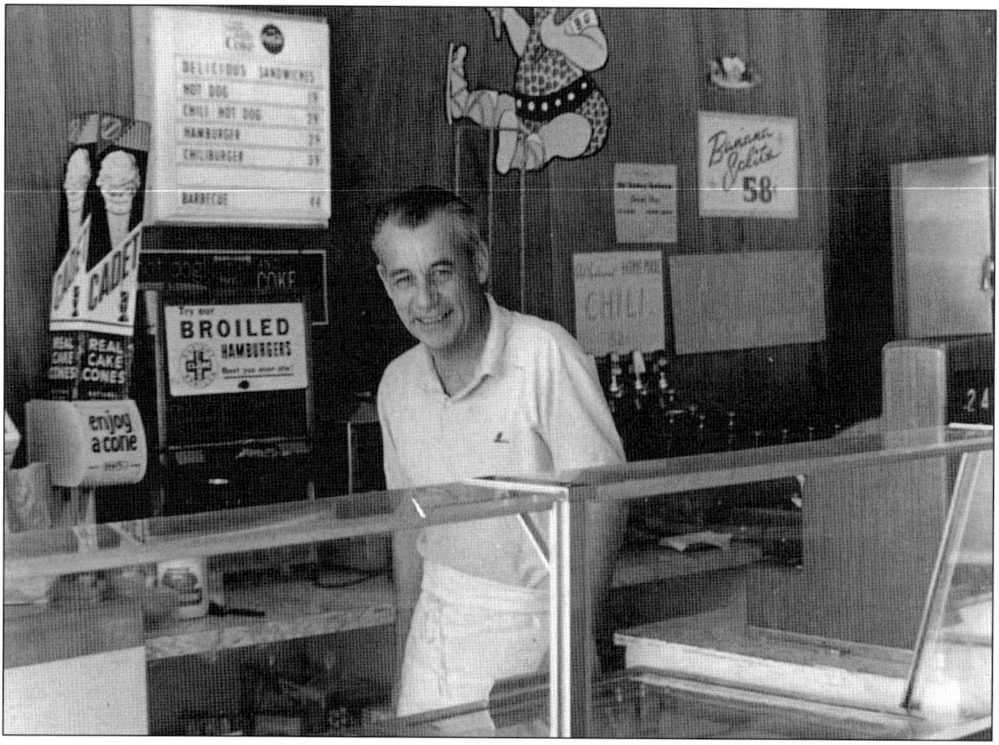

Many area businesses were owned and operated by Southside Place families. William Suhler (pictured above) and his family of 3728 Garnet Street operated a Baby Giant ice cream shop on University Boulevard. At the time, Baby Giant boasted more flavor choices than Baskin-Robbins. It was a popular after-school destination for West University Elementary schoolchildren. (Both courtesy of the Suhler family.)

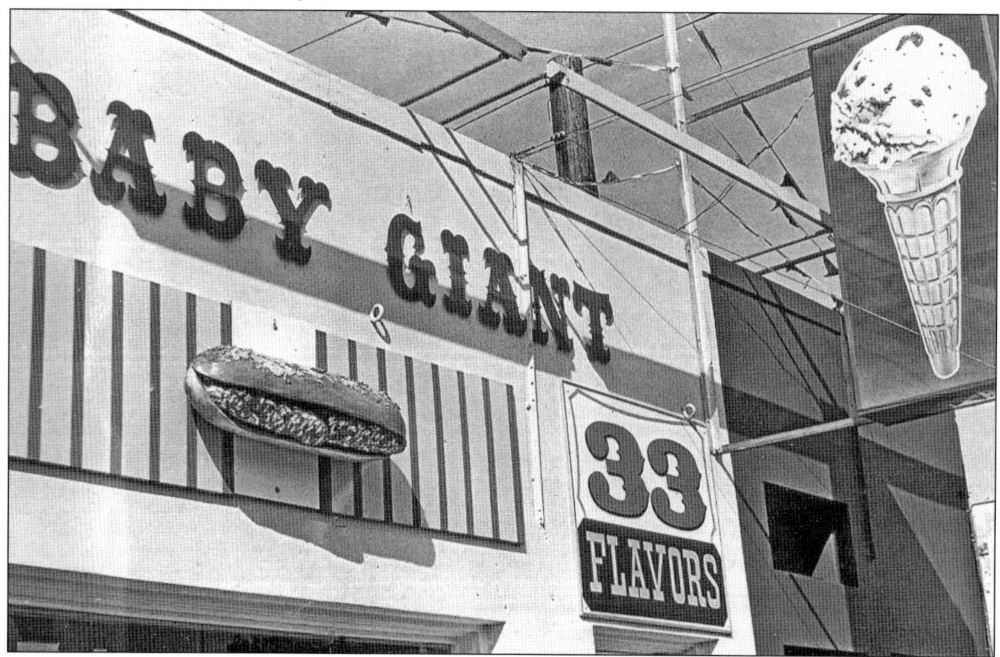

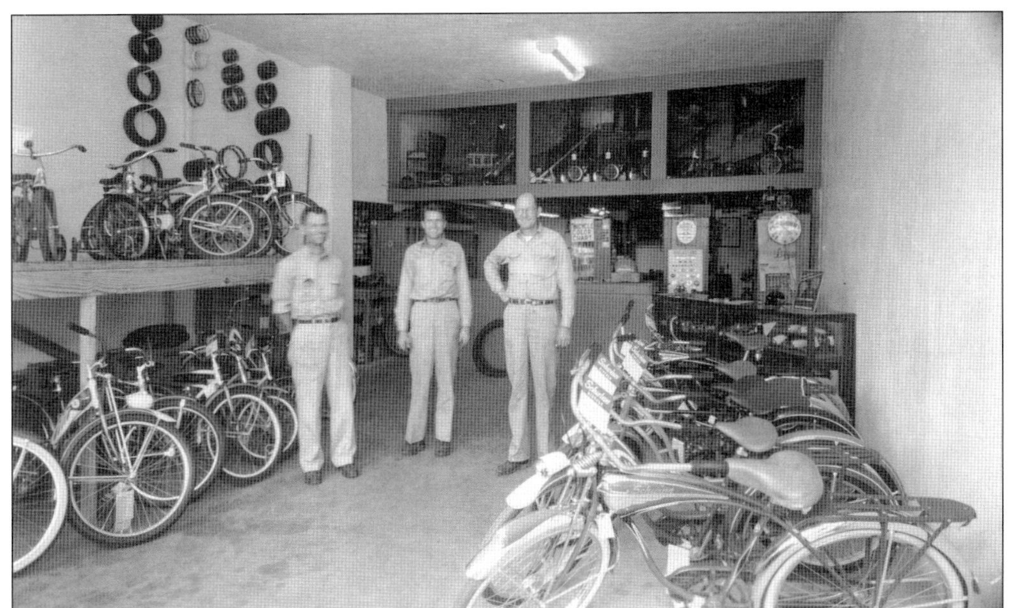

Arthur Ireson (pictured above, middle) purchased University Cycle and Lawnmower Shop in the Rice Village in 1947 and operated it for 56 years. With the war over and the government ban on peacetime luxury goods a thing of the past, pent-up demand for consumer goods kept factory assembly lines moving. From bicycles to lawn mowers and refrigerators to clothes dryers, domestic life was greatly improved with an influx of time-saving conveniences. The Skeltons' kitchen on Garnet Street (pictured below in the 1940s) shows the iron press and the variety of chores once done by hand. (Above, courtesy of Mary Ireson; below, Kelly Mears.)

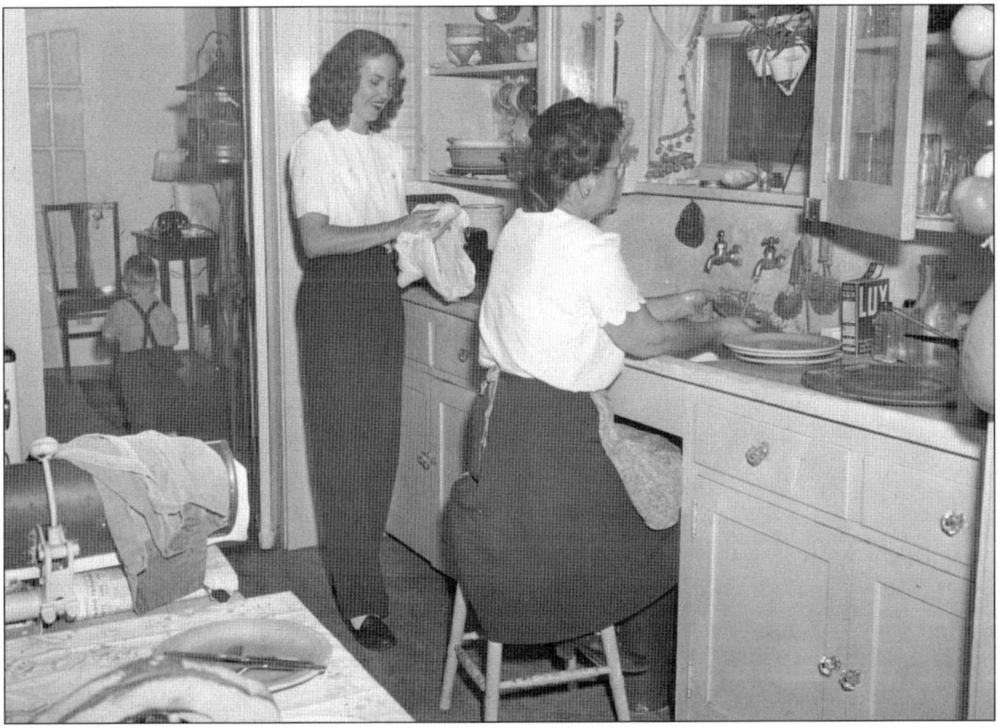

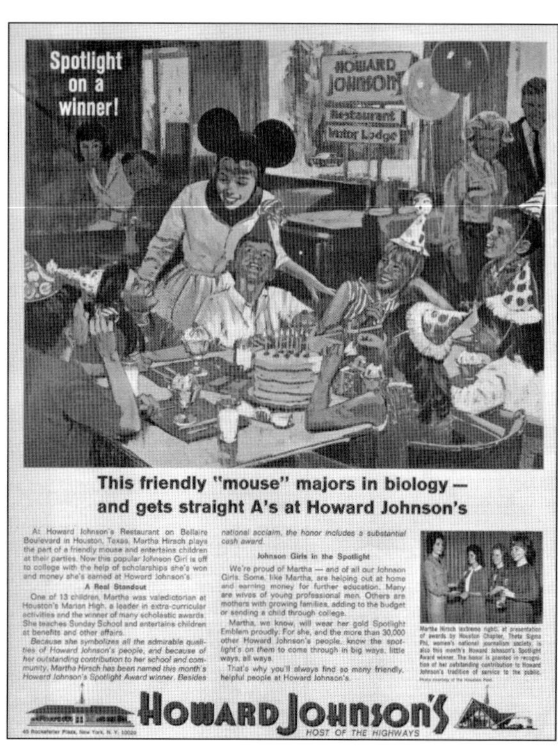

Commercial development on Bellaire Boulevard, Southside Place's southern border, was also in full swing. Howard Johnson's, known for its affordable restaurants and motor courts across the country, operated a restaurant at 4201 Bellaire Boulevard. Gramercy Street resident Martha Hirsch, one of 13 children, was featured in this classic advertisement as part of the restaurant's student scholarship program. The building has been home to Moeller's Bakery since 1990. (Courtesy of Kate McCormick.)

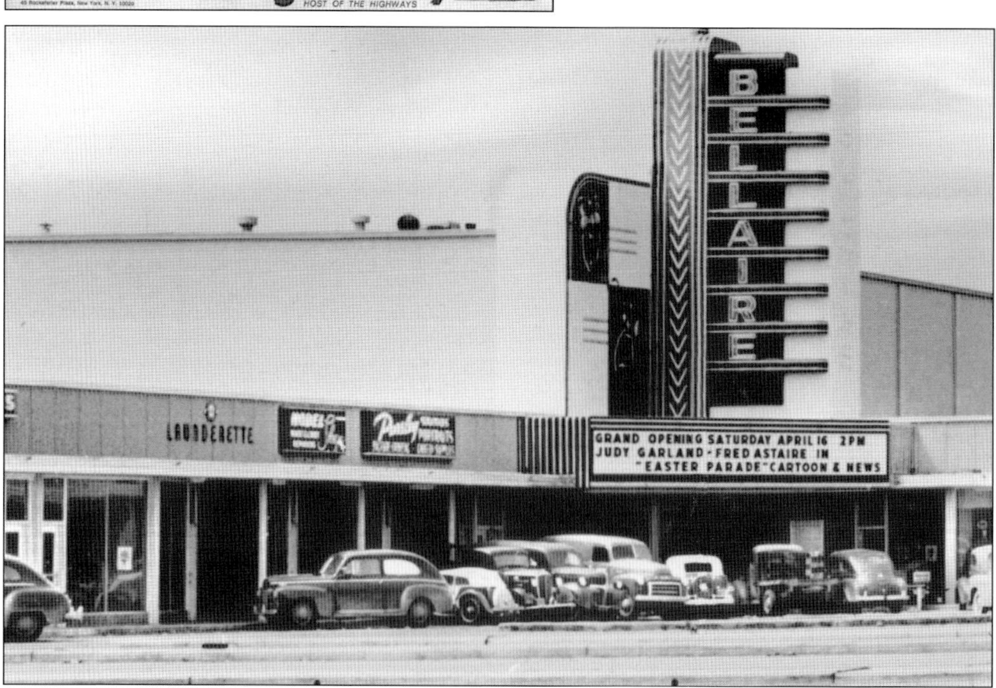

In 1949, the Bellaire Theatre opened on the 4000 block of Bellaire Boulevard. The closest movie theater, University Theatre on the 3600 block of University Boulevard, had closed the year before. The interior of the Bellaire Theatre featured murals by local artist Nione Carlson, who also designed the marquee. The theater operated until 1990 and is currently home to Whole Foods Market. (Courtesy of Mike McCorkle.)

TEN COMMANDMENTS

For Little League Parents

1. I shall not criticize the umpire unless ready to assume his duties.
2. I shall not complain about anyone unless I have labored more hours on the Little League program than they have.
3. I shall remember that only nine boys can play at any one time.
4. I shall not be a grandstand manager.
5. I shall set an example of sportsmanship for my son to follow.
6. I shall not be critical unless willing to put out necessary effort to correct my criticism.
7. I shall remember that all managers, officers, and ladies are volunteer workers.
8. I shall remember that all officers of the League must earn a living and cannot work on Little League full time.
9. I shall offer my services for work whenever possible.
10. I shall take my boy to Church on Sunday.

By the mid-1950s, a youth-oriented sports agenda took shape, and the Houston Little League was formed. In 1954, the name of the league changed to the West University Little League. The Ten Commandments for Little League Parents (right) was published in the 1958 Baseball League Book, which listed 60 Major League boys (4 teams), 164 Minor League boys (6 teams), and 76 Pee Wee League boys (4 teams). Games were played at the Coca-Cola Field located on the West University Elementary School grounds. Today, the West University Little League is one of the largest leagues in the country, with more than 1,300 boys and girls on its rosters. (Right, courtesy of Kris Holt; below, Ann Young.)

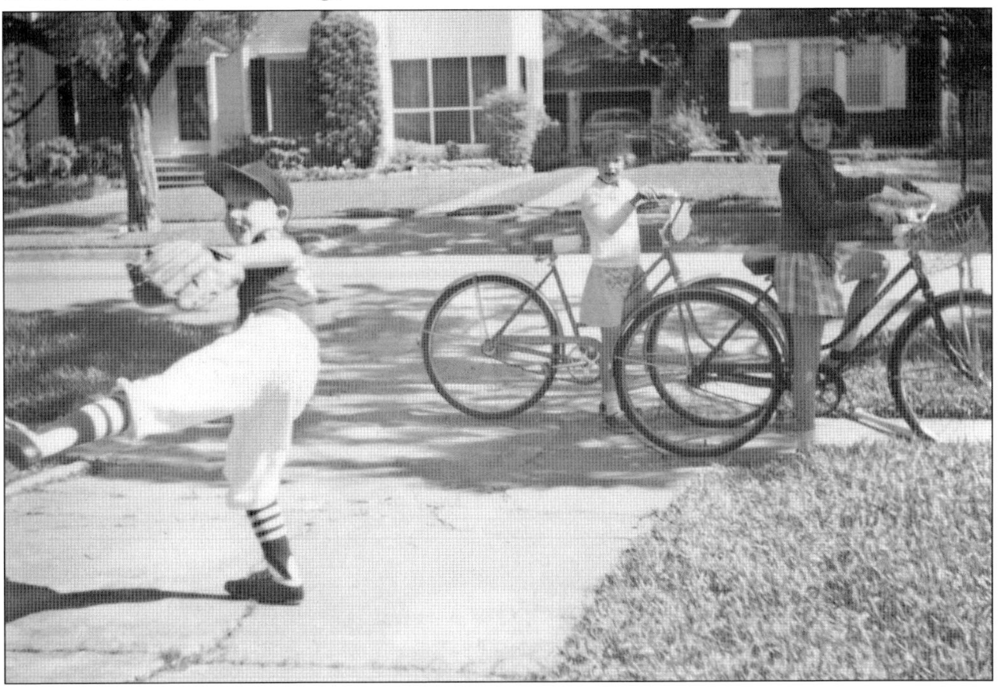

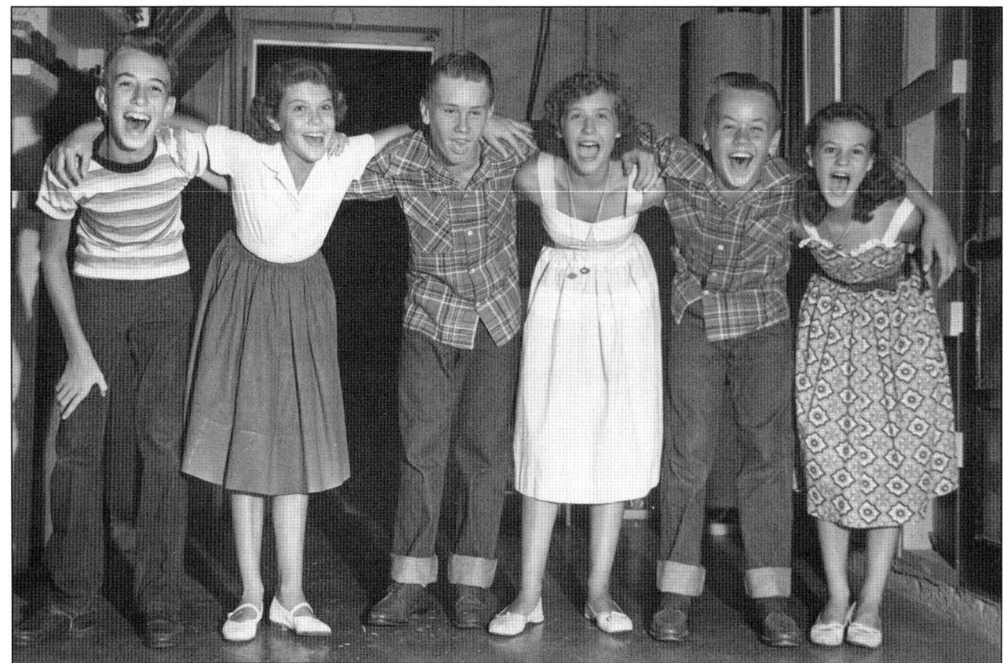

Postwar growth and prosperity influenced most American households, and Southside Place was no different. These quintessential images of a garage theater performance on Darcus Street in the 1950s, and Christmas Day on University Boulevard in the 1960s, reflect the influences of a robust economy and depict happy prosperous times. (Above, courtesy of Kelly Mears; below, Roger Judson.)

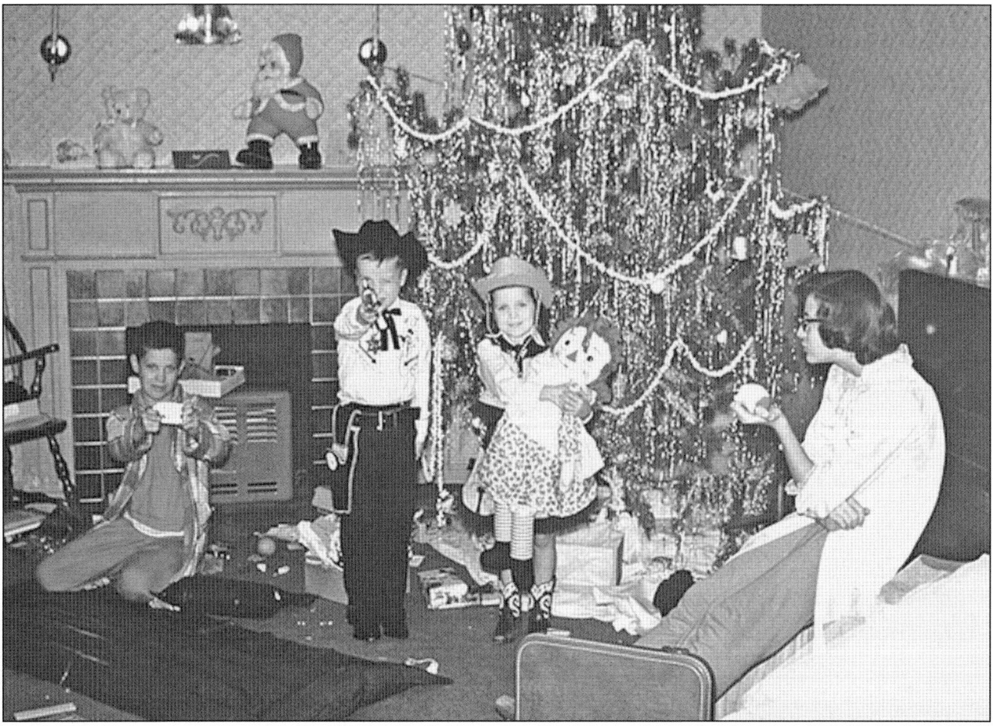

Seven

Southside Place Celebrates America's Bicentennial

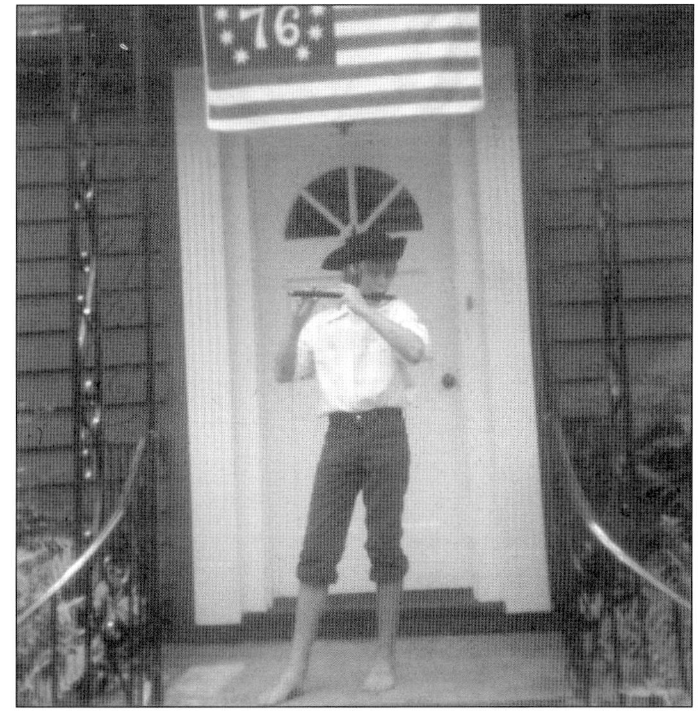

Initially, the federal government's plans to commemorate the US Bicentennial focused on a single-city, national event. The idea of one event to commemorate the anniversary of the country's founding was ultimately rejected in favor of local observances. The American Revolution Bicentennial Administration developed a program to allow a locality to be designated a "Bicentennial Community" if it engaged in activities to promote the bicentennial. Southside Place enthusiastically accepted the challenge. (Courtesy of Ann Young.)

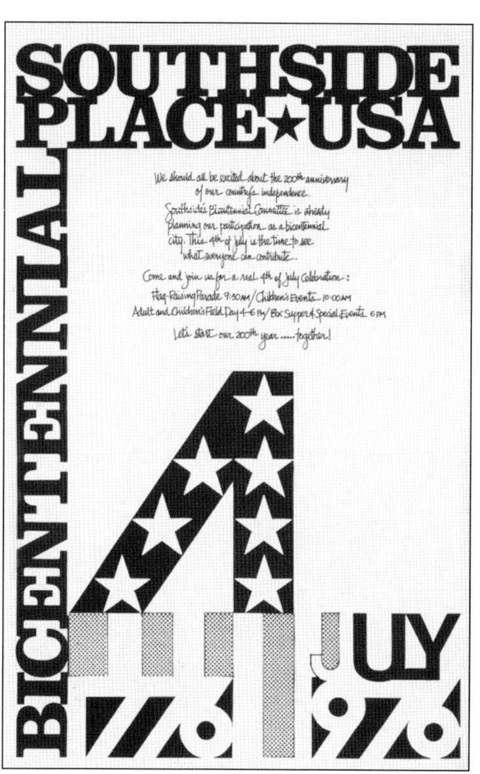

In 1975, Southside Place began its efforts to receive the Bicentennial Community designation. It created a Bicentennial Committee to identify projects that furthered the enumerated goals of the bicentennial: heritage, horizons, and festival. The city's festival projects were numerous and diverse. This 1975 poster announced the initial wave of festivities to Southside Place residents and began the community's yearlong commemoration. In addition to painting the fire hydrants and the city water tower red, white, and blue, the committee hosted a July 4, 1975, flag-raising parade, as well as swimming and field events at the park, a picnic, and a square dance. (Left, courtesy of Ann Young; below, Harriett Bevil.)

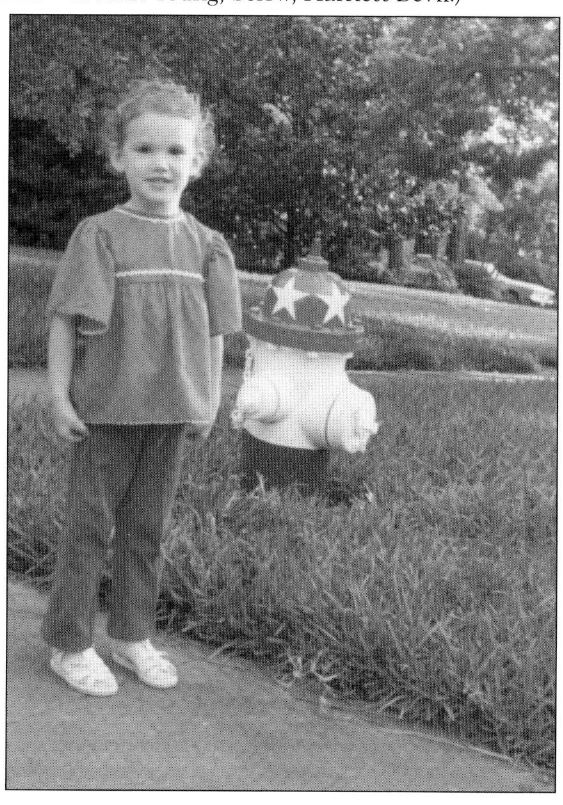

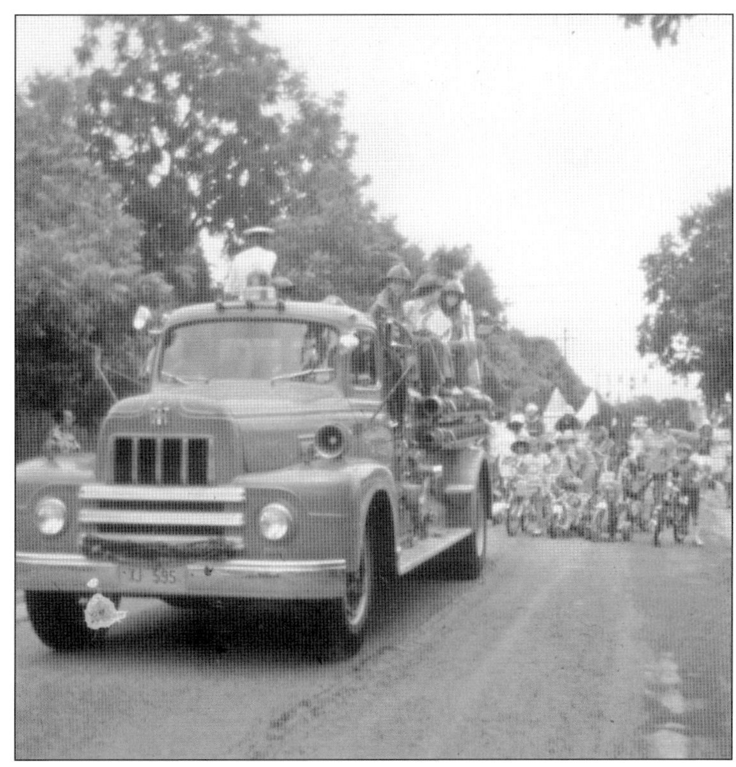

The flag-raising parade evolved into a bike and wagon parade that became a Fourth of July neighborhood tradition. This photograph from the 1976 bike parade shows Engine One from the Southside Place Fire Department leading the parade from Southside Place City Hall down Edloe Street to Fire Truck Park. (Courtesy of Ann Young.)

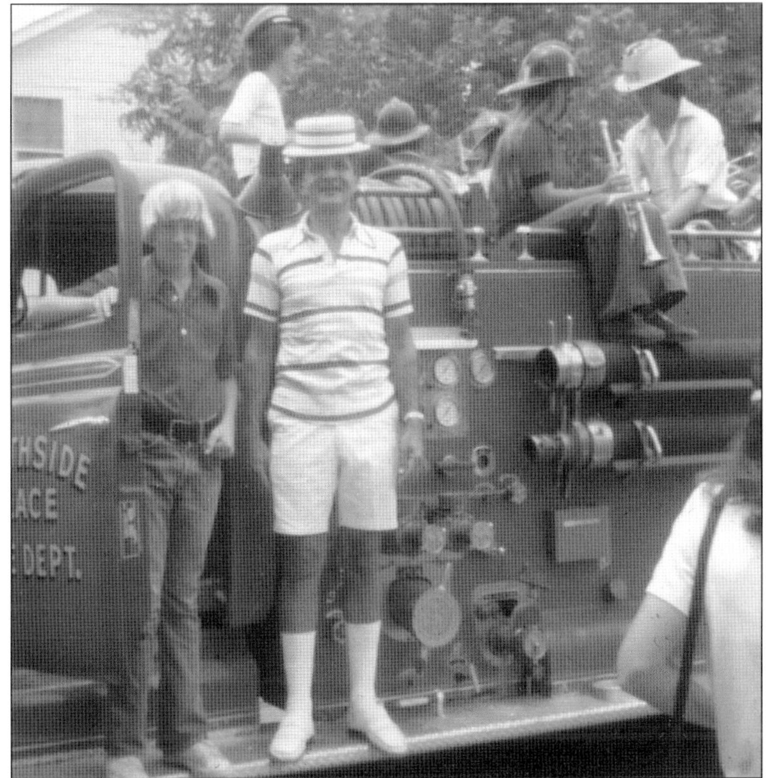

Allan Young and his father, Seth, posed for a picture on Engine One at the 1976 July Fourth parade. Seth Young would later become a three-term mayor, council member, and city manager until his retirement in 1999. The Youngs have called Southside Place home since 1967. (Courtesy of Ann Young.)

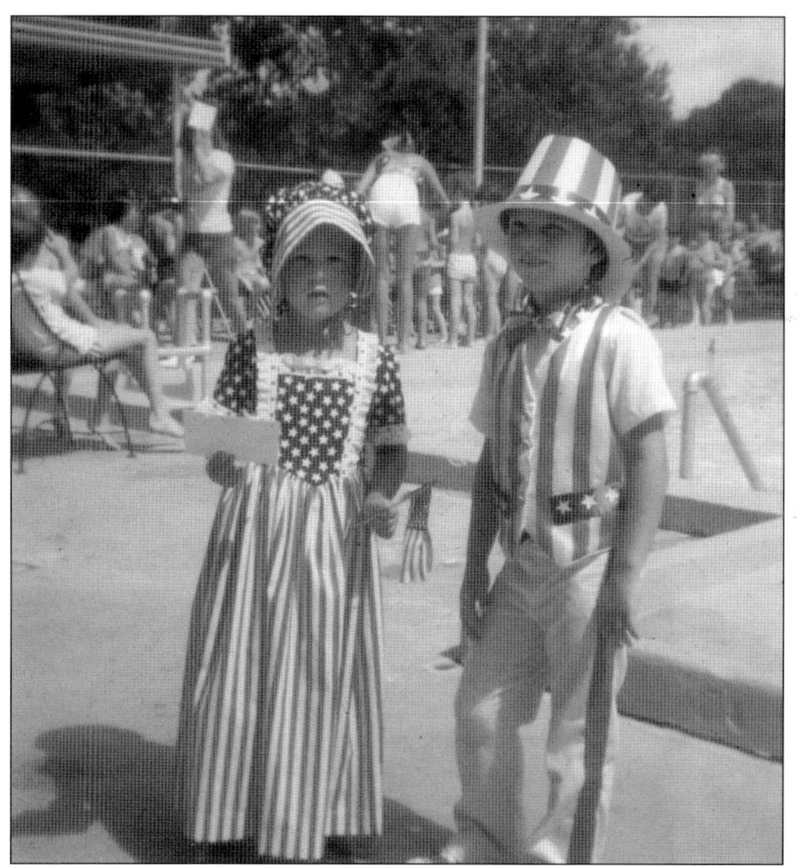

The parade ended at the park, where awards were given to the "most creative," "most decorated," and "most patriotic" contestants in the bike parade. The July Fourth festivities that began in 1975 continue to the present. This bike contestant shows his red, white, and blue in 1995. (Left, courtesy of Ann Young; below, Kris Holt.)

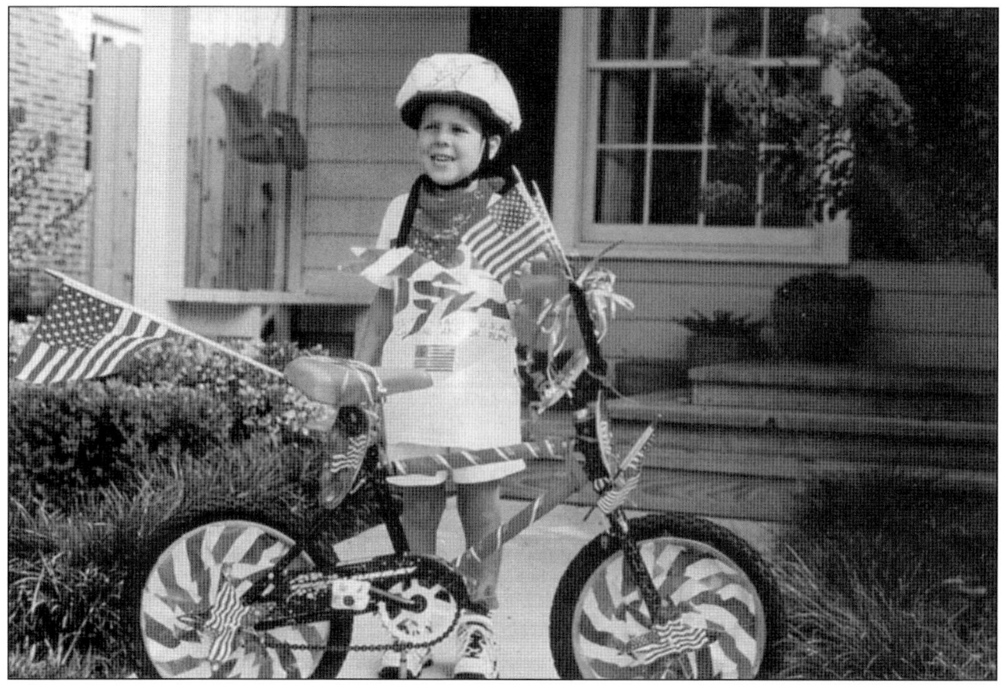

Although the square dance has fallen out of favor with residents, the July Fourth swimming and field events organized as part of the bicentennial remain popular. Residents of all ages continue to gather at the park after the parade for an afternoon of swimming, pool games, and activities. "Lady Liberty," in full regalia, kicked off the pool events in 1975 by floating on water, while in 1999, it was the greased watermelon toss that got the crowd to jump in. (Right, courtesy of Ann Young; below, Kris Holt.)

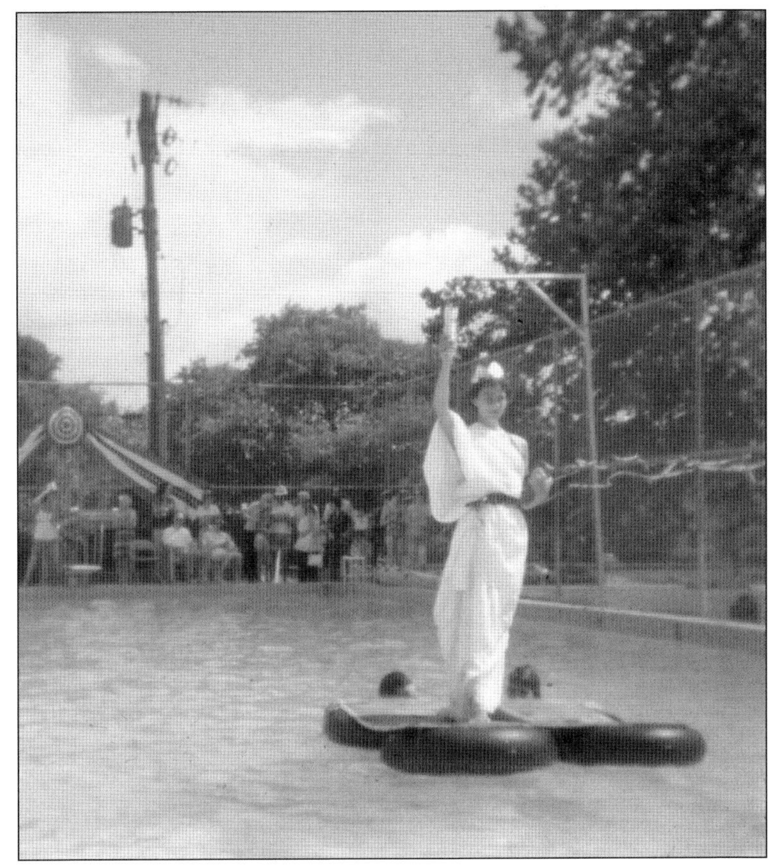

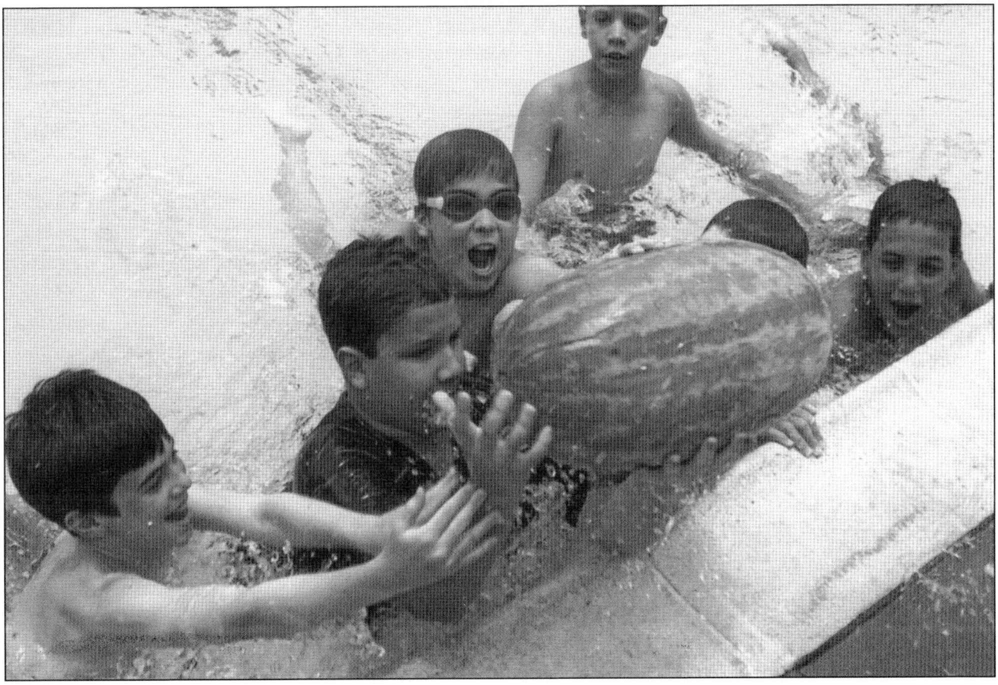

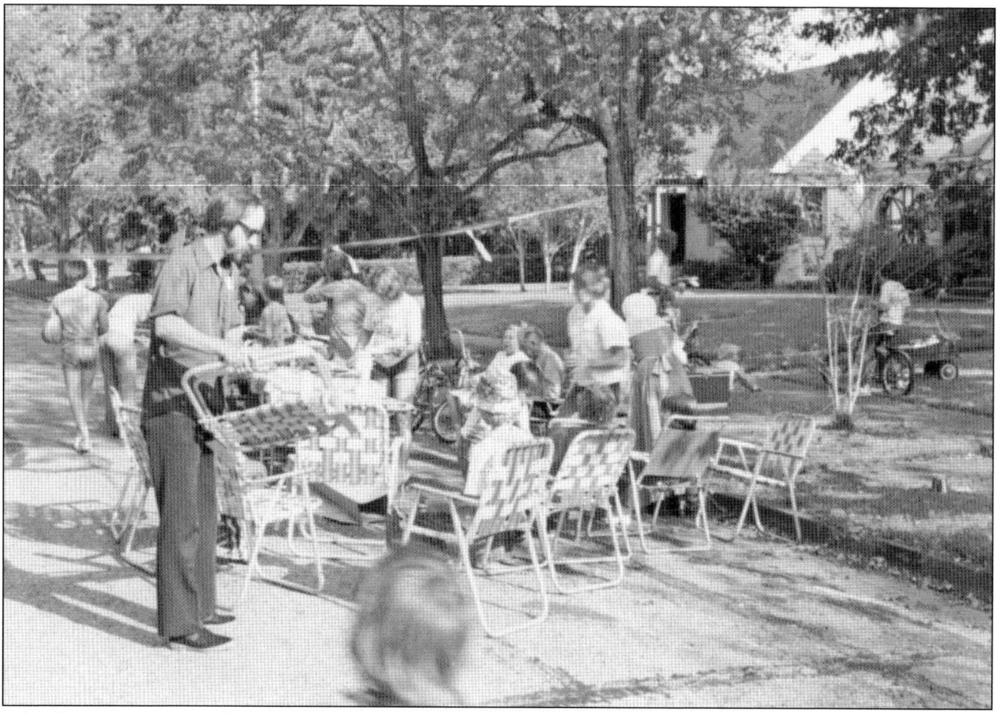

The first community block party was held in the fall of 1975, with the original 13 US Colonies represented by each of the 13 streets in Southside Place. Each street had its own block party, and then, displaying original flags and banners, they "united" at the park for dessert, a concert, and a chance to meet and greet their neighbors. (Above, courtesy of Harriett Bevil; below, Ann Young.)

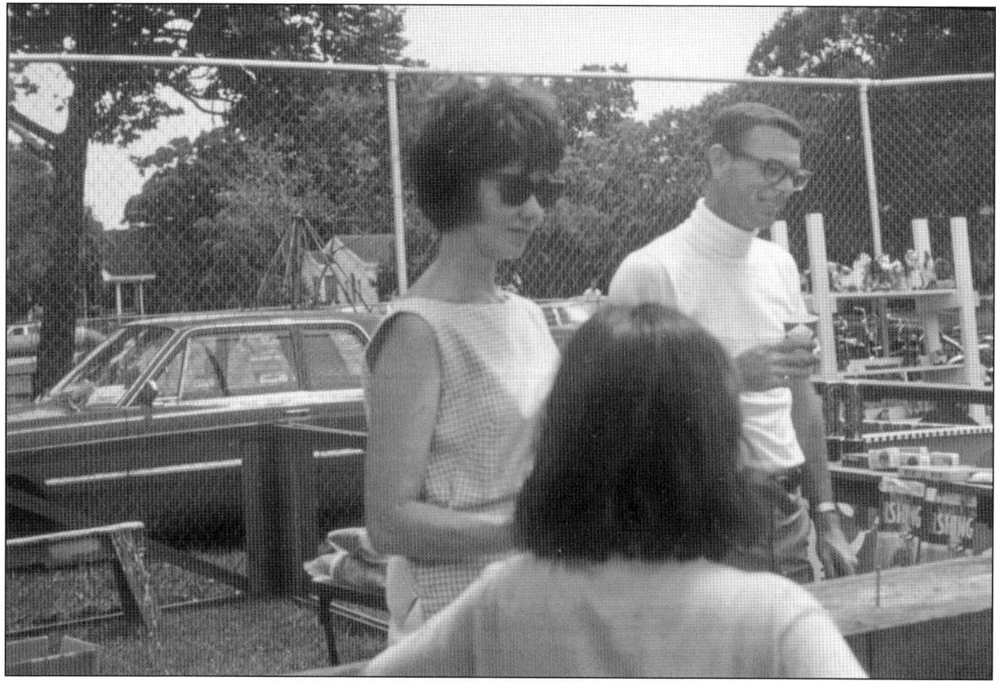

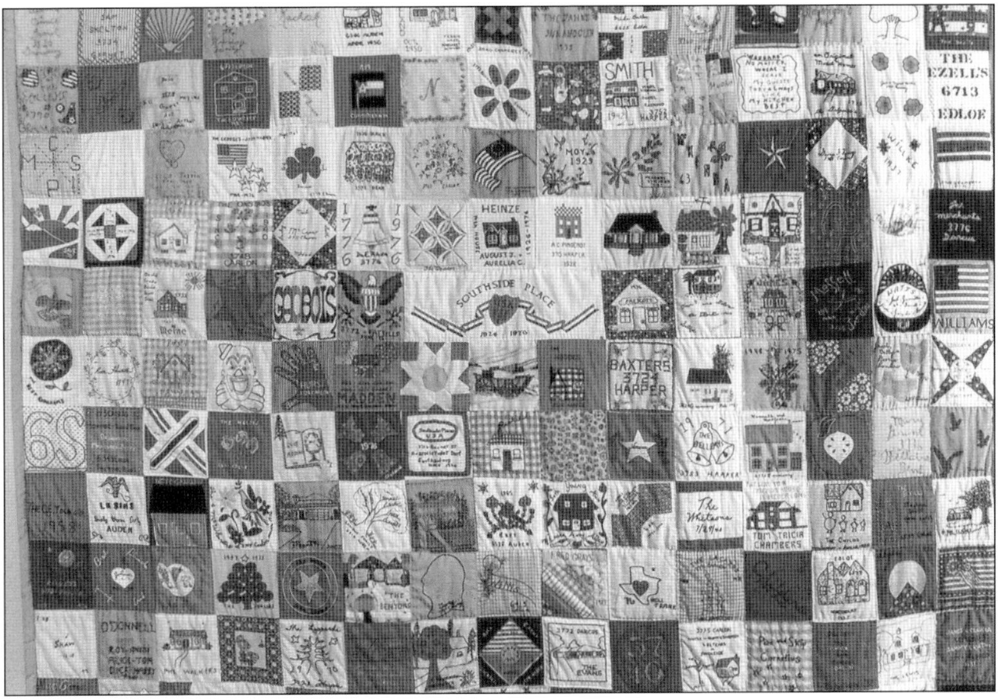

The legacy of the Bicentennial Committee's festival project was a "friendship quilt." Spearheaded by Carlon Street resident Ann Young and crafted in part by the 1975–1976 Women's Club, the quilt was assembled by residents in commemoration of the bicentennial. Each household was sent a quilt pattern with a request to create a five-inch square both memorable and personal. The response was tremendous. Unique, colorful, and thoughtfully considered, 225 individually quilted squares were collected and sewn together by a team of neighborhood women in the park clubhouse. The quilt proudly hung in the clubhouse meeting room until 2011. It is now on public display at the Southside Place City Hall. (Above, courtesy of Joe Gayle; right, Ann Young.)

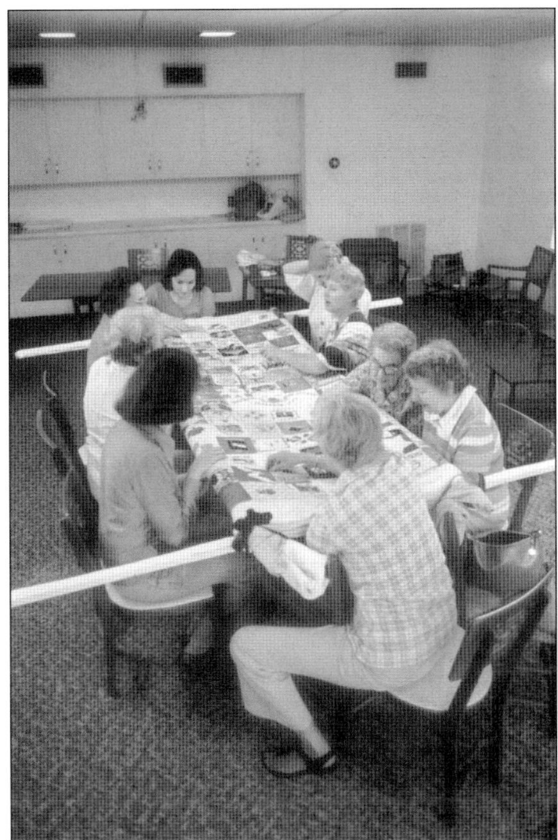

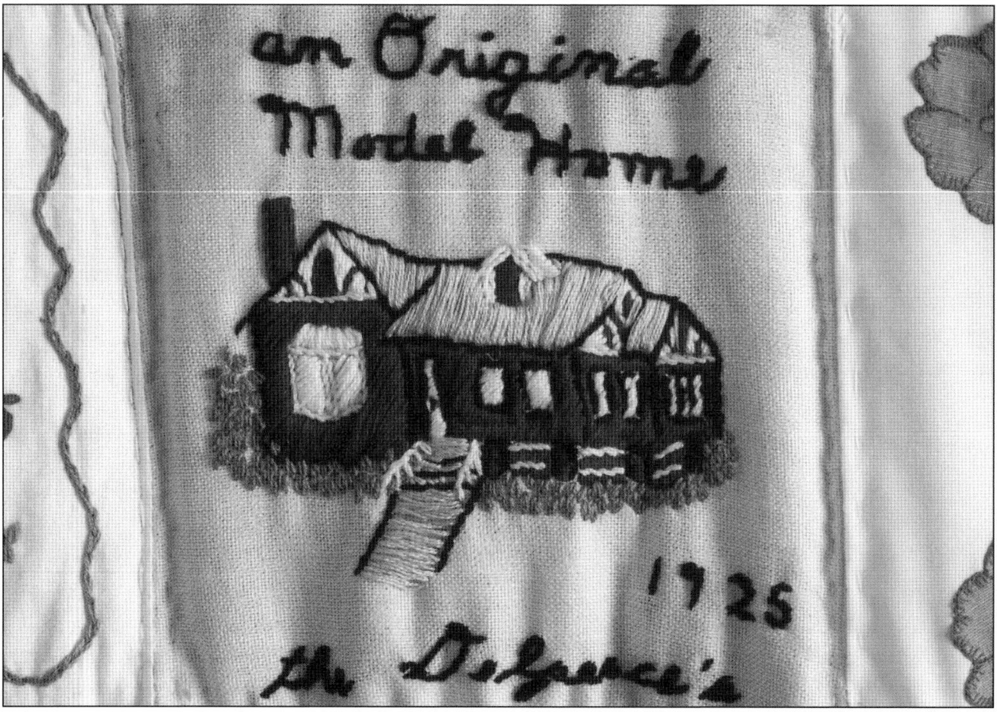

The friendship quilt offers an inimitable perspective on the history of Southside Place. These two quilt squares are key to weaving the narrative of the city's early beginnings. The square of the original 1925 Crain Ready-Cut model home (above) was handsomely stitched by Shirley Delpesce, who acquired the house at 3734 Elmora Street after she married. Her parents, August and Aurelia Heinze, lived just around the corner at 3757 Farbar Street. The square below shows her parents' home as the 14th house built by the Crain Ready-Cut House Company in 1926. Shirley's childhood years on Farbar Street allotted her and her family the distinction of being one of the first families of Southside Place. (Both courtesy of Joe Gayle.)

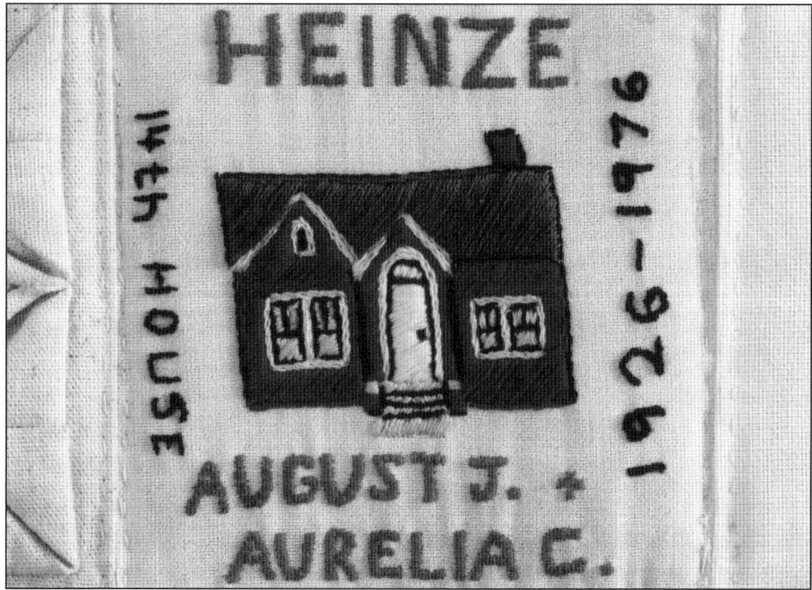

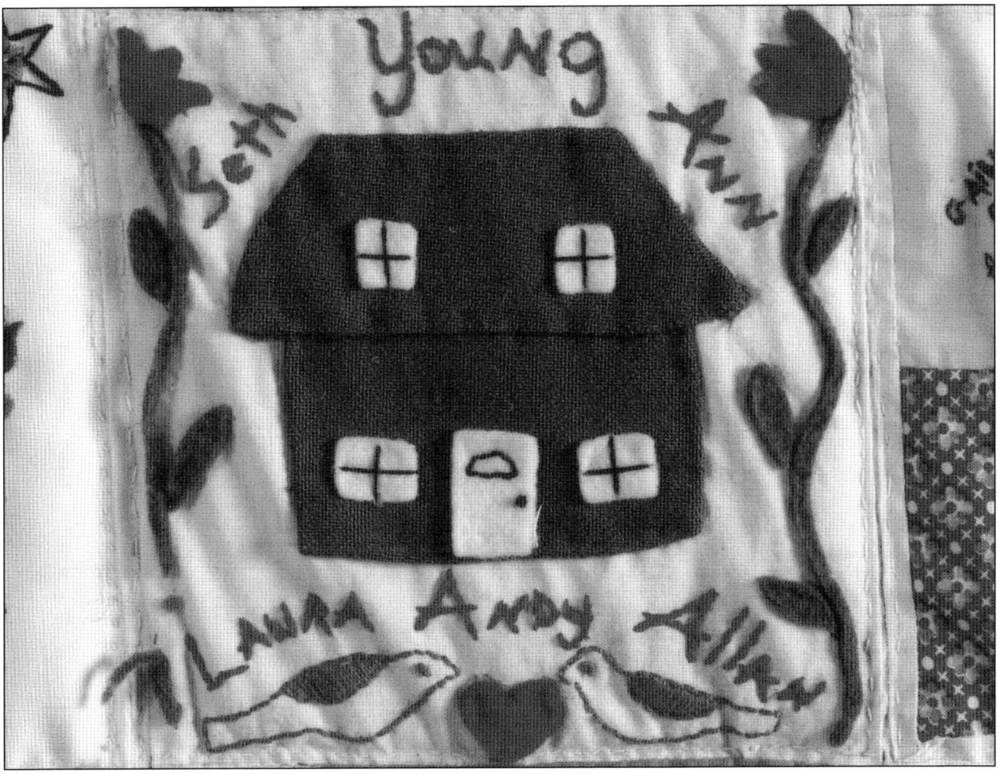

The quilt square that a family contributed often represented the home they lived in. Bicentennial quilt creator Ann Young and her family contributed the square above. Many branded their squares with their family surname. (Both courtesy of Joe Gayle.)

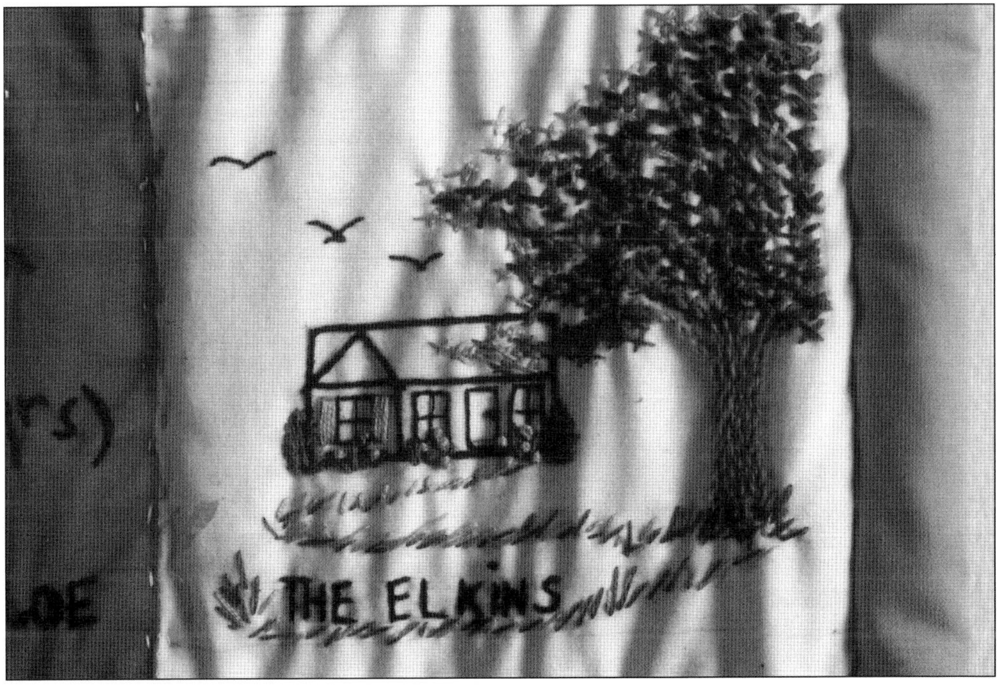

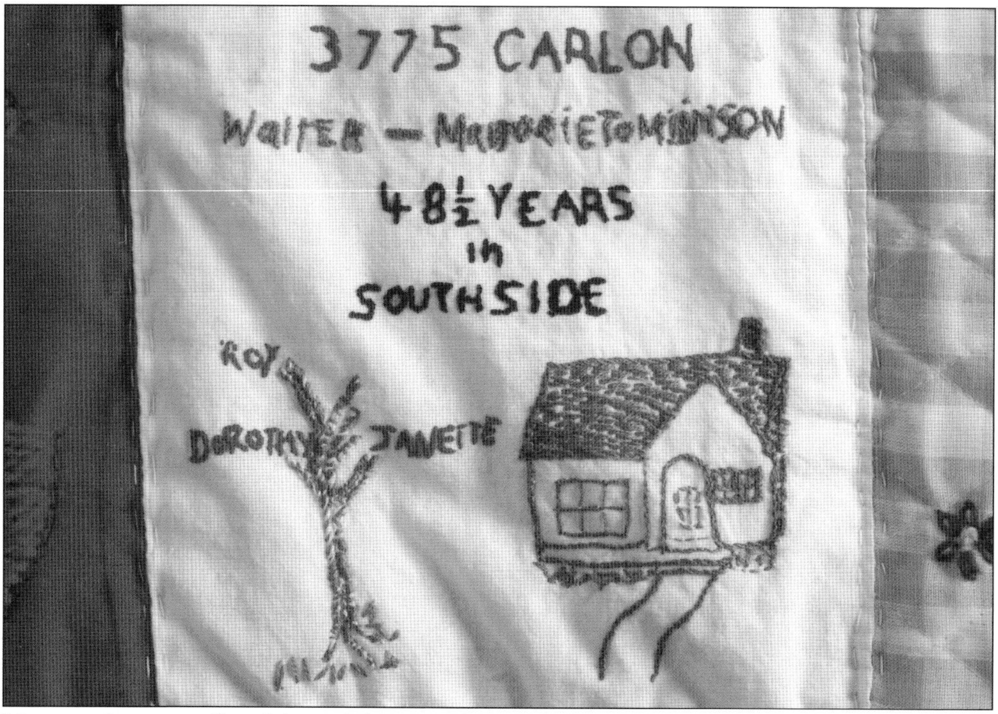

Many residents proudly celebrated the years they resided at their Southside Place address. Crafted with great care, the quilt squares provide a rare glimpse of the early architecture in the city. (Both courtesy of Joe Gayle.)

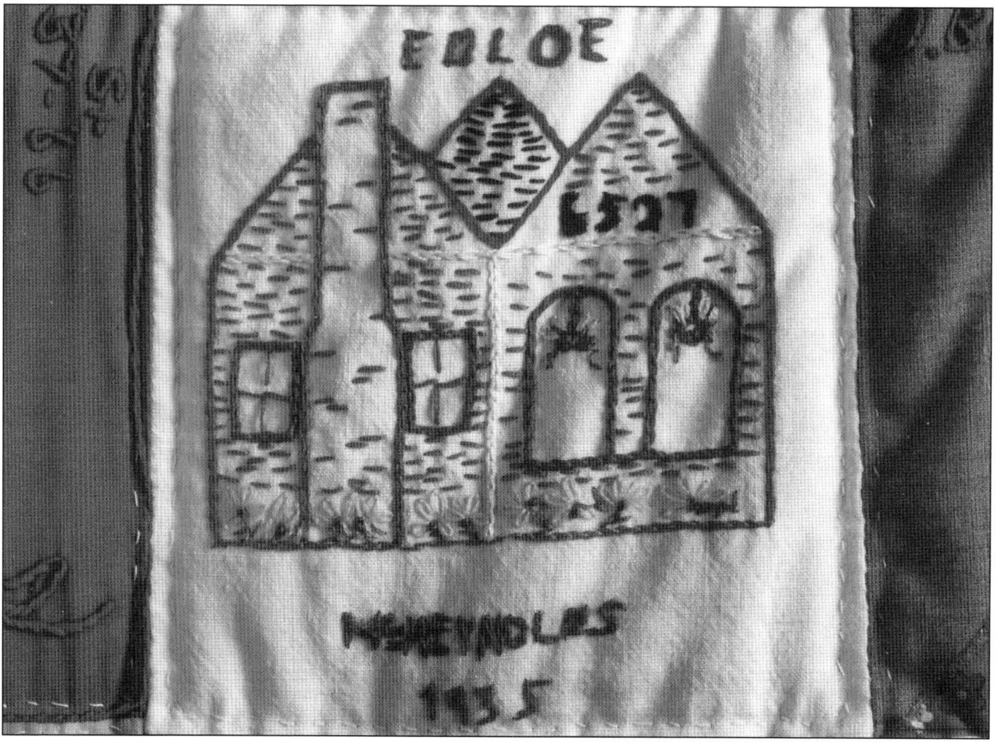

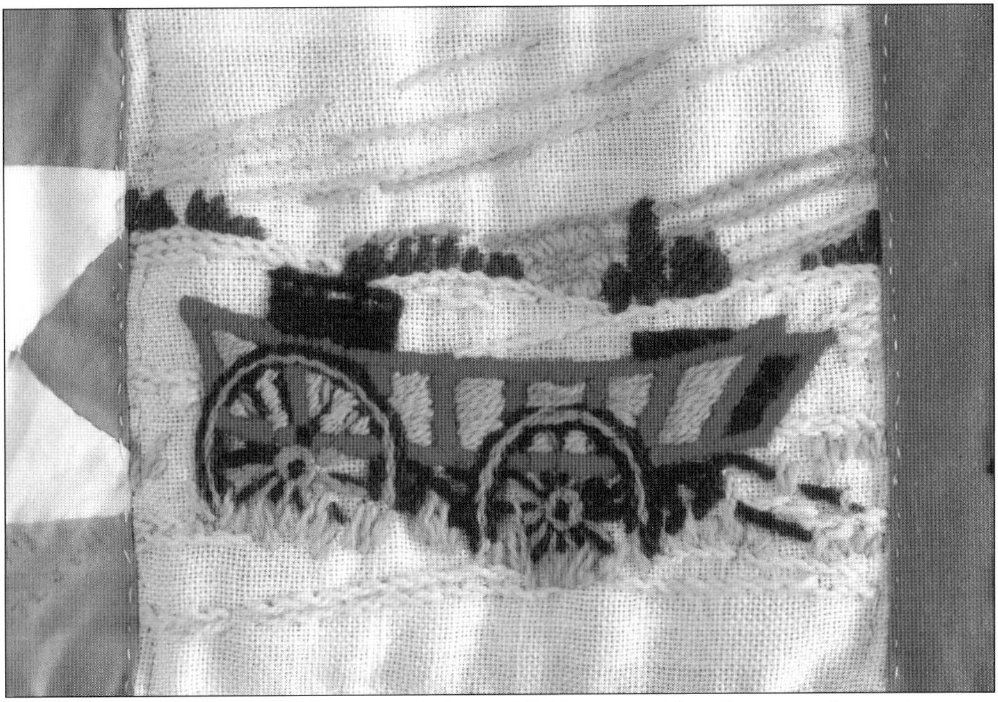

Many quilt squares are symbolic or simply beautiful. The peaceful quilt square of a sturdy wagon at rest under a sunset sky above shows superb skill with the needle. It was lovingly sewn by Ruth Stillwagon, a longtime resident and volunteer. The square below represents a home built in 1926 at 3709 Garnet Street, currently the oldest Ready-Cut home remaining in the city. This tightly stitched square is notable, as it strongly resembles the well-preserved home as it is known today. (Both courtesy of Joe Gayle.)

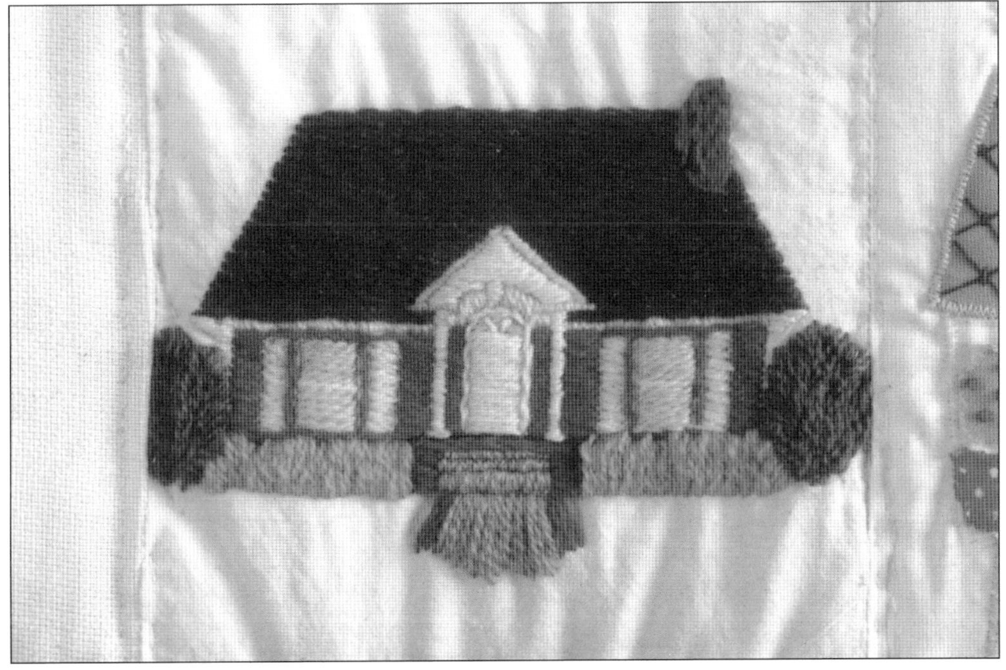

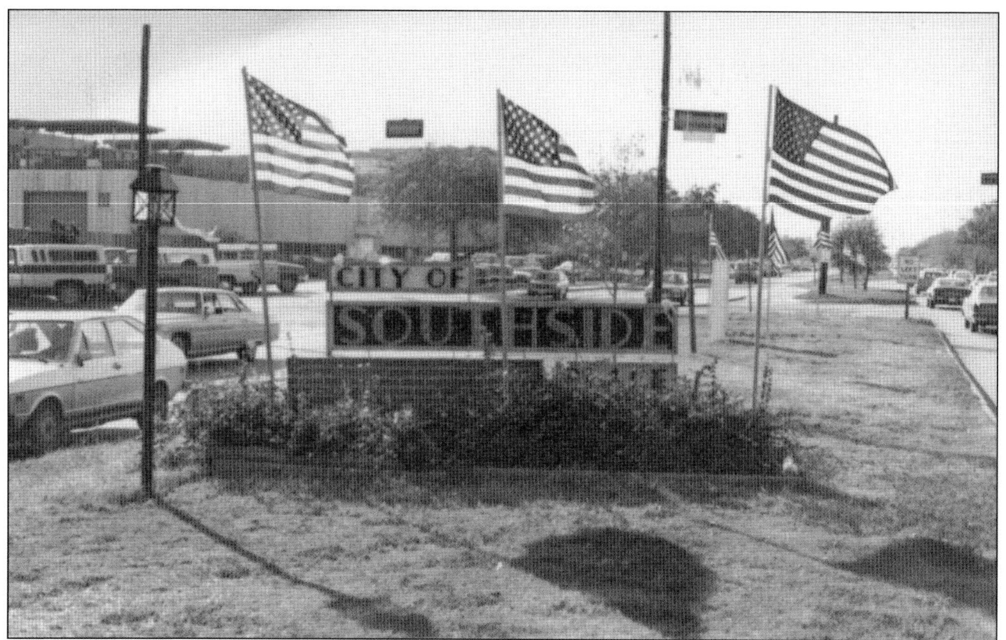

Local businesses also participated in the festival project in 1976 by creating a "parade of flags" along Bellaire Boulevard, Southside Place's business district. Here, flags flank the signage identifying the beginning of Southside Place along Bellaire Boulevard near Edloe Street. (Courtesy of SSP.)

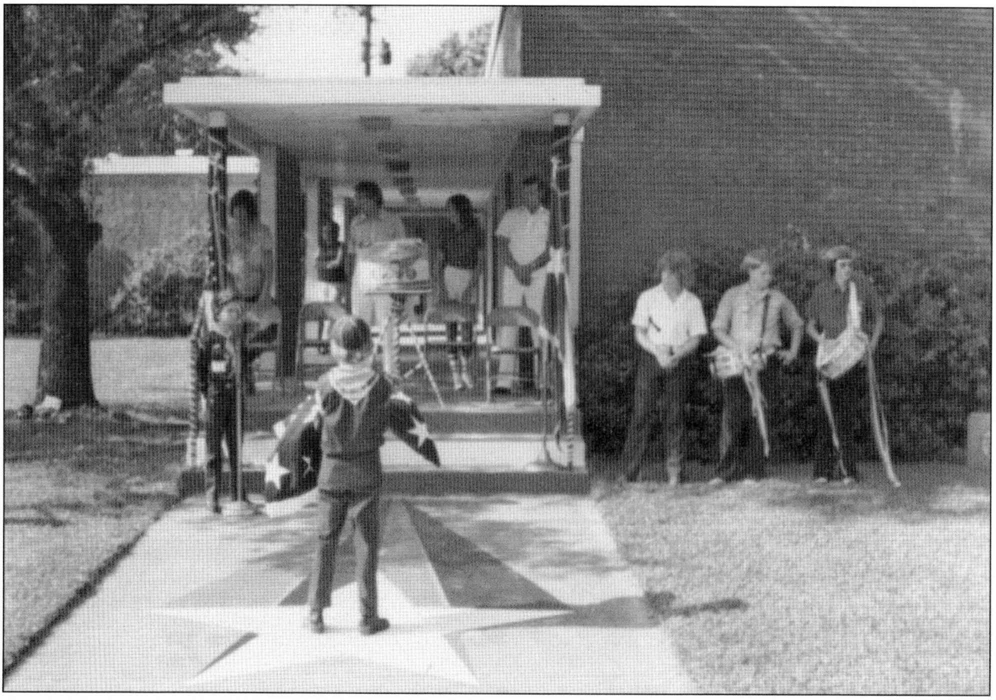

A Junior Bicentennial Committee comprised of neighborhood children and youth organizations participated in ceremonies at the clubhouse recognizing Southside Place's designation as a Bicentennial Community on July 4, 1976. The committee created a time capsule that was buried in the park with instructions that it be opened in 100 years. (Courtesy of Harriett Bevil.)

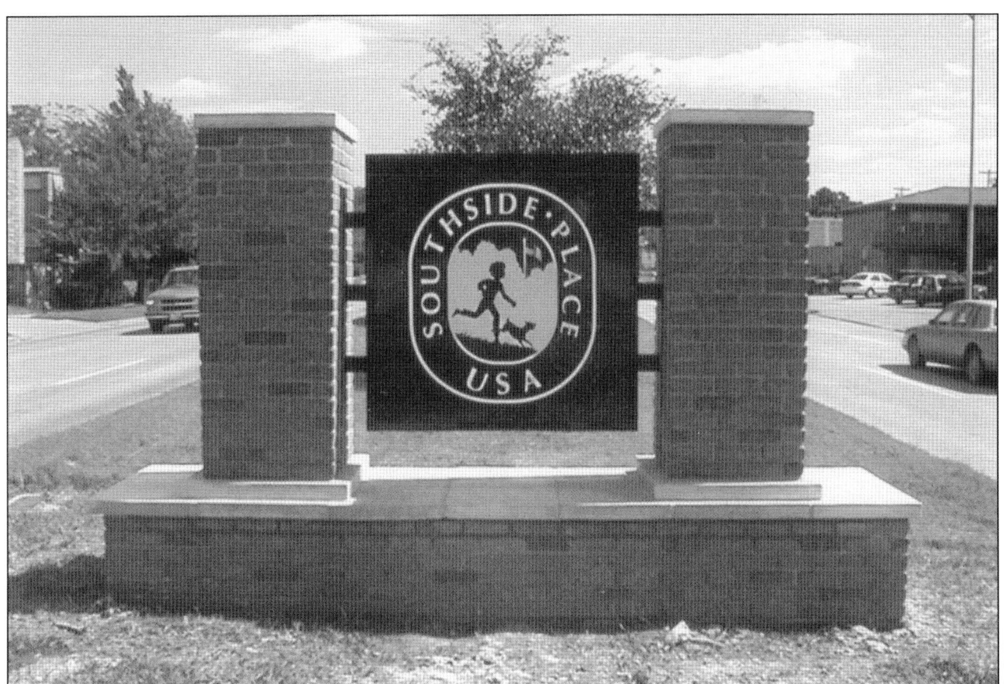

For its horizon project, the committee chose to make improvements to the park, including building a brick patio between the pool and the clubhouse and renovating the tennis courts. To raise funds, local graphic designer and resident Jerry Herring created a Southside Place logo that was put on T-shirts sold in the community. This was the first time the city began referring to itself as "Southside Place, USA." The now-iconic logo of a silhouetted child running with his dog and the American flag in the distance still graces T-shirts, as well as the signage on Bellaire Boulevard. (Both courtesy of Kris Holt.)

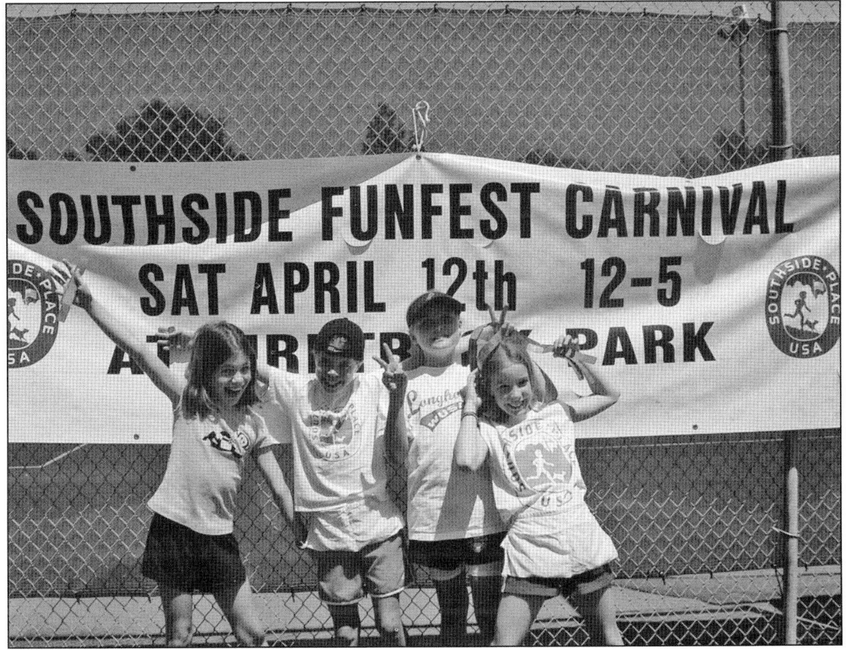

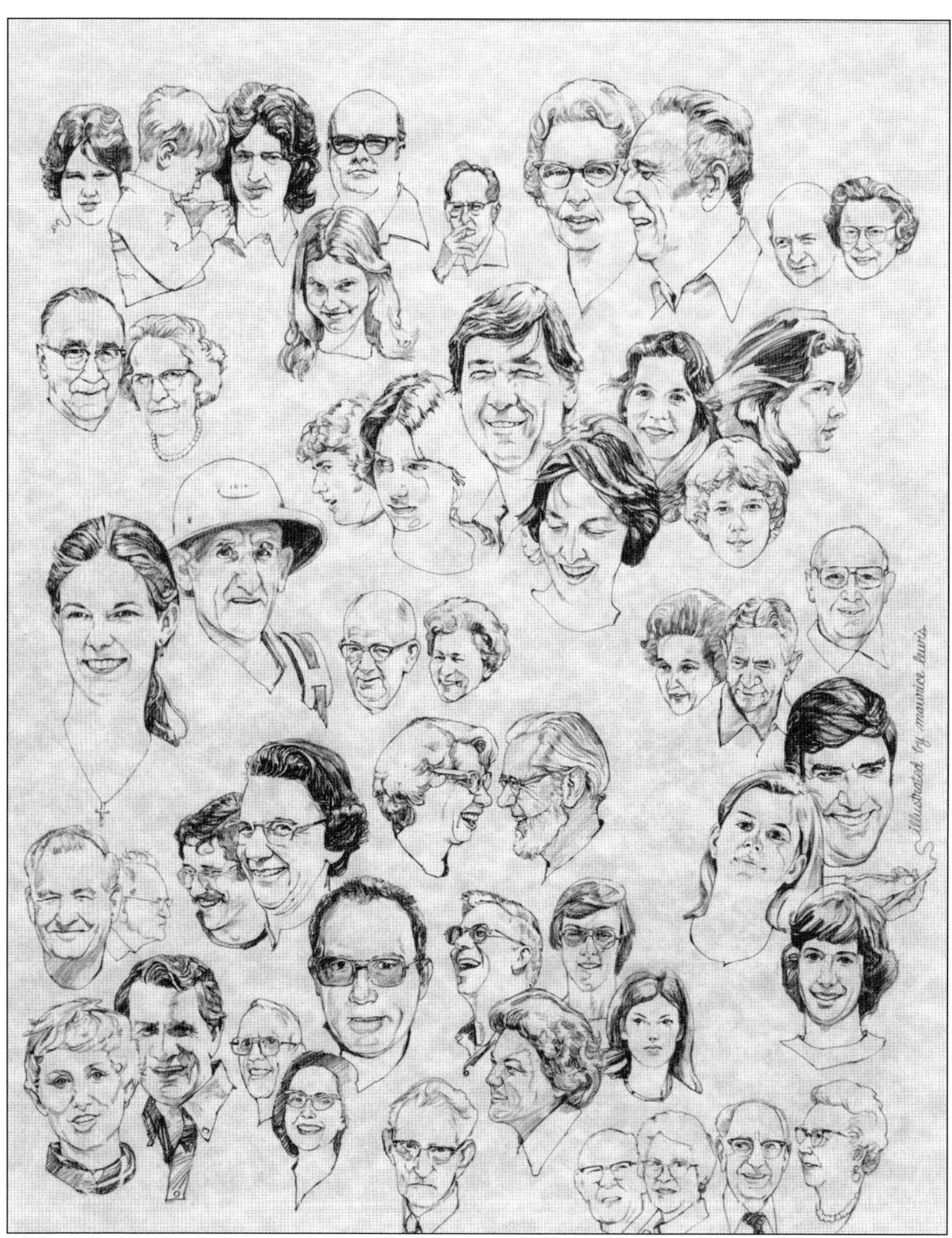

The heritage project and the culmination of the city's efforts to be designated as a Bicentennial Community was a detailed history of Southside Place. From the 1831 land grant to Allen C. Reynolds to the establishment of the subdivision by E.L. Crain in 1924 and ending with the city's efforts to commemorate the bicentennial, the city's history and related photographs were bound in a book as a keepsake for residents. The book includes character illustrations throughout by artist and Southside Place resident Maurice Lewis, who noted at the time, "Southside Place is like a small town. All of the characters in my mythical all-American community are right here." (Courtesy of Maurice Lewis.)

Eight

Pool, Park, Clubhouse, and Social Clubs

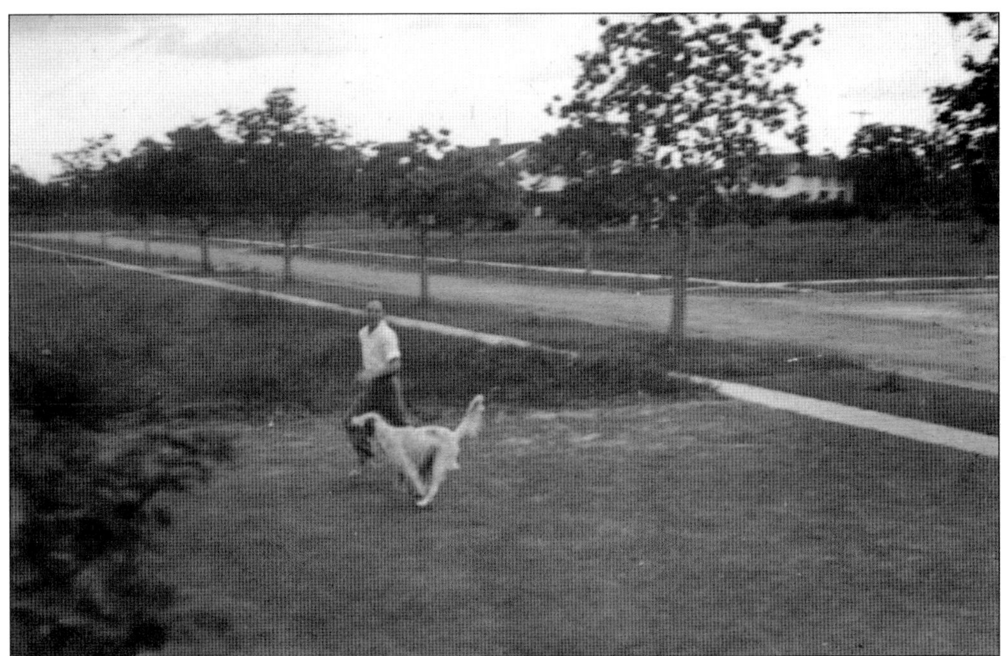

When E.L. Crain platted Southside Place in 1924, he carved out a 1.5-acre park as its civic center. Nestled between Garnet and Farbar Streets, the park was considered extraordinary for its time. Eagerly promoted in marketing brochures, the park boasted a tennis court, swimming pool, bathhouse, clubhouse, and an open field for play. This image of a boy running with his dog in the 1930s may have been the inspiration for the city logo. The park remains the neighborhood's most defining attribute. (Courtesy of Kelly Mears.)

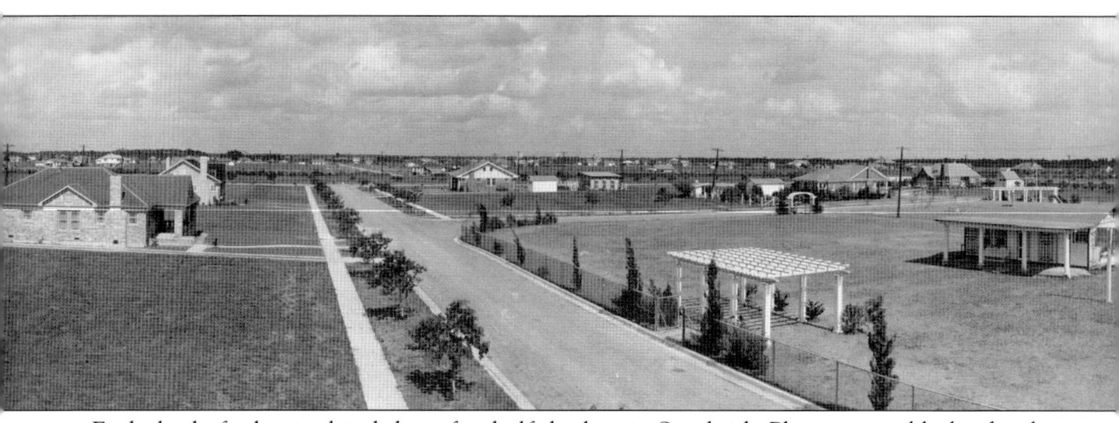

Each deed of sale stipulated that after half the lots in Southside Place were sold, the developer would deed the park to a neighborhood association of property owners to operate and maintain. In 1932, Crain deeded the park to the Southside Park Association. Managing the park, however, proved no easy task and required the efforts of many. Property owners were assessed an annual

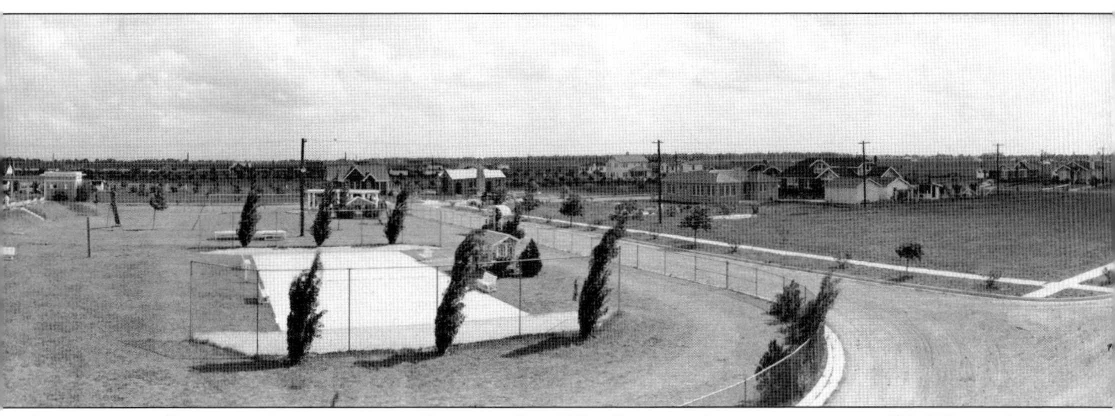

fee to cover the cost of maintaining the complex. The first year's assessment was $6. Through the years, the park fee gradually increased, topping out at $425 per year in 2013. Today, park maintenance is covered by a user fee and property taxes. (Courtesy of SSP.)

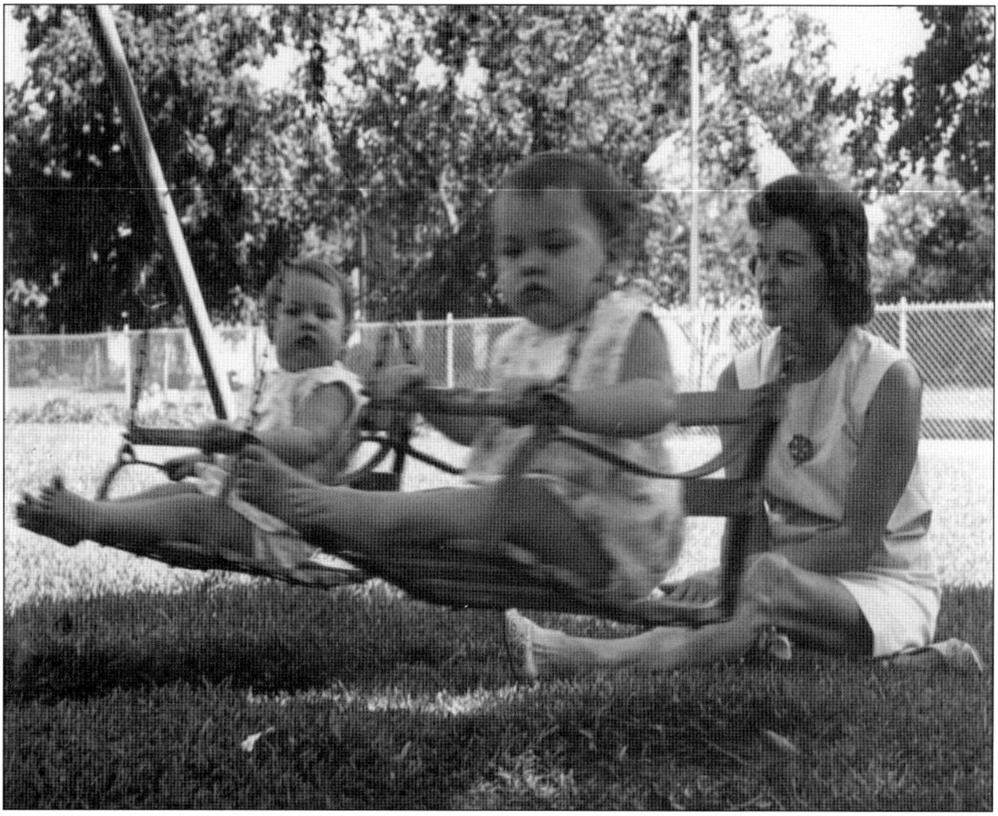

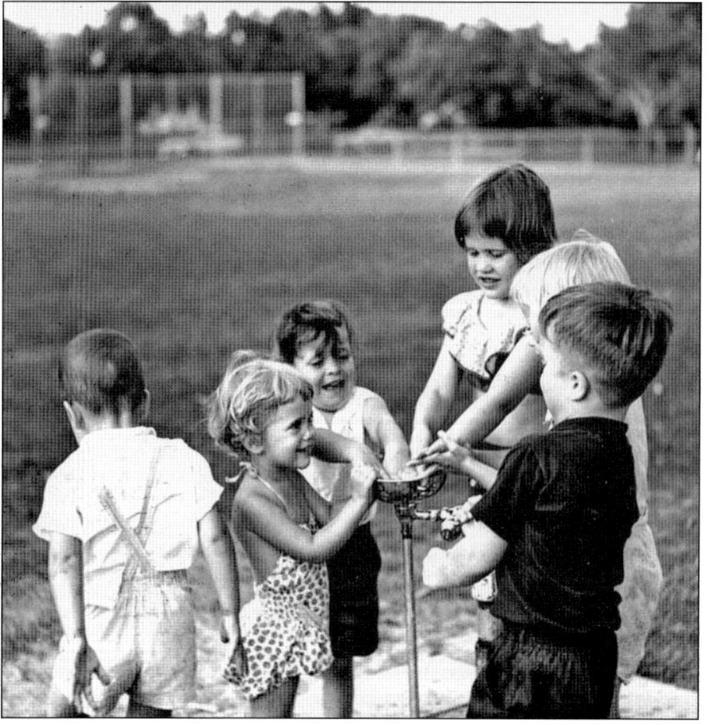

The Southside Park Association was initially represented by five board members. In 1942, the bylaws were amended to provide for seven board members, elected by residents for a two-year term. In 2012, the park association, burdened by increased costs for park upkeep and unable to consistently secure a committed roster of citizen volunteers, voted to transfer stewardship of the park complex to the city's newly established park department. The decision formally ended 80 years of citizen-directed management of the park. (Above, courtesy of Kelly Mears; left, Roger Judson.)

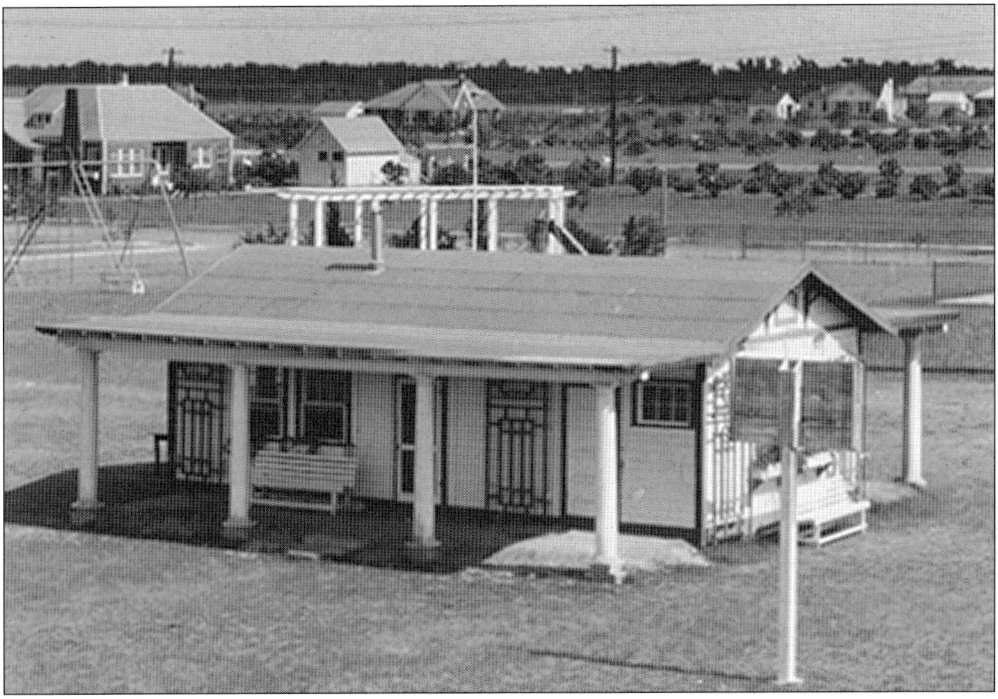

The park's first clubhouse (above) was the builder's construction shack, which was moved from Bellaire Boulevard to 3743 Garnet Street and repurposed to serve as the community clubhouse. It was remodeled and expanded several times over the years to accommodate the needs of a growing population. A 1936 evening photograph (below) shows a revamped clubhouse without frills. It was a popular meeting place for neighborhood children. In the 1950s, the clubhouse had a jukebox, and the neighborhood hosted root-beer socials, storytelling, ping-pong, Boy Scout functions, and community suppers. (Above, courtesy of SSP; below, Kris Holt.)

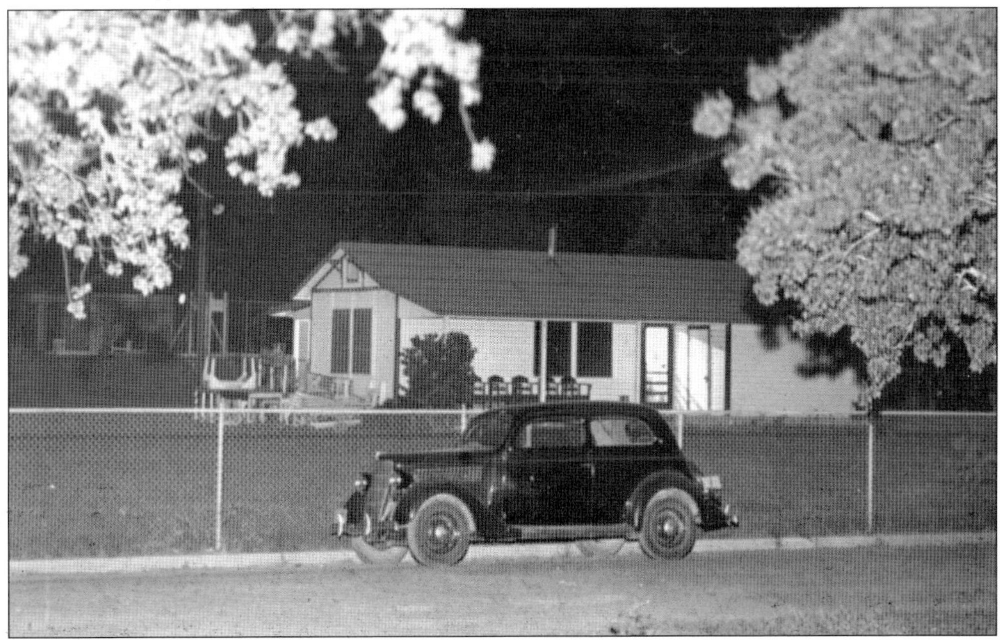

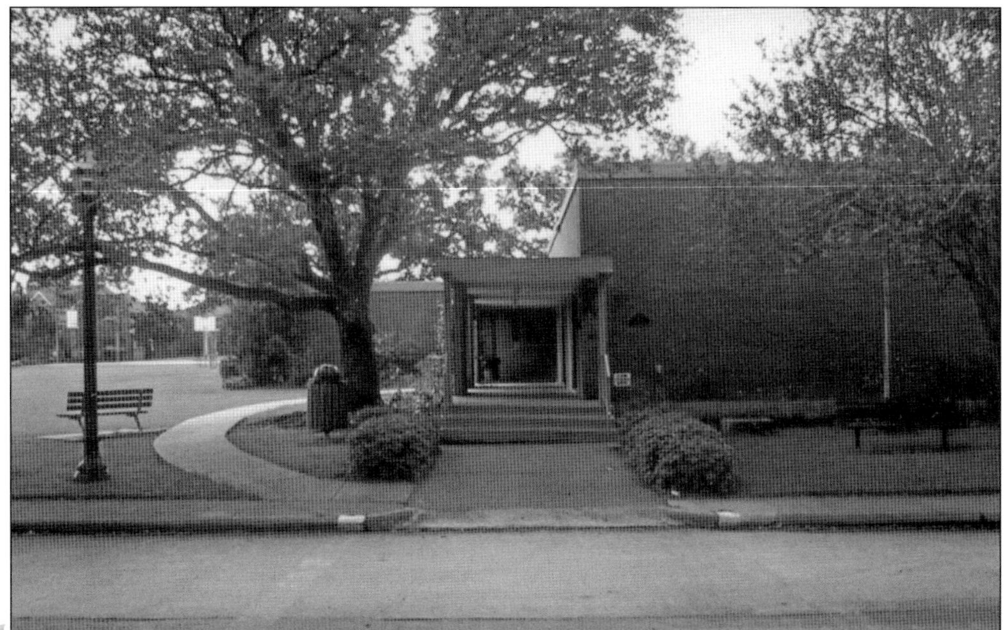

In 1959, plans were approved for a new clubhouse that would be larger and have air-conditioning, separate meeting rooms, and a full kitchen. The construction contract was awarded to Donald Cook, a Southside Place resident who labored at the park as a volunteer. Cook Construction Company completed the 3,000-square-foot building in 1960. (Courtesy of Val Glitch.)

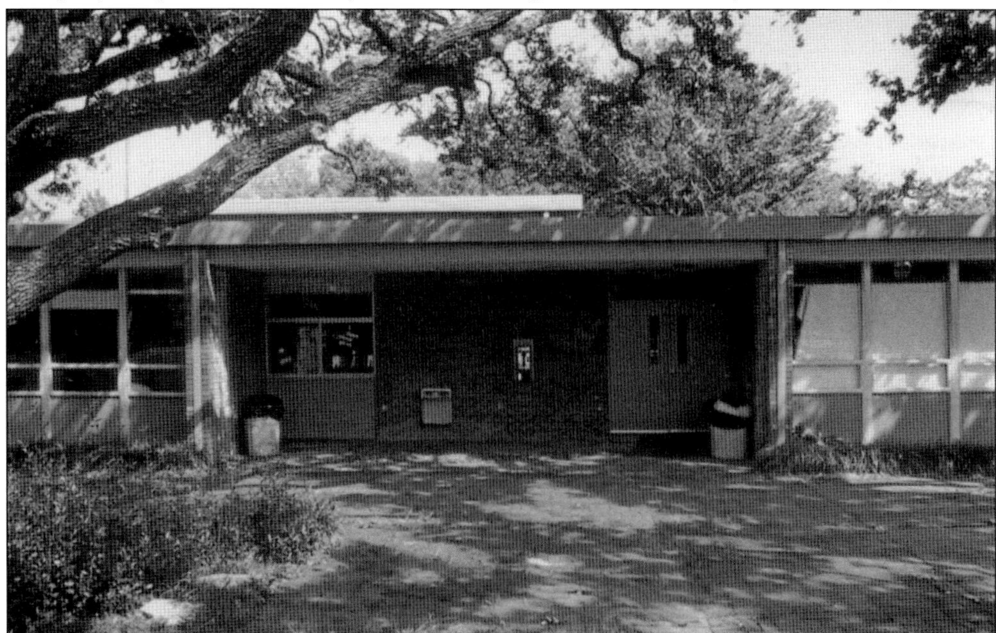

The flat roofed, single-story building was made of brick, with a large covered breezeway serving the main entrance. The back of the clubhouse (shown here) led to a shaded courtyard, with the pool and the playground just a few short steps away. The mid-century interior was simple: cinder block walls, aluminum-framed sliding glass doors, and a linoleum floor. A full calendar of activities kept the community vibrant, engaged, and alive. (Courtesy of Val Glitch.)

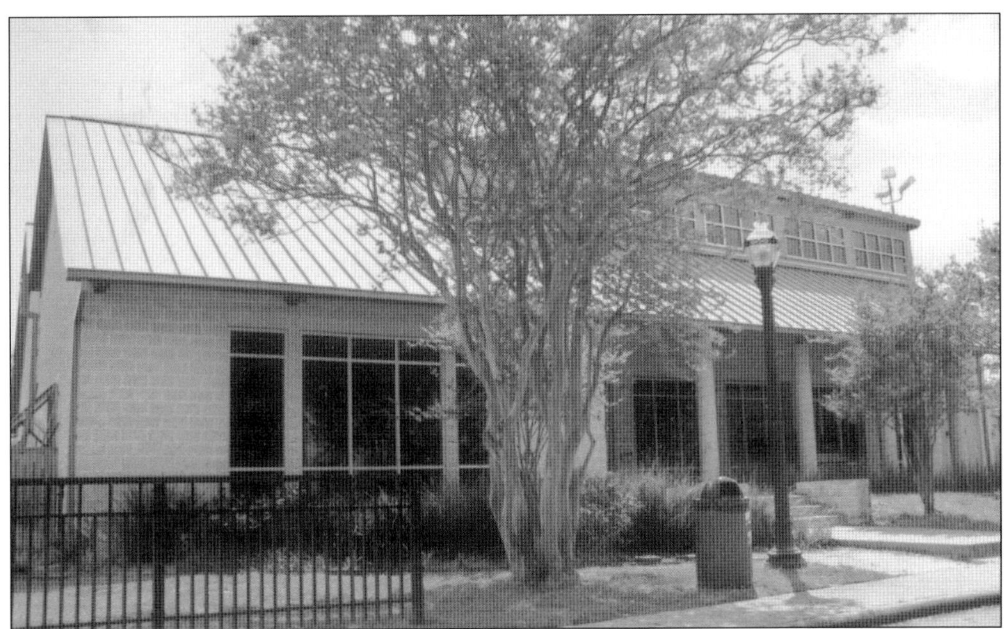

Forty-two years later, in 2002, the Southside Park Association made plans to build anew. After two years of aggressive fundraising and a bank note secured, a new clubhouse made its debut. The firm of Val Glitch Architects worked closely with clubhouse committee members to design a space to meet the community's needs. The front elevation (above) boasts a large porch, while the back of the building (below) opens onto a large, shaded deck. The interior has concrete floors, a great room, separate craft and meeting rooms, a commercial kitchen, and storage both inside and out. The facility's main room can accommodate more than 150 guests and is a welcoming host to the popular summer camp program that fills the space to capacity each year. (Both courtesy of Kris Holt.)

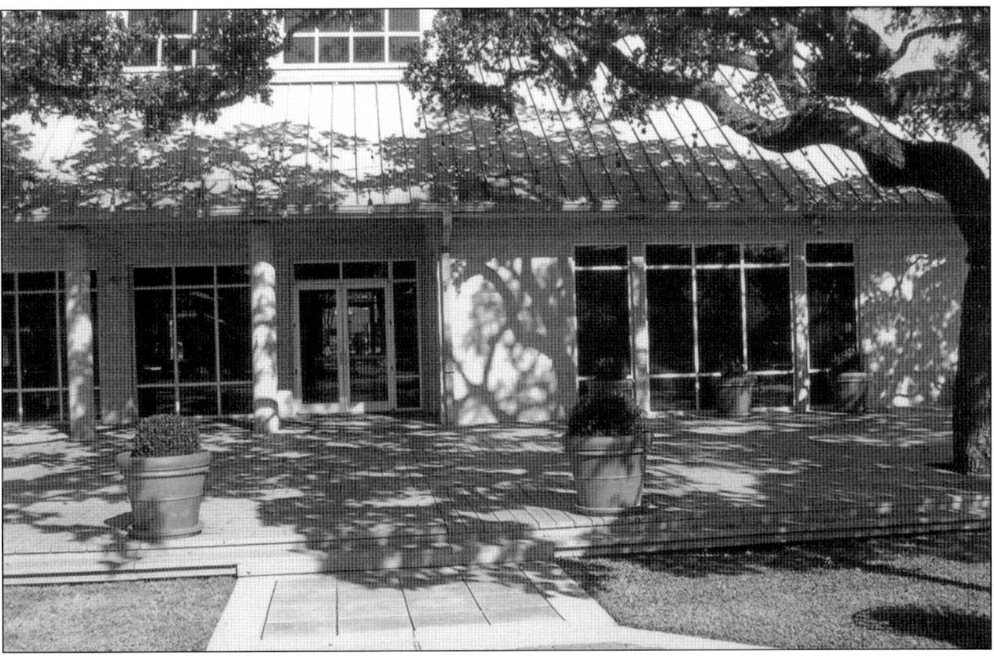

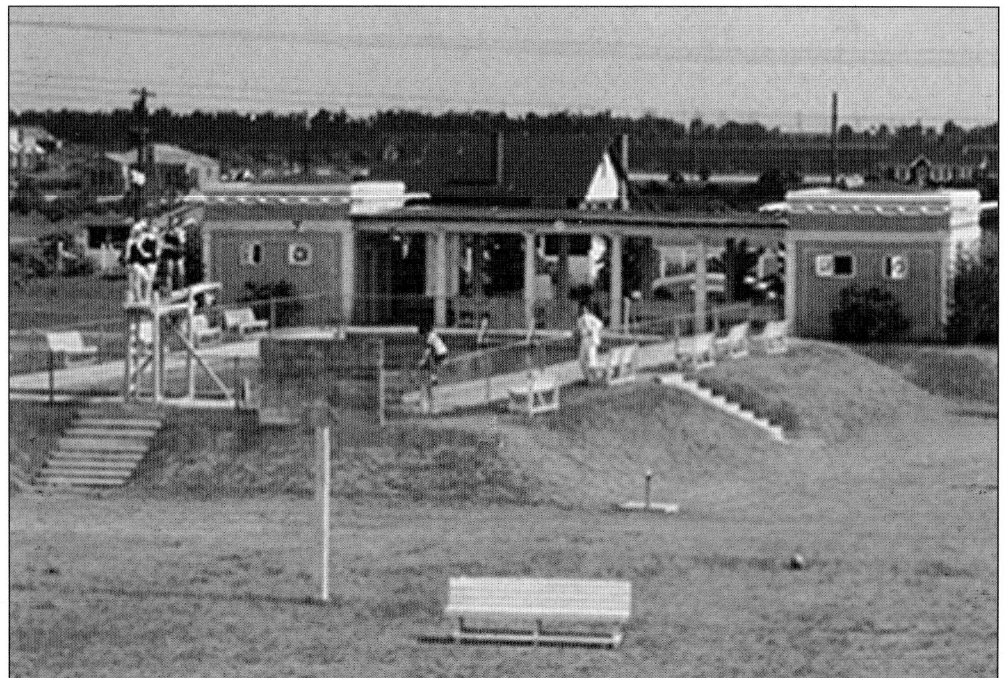

The original design of the Southside Place swimming pool was both impressive and grand. The pool was elevated from the rest of the park on a small grassy hill. The pillared pool entry was neoclassical in design, with two airy bathhouses on either side and a tiered front entrance on Farbar Street. Olympic diver Georgia Coleman, a medalist in the 1928 and 1932 Olympics, coached neighborhood children on the high board (visible in this photograph) in the 1920s. (Courtesy of SSP.)

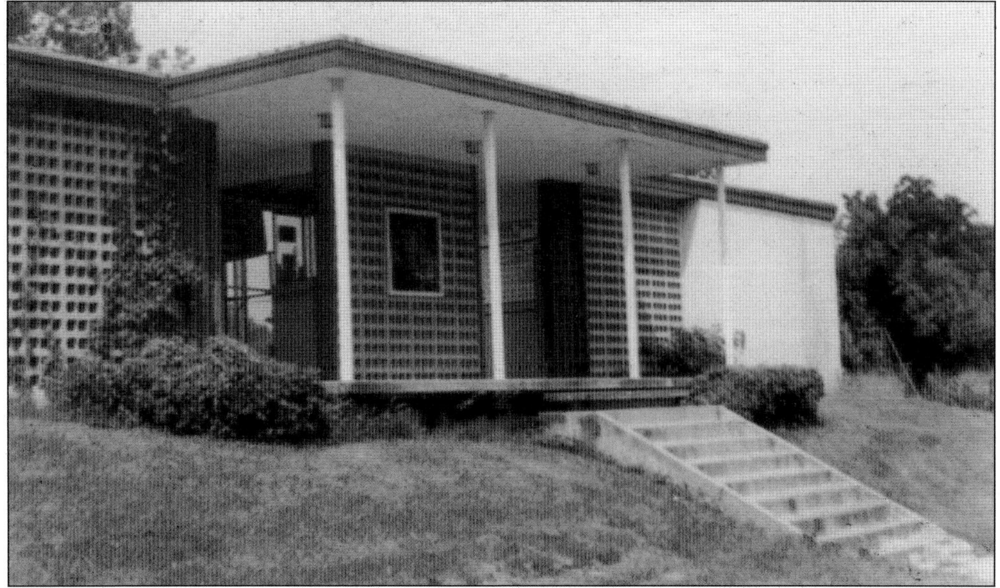

Regrettably, the entry and bath houses underwent a dubious stylistic change in 1960, and few photographs remain to document the original architecture. In this photograph, the original neoclassical entry and bath houses are unrecognizable. (Courtesy of SSP.)

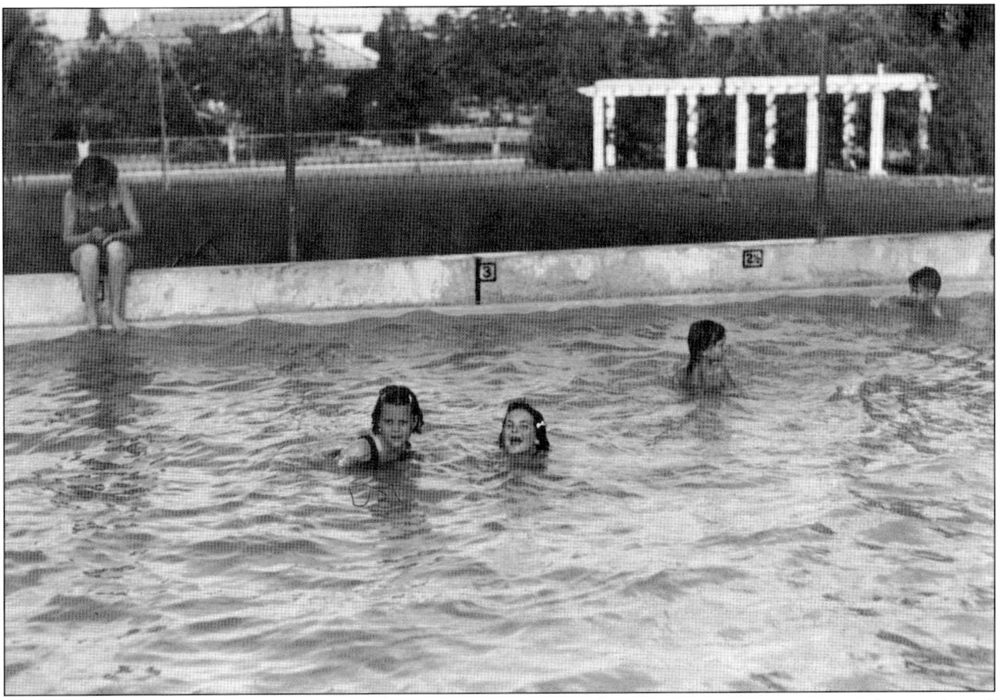

Prior to effective chlorination, the Southside Place Volunteer Fire Department drained and filled the pool twice weekly from the city's 1,200-foot water well located on Bellaire Boulevard. Children delighted in swimming soon after a refill, as shown in these c. 1935 (above) and 1940 (below) photographs, as the water was sure to be clear and cold. A filter system was installed in 1965, ending the routine practice. (Above, courtesy of Kelly Mears; below, Jackie Duffie.)

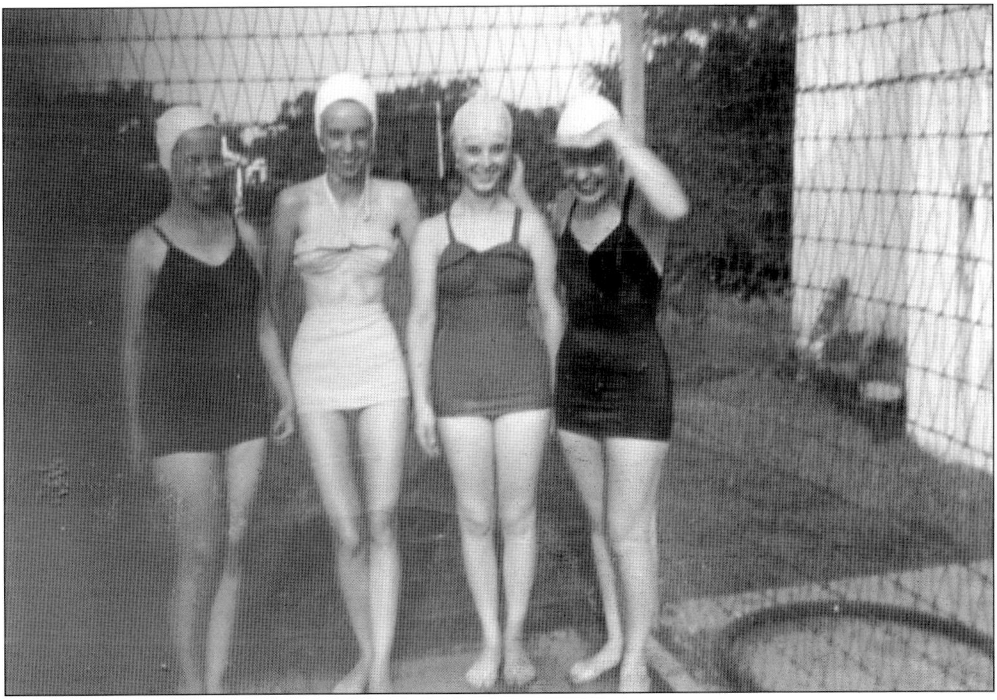

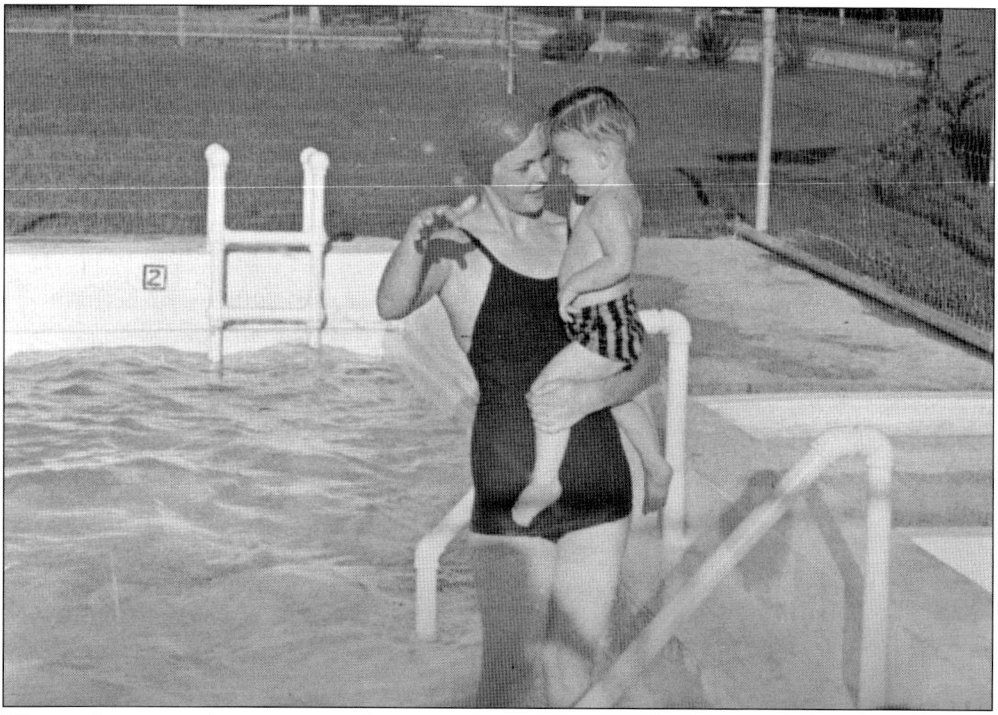

The pool remains the epicenter of summer activities in Southside Place. Children who grew up swimming in the pool each summer often returned to work as lifeguards in their teen years. Teenagers serve as role models to the younger children, and the cycle continues from one generation to the next. The photographs on this page of the Evans family enjoying the pool are believed to be among the earliest images of the pool. (Both courtesy of Kelly Mears.)

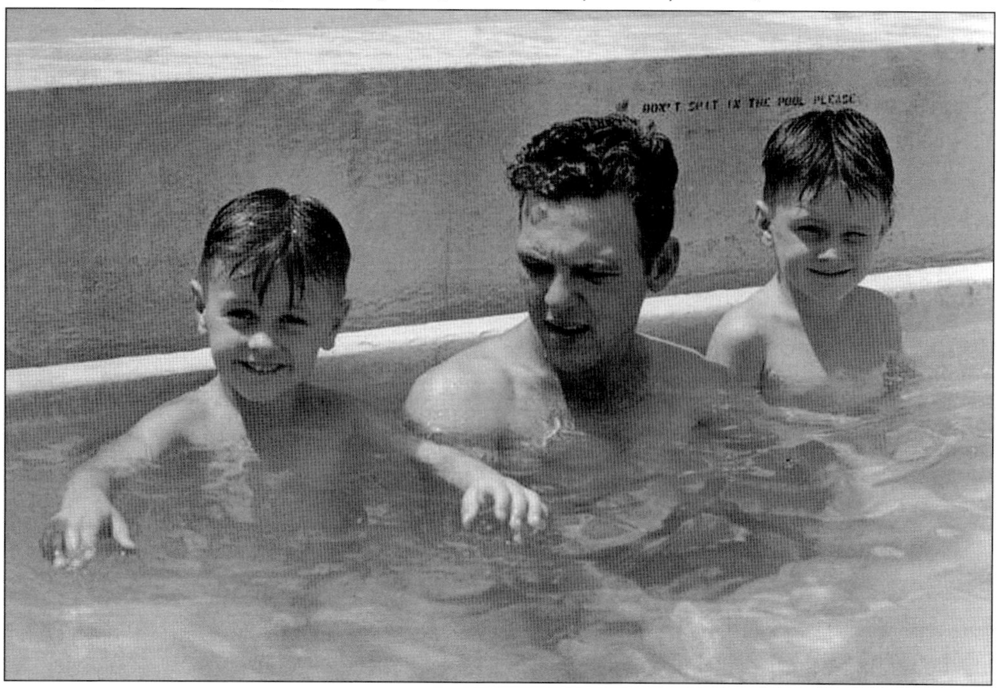

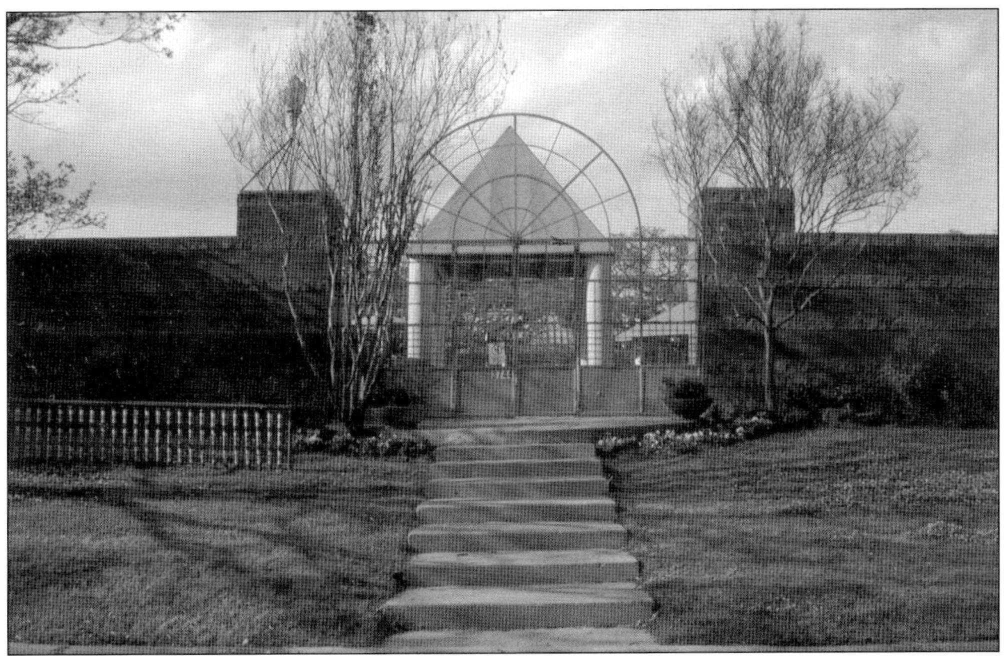

In 1983, Taft Architects reimagined the pool's entrance on Farbar Street (above), replacing the 1960s facade with a design considered both complementary and conforming to the clubhouse and surrounding homes. A new 25-yard inground pool with swimming lanes (visible in the photograph below from the back of the clubhouse) was also installed, eliminating the grassy berm. The new pool became home to the neighborhood "All-Stars" swim team, in which more than 100 children participate each summer. (Both courtesy of Kris Holt.)

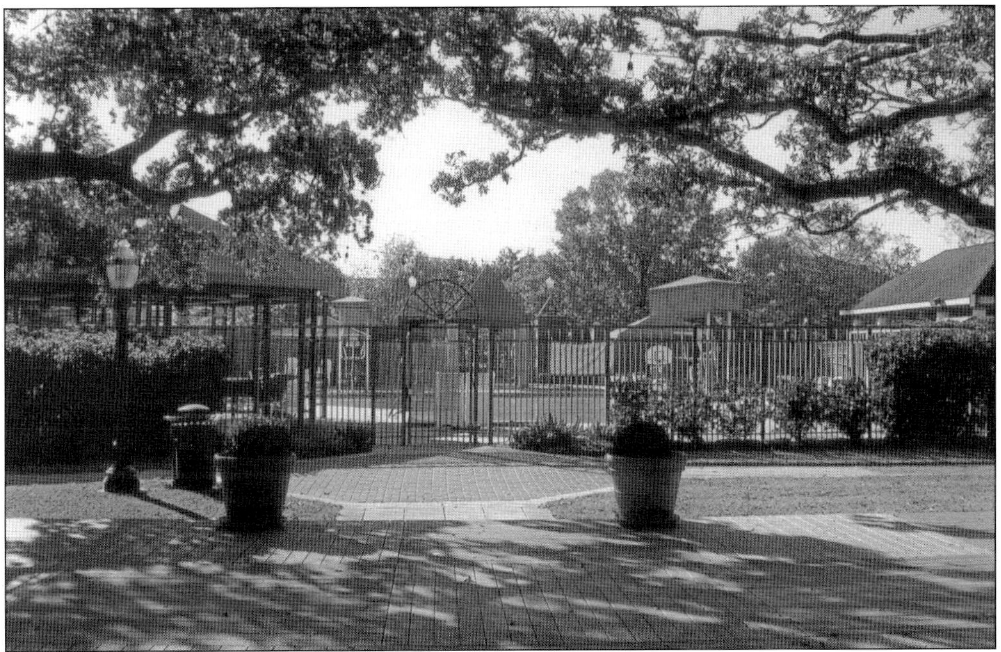

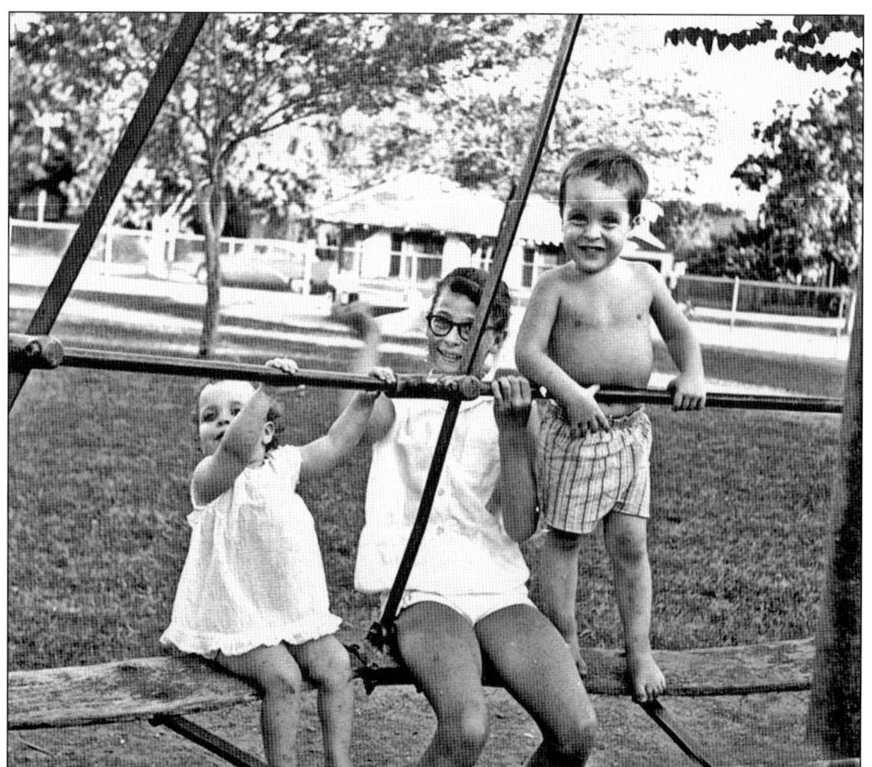

The play area of the park anchored generations of neighborhood children. The park's original plans included a swing set, climbing bars, slide, wading pool, and a maypole as seen in the rendering on page 24. These photographs depict the vintage playground equipment in full swing. (Both courtesy of Roger Judson.)

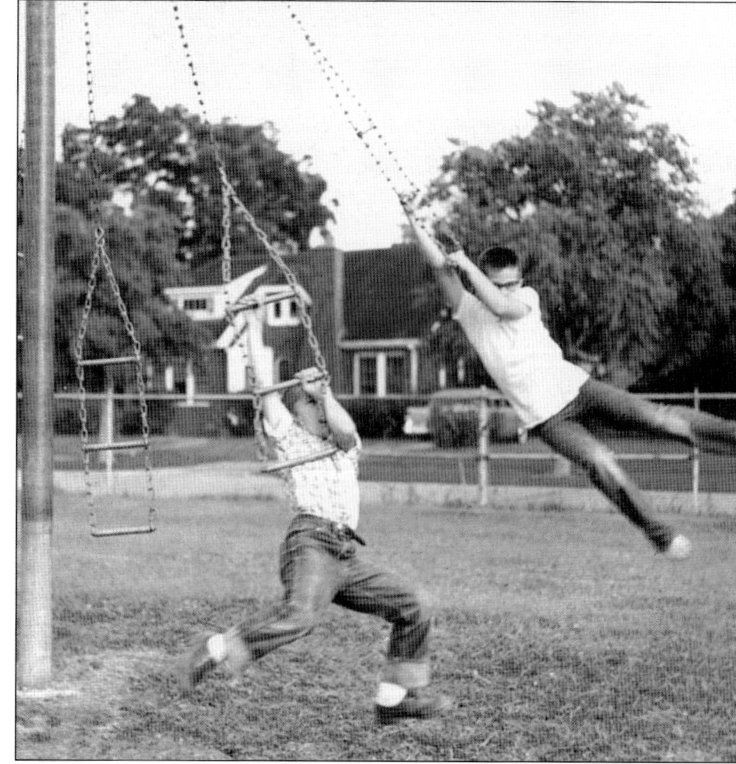

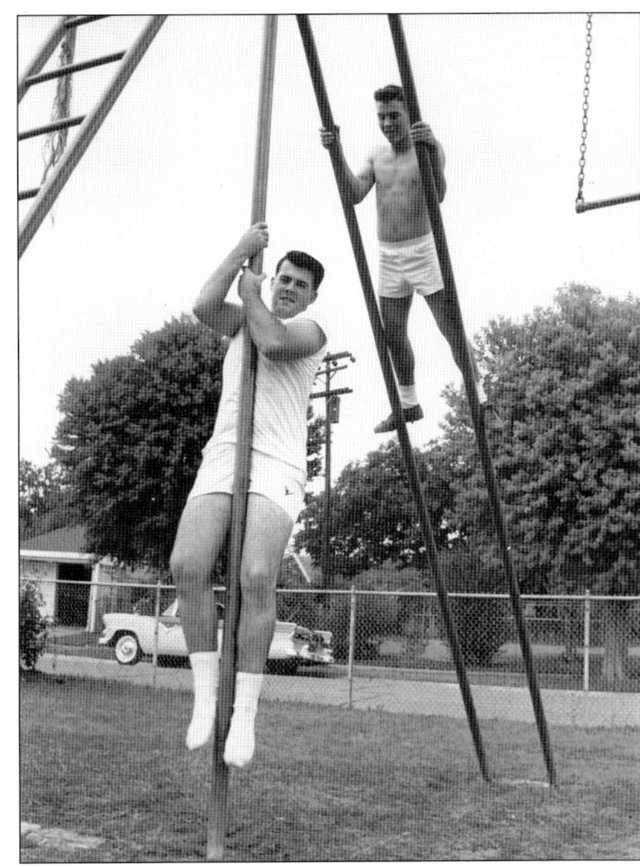

Much of the original play equipment far outlived its lifespan and served the park for more than 50 years. The playground underwent a series of large-scale renovations in 1980, 1995, and 2012 as a result of grassroots funding efforts and neighborhood volunteers. In addition to park equipment, organized outdoor activities have evolved as well. Potato-sack and three-legged races have been replaced with ringalevio on summer nights. (Right, courtesy of Kelly Mears; below, Roger Judson.)

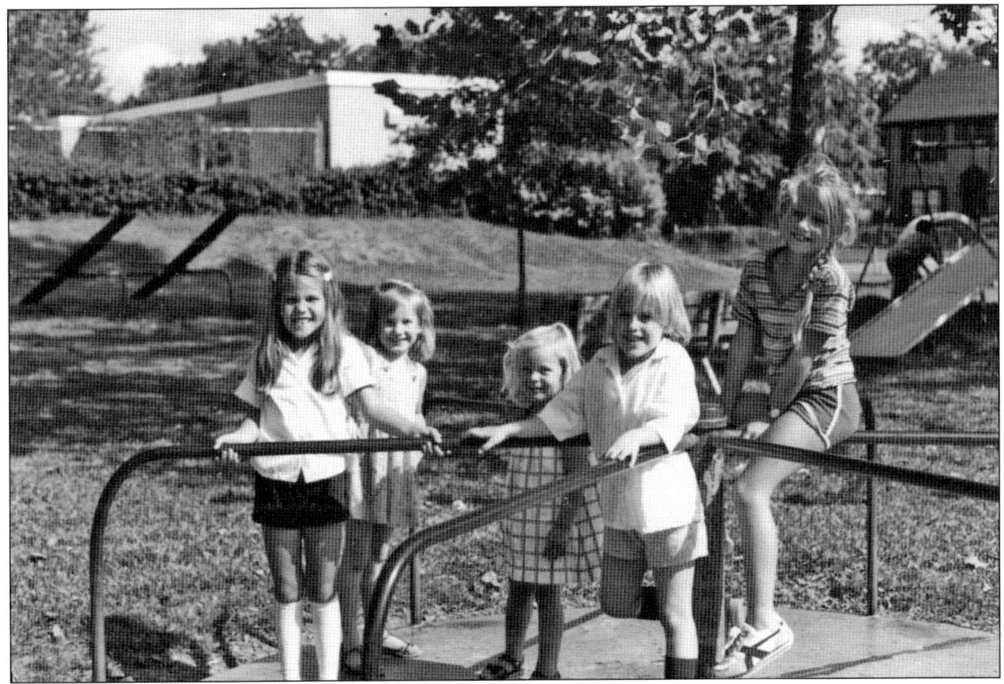

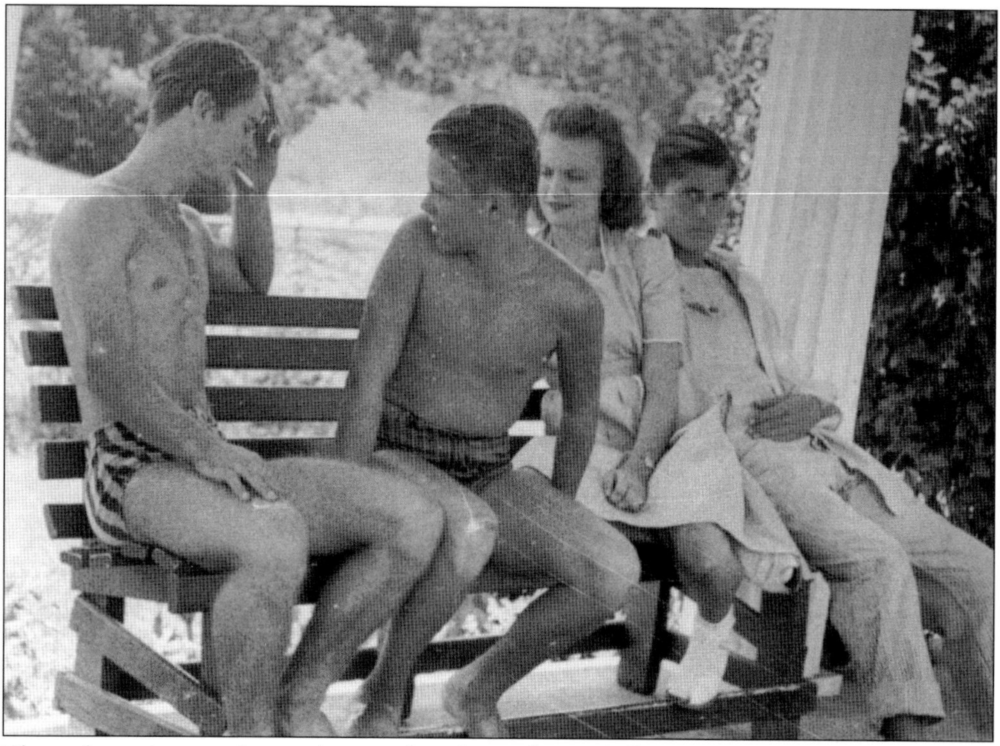

The park continues to be a gathering place for residents of all ages. The 1937 photograph above shows young teens enjoying the shade trellis at the park's southeast corner. The same seating area today offers a view of the park's basketball court. The Judson family, seen below, is enjoying a park picnic in the 1940s. Today, there is a large covered pavilion for picnics and social functions. (Above, courtesy of Kelly Mears; below, Roger Judson.)

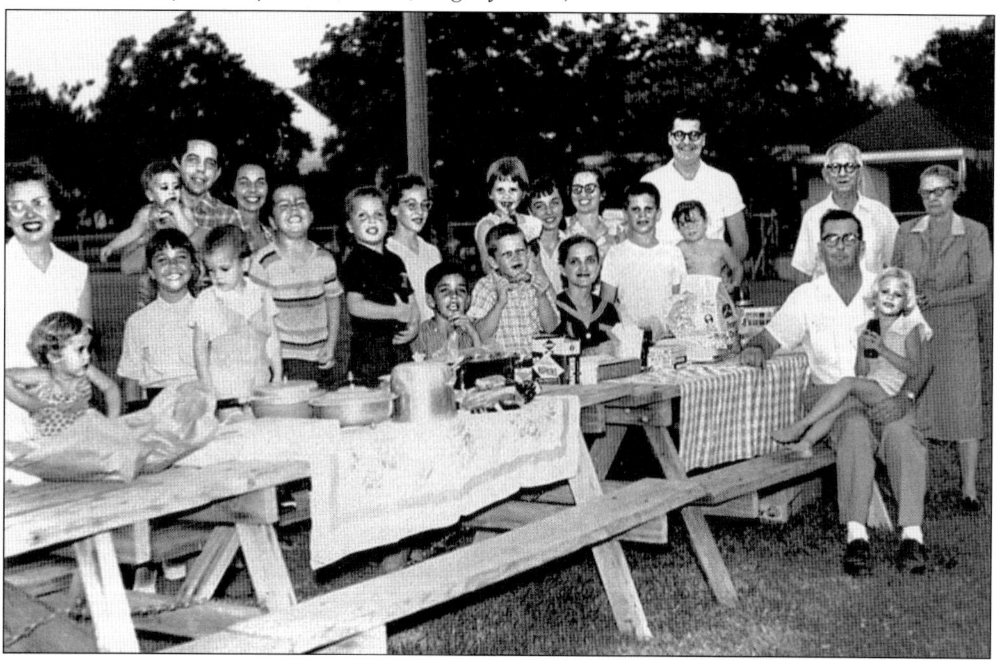

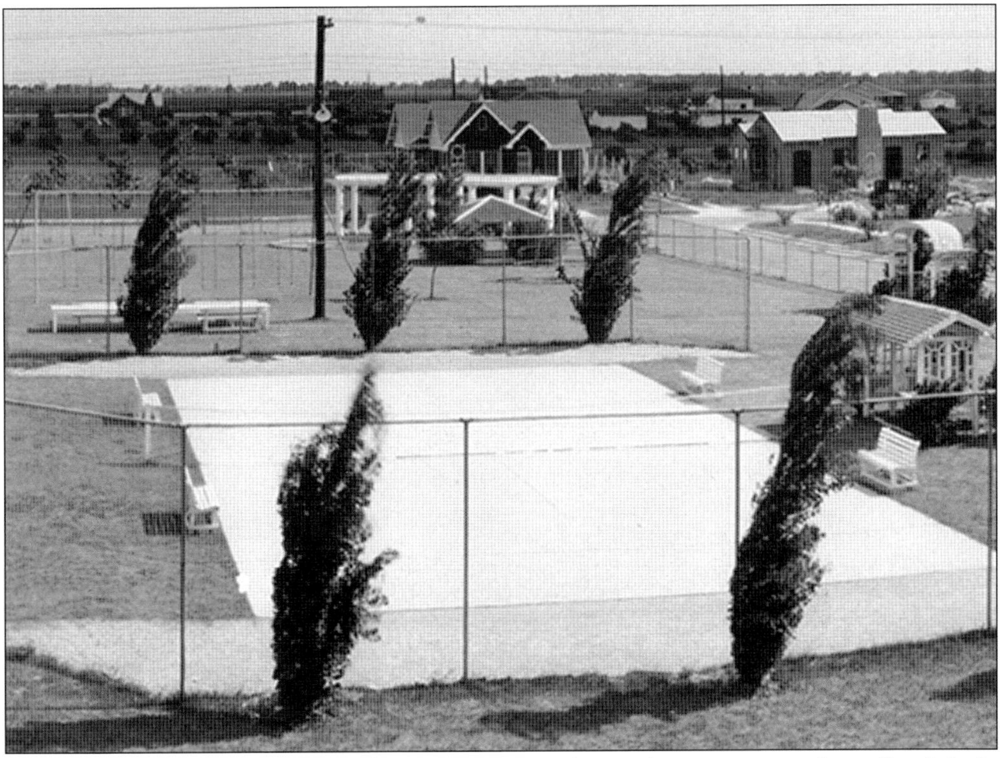

The original park design had a single tennis court on the northwest corner and a trellised shade structure (pictured above on the right) for resting between matches that complemented the park entrances. Lights allowed for evening play, and for decades dances were held on the courts on summer nights. (Above, courtesy of SSP; below, Kelly Mears.)

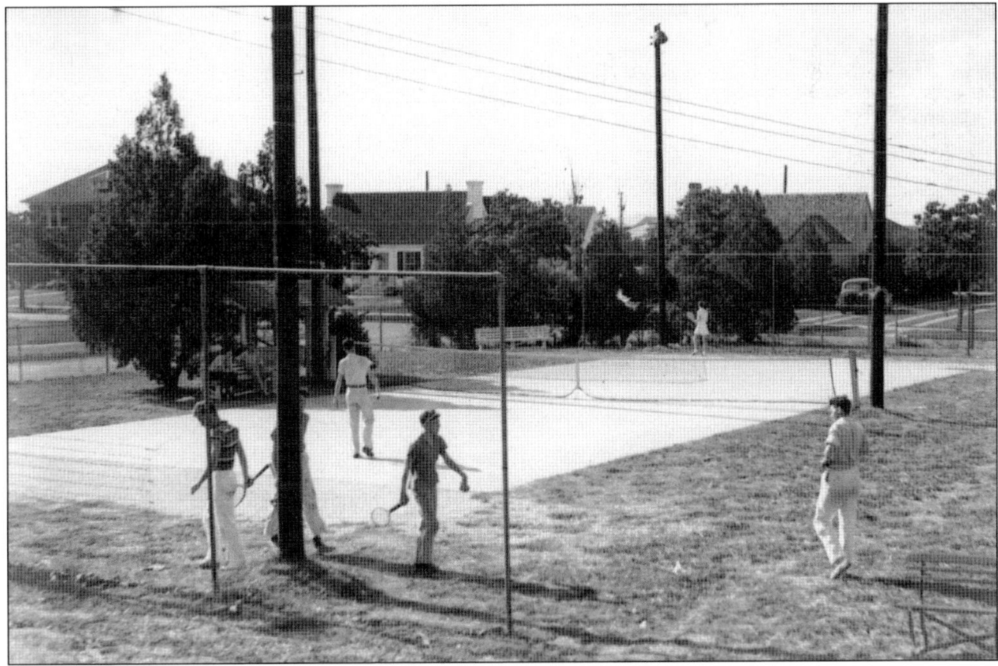

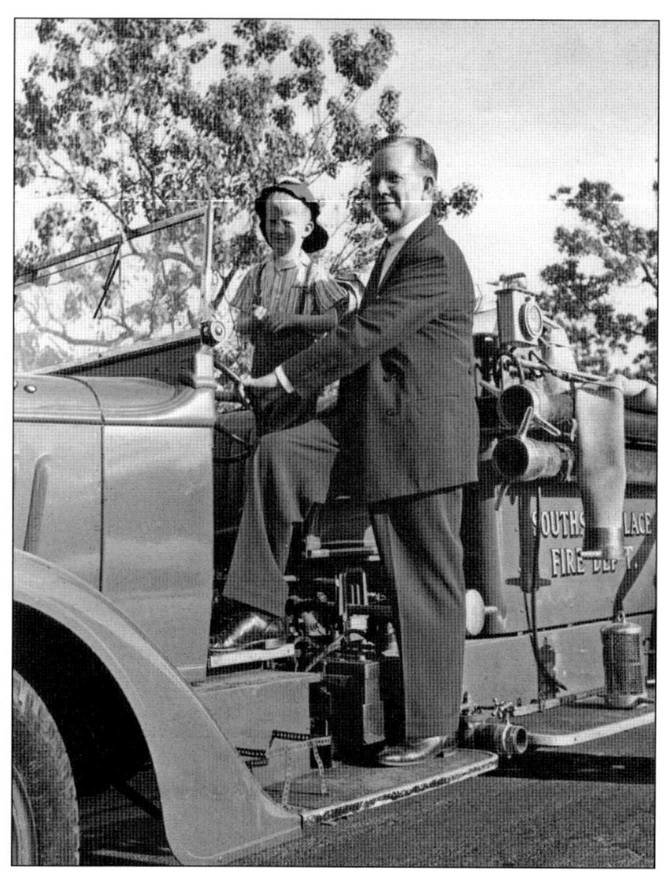

After the familiar 1935 Seagrave fire truck was retired from city service in 1970, it was retrofitted for playground use and placed in the park. Countless children have climbed on, under, and through the revered vehicle, and over time, the park became known as "Fire Truck Park." In 2012, the vintage red fire truck (seen below) was removed and replaced with a mock version. (Left, courtesy of Paul Brewer; below, Kris Holt.)

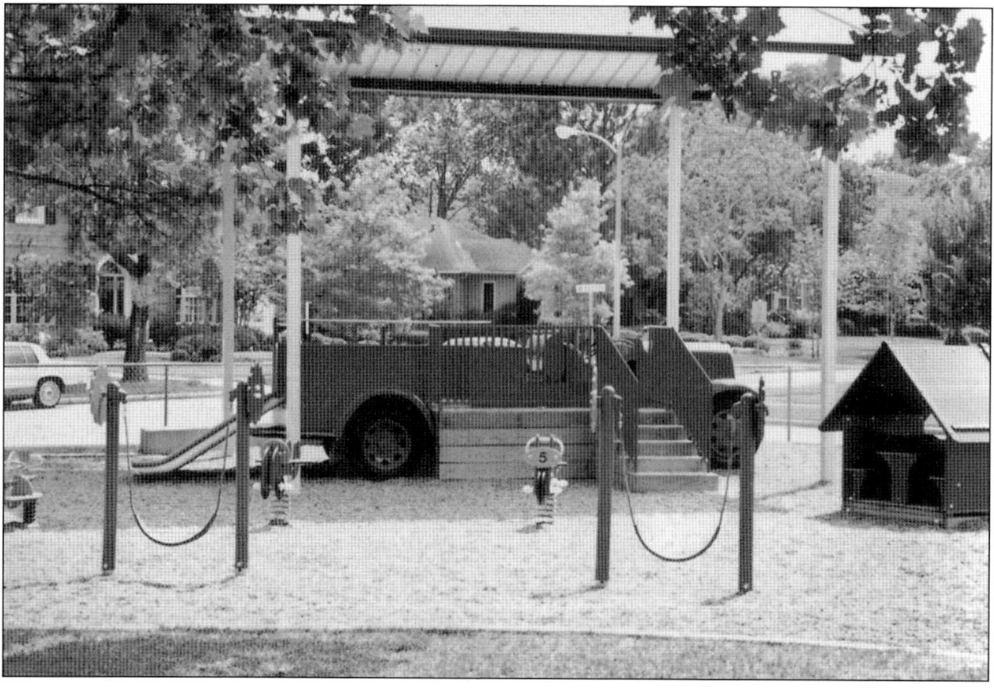

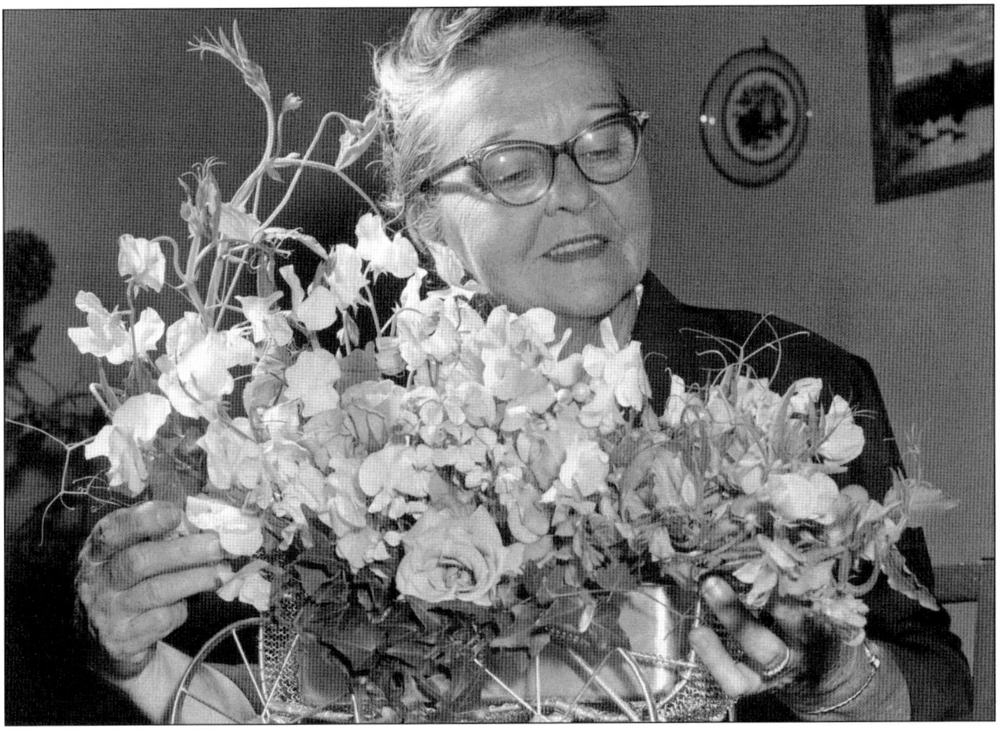

Southside Place's civic clubs have always played an important role in supporting the park and uniting the community. Founded in 1935, the Garden Club was an active gardening organization, winning awards in Houston flower shows. Elizabeth Skelton, a founding member of the club, admires an arrangement in this undated photograph. The Men's Club took care of the city's civic areas. As a social club, it supported the volunteer fire department and nominated candidates for city council and mayor. (Courtesy of Kelly Mears.)

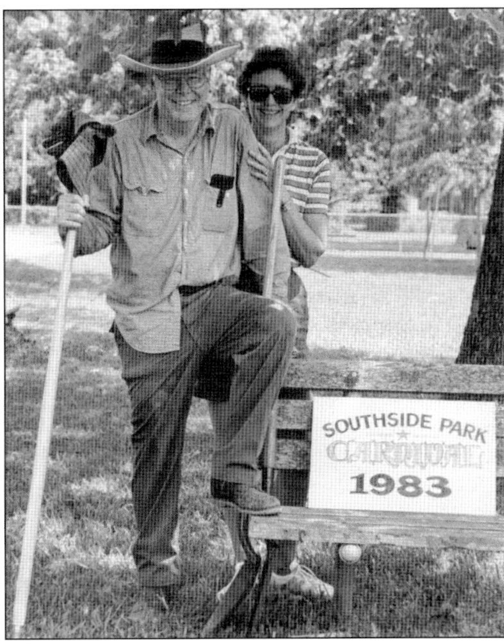

In the spring of 1936, the Men's Club and Garden Club organized the first carnival to raise funds for social activities and park improvements. The carnival lasted from morning until late evening, with activities for all ages and interests. The carnival became an annual event due to an outpouring of community volunteers who ensured its success over the years, as shown in this 1983 photograph of Ingold Street residents Martha and Bob Strawn. Proceeds from the annual carnival (now reimagined as a winter carnival) continue to support park maintenance today. Both the Garden Club and the Men's Club remained active in the community for more than 65 years. (Courtesy of Maurice Lewis.)

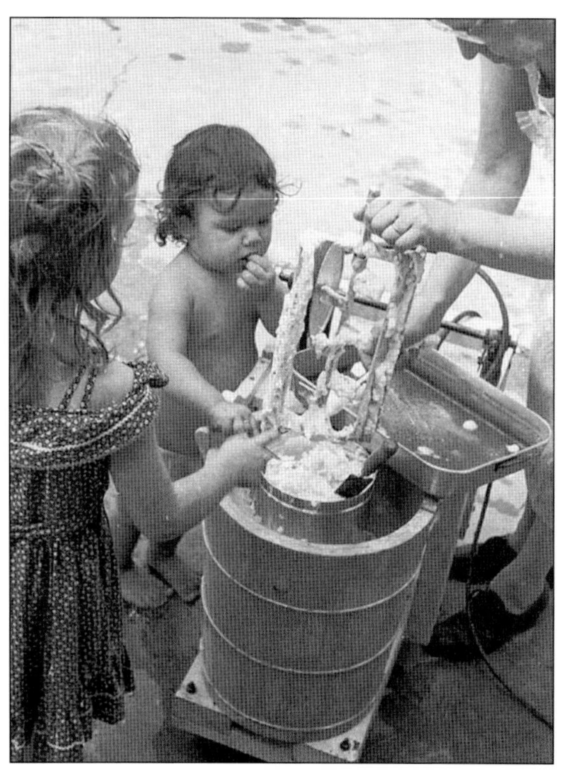

The Women's Civic Club was a later entry in the city's philanthropic timeline. Established in 1945, the club was started by a group of mothers seeking shared play dates and supervised activities for their children. It soon grew beyond park activities to include monthly meetings, luncheons, and community projects. The organization's first project in 1947 was to chlorinate the pool. Later that same year, the club planned a neighborhood spaghetti dinner to celebrate the completion of road paving in the city. (Courtesy of Roger Judson.)

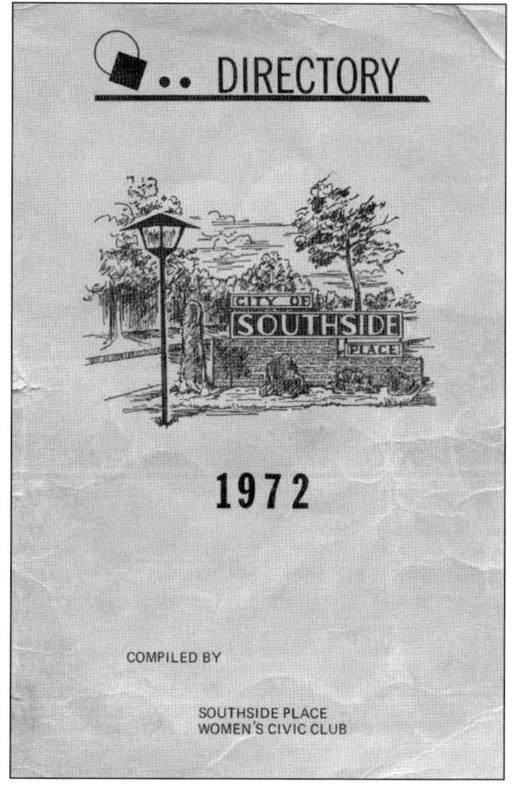

The Women's Civic Club's lasting legacy, however, is its biennial neighborhood directory. Although the Garden Club compiled a city yearbook in the 1940s, it ceased publication during the war due to paper shortages. After the war, the civic club began publishing a neighborhood directory that contained the names, addresses, and phone numbers of all adult residents, as well as the names and ages of their children, and the husband's employer. Beginning in 1951, the directory evolved from a simple set of papers stapled together to a professionally printed booklet containing information about residents as well as city services and local businesses. The 1972 directory (right) shows the city logo in use at the time. A modern version of the directory is published today. Beginning in 2014, the Women's Civic Club opened membership to both men and women and was renamed the Southside Place Civic. The club remains active, keeping neighborhood traditions alive by hosting a progressive dinner, a block party, speakers, and holiday activities. (Courtesy of SSP.)

Nine

Housing Styles and Trends

WOLF'S WEEKLY SPECIAL

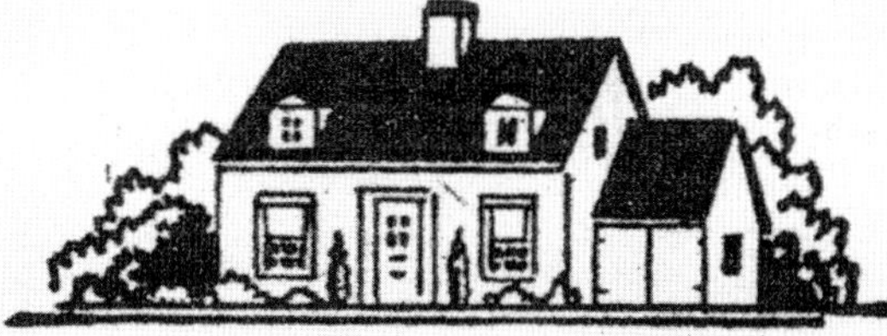

SOUTHSIDE PLACE

Bungalow—$7,450

A wonderful place for the kiddies. There is a well-supervised playground where they can play and swim and it is also near school, bus and stores. You will enjoy this cozy, five-room bungalow with a delightful screened porch. Call now for an appointment.

Real estate firms coined clever advertising phrases over the years to entice buyers to the idyllic neighborhood, as reflected in this 1945 advertisement by Wolf Realty Company. Certainly unique to Southside Place were the amenities marketed by salesmen at every opportunity. Although E.L. Crain's vision of a neighborhood filled to capacity with his specialty homes never came to pass, trends emerged over time. Homes in the city today reflect architectural styles from nearly every decade from 1920 to the present. (Courtesy of SSP.)

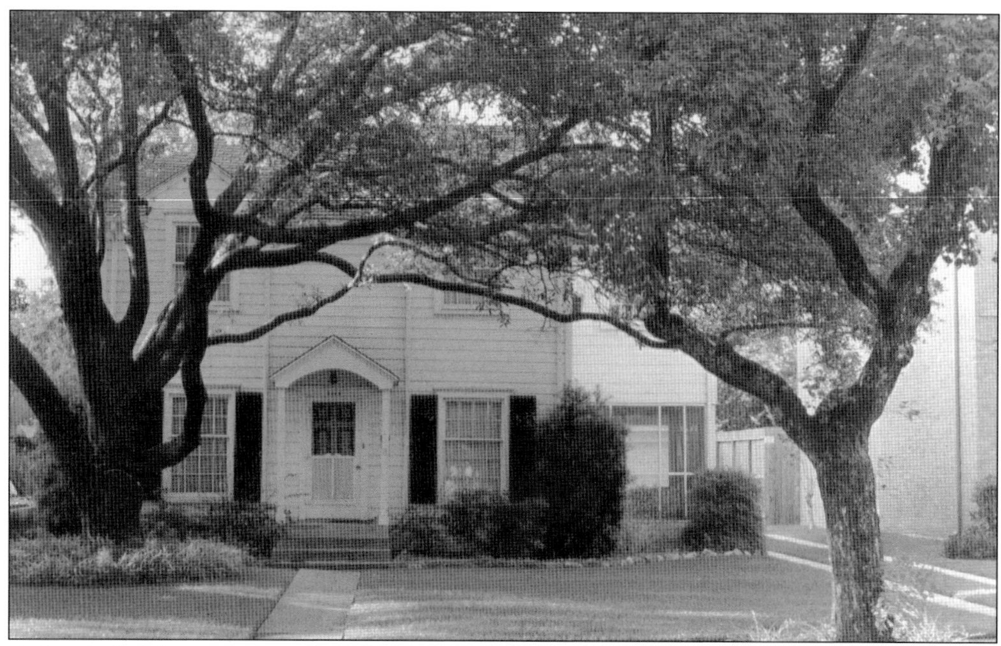

Early sales brochures promoted Southside Place as a "sound investment," and many of the lots were sold to speculators. In 1928, Philip Helfrich, a meter clerk for the Houston Water Department, bought contiguous lots on Carlon Street for $1,950 each, a $400 premium over the initial 1924 marketed price. Unfortunately, the Depression hit, and Helfrich's once-promising investment suffered. Nine years later, he sold both properties to two sisters and their husbands for $750 each. In two months, the couples built identical homes with the exception of some exterior stylistic differences at 3740 (above) and 3744 (below) Carlon Street. According to tax records, the modest 1,406-square-foot, two-bedroom, one-bath homes were valued at $1,290 each. (Both courtesy of Thomas McWhorter.)

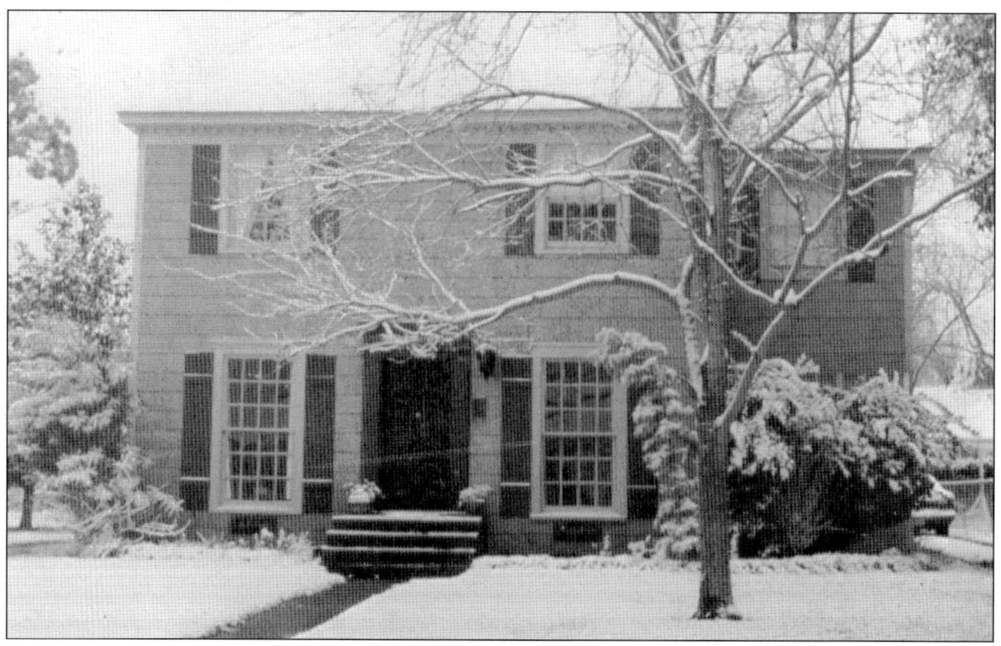

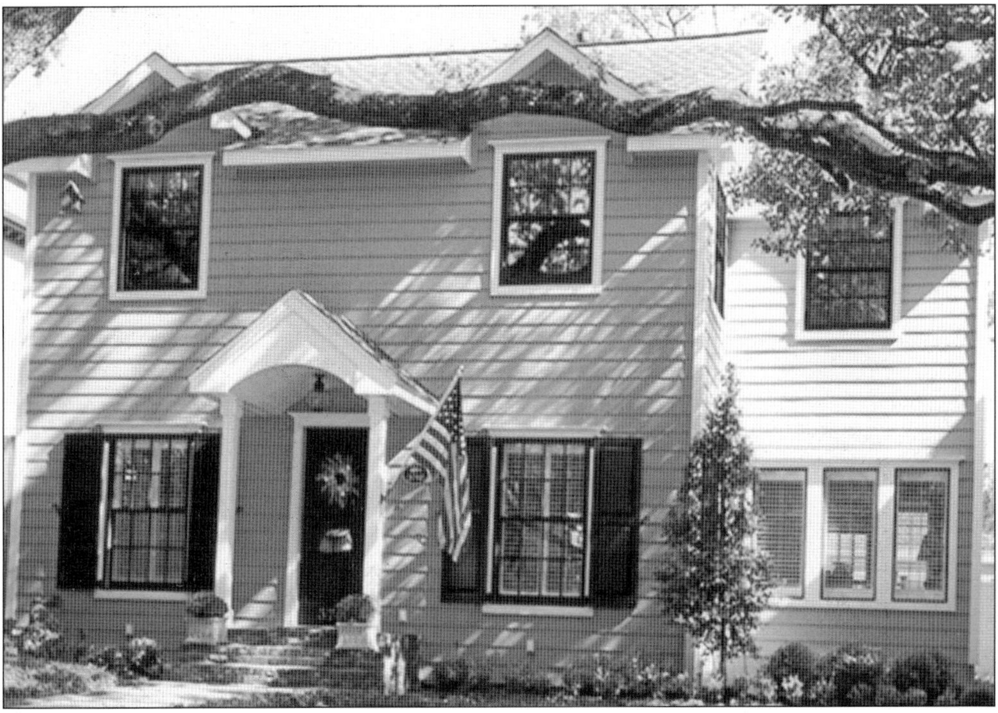

The home at 3744 Carlon Street was torn down in the 1990s. In 1987, Florence Gray, the original owner of 3740 Carlon Street (above), sold her home under the condition that it was not to be torn down. The home exchanged hands several more times until it was purchased in 1996 and fully restored 12 years later. Its restoration and sensitive addition earned its owners a 2011 Good Brick Award for excellence in historic preservation from the Greater Houston Preservation Alliance (now Preservation Houston). Other properties have been renovated and reimagined from the original housing stock for today's needs, such as this home at 3748 Carlon Street. (Both courtesy of Kate McCormick.)

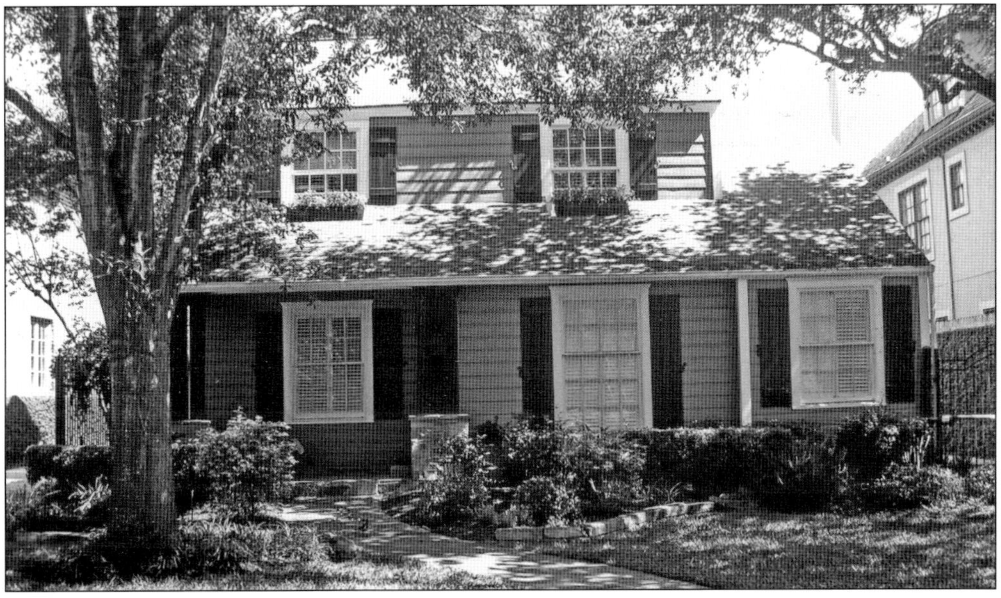

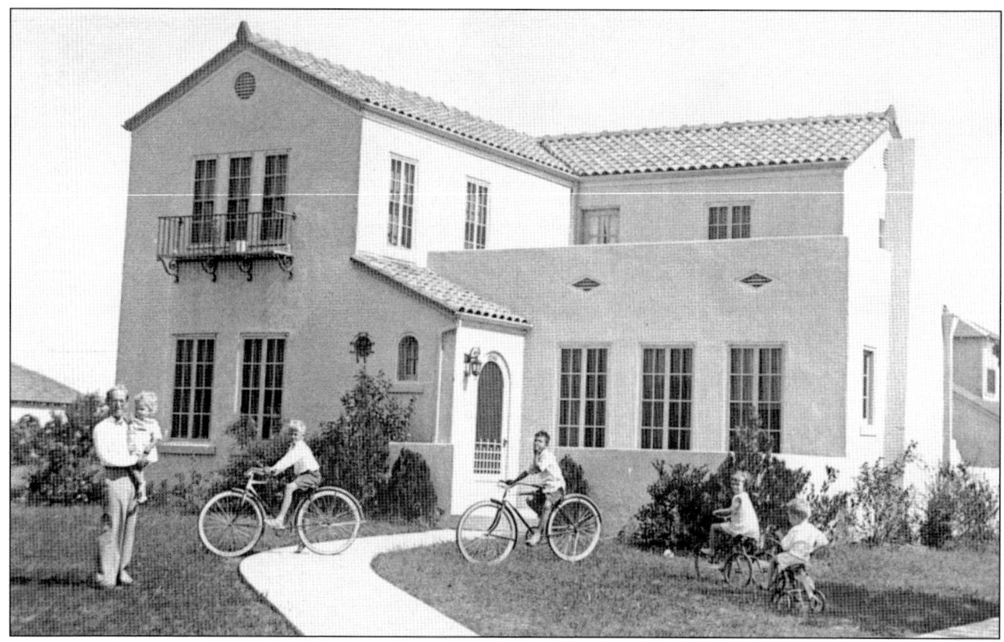

This Mediterranean-style home at 3783 Carlon Street (pictured above), believed to have been built by Louis Spaw Sr. in 1930, used load-bearing clay blocks for its primary construction. The blocks were then sealed with layers of masonry stucco. Typically a technique considered for more expensive residential neighborhoods, it was the only one of its kind in Southside Place during that time. Regrettably, the house was plagued by moisture and was torn down in the 1990s. New owners, inspired by its stylistic past, incorporated a portion of the stucco perimeter wall, retained the arched Spanish-style front door, and added a twist to the property's Mediterranean heritage. (Above, courtesy of Roger Judson; below, Kris Holt.)

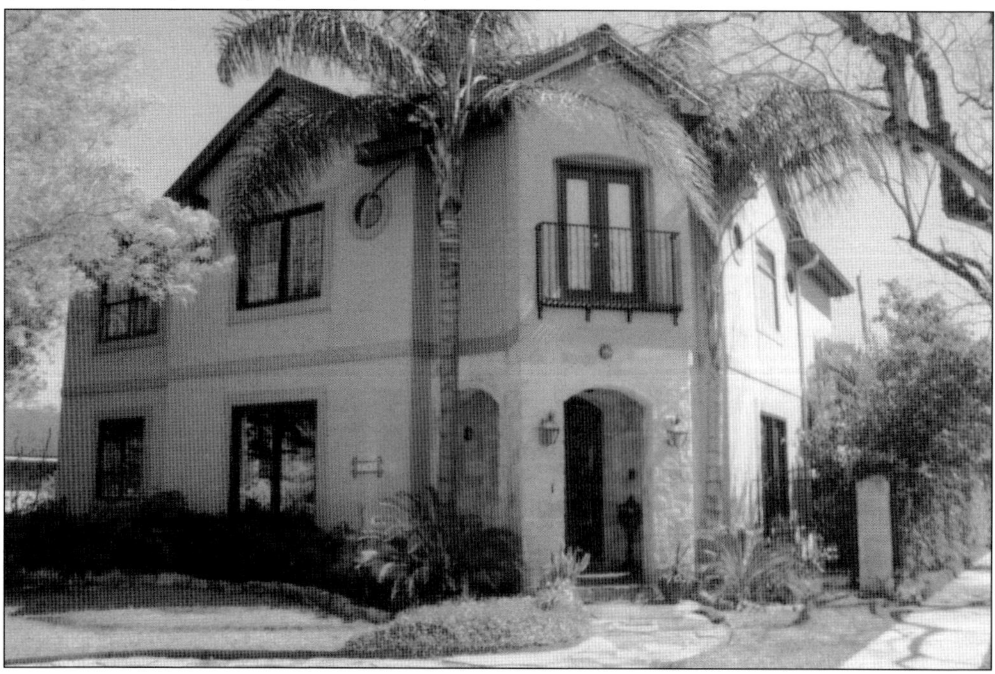

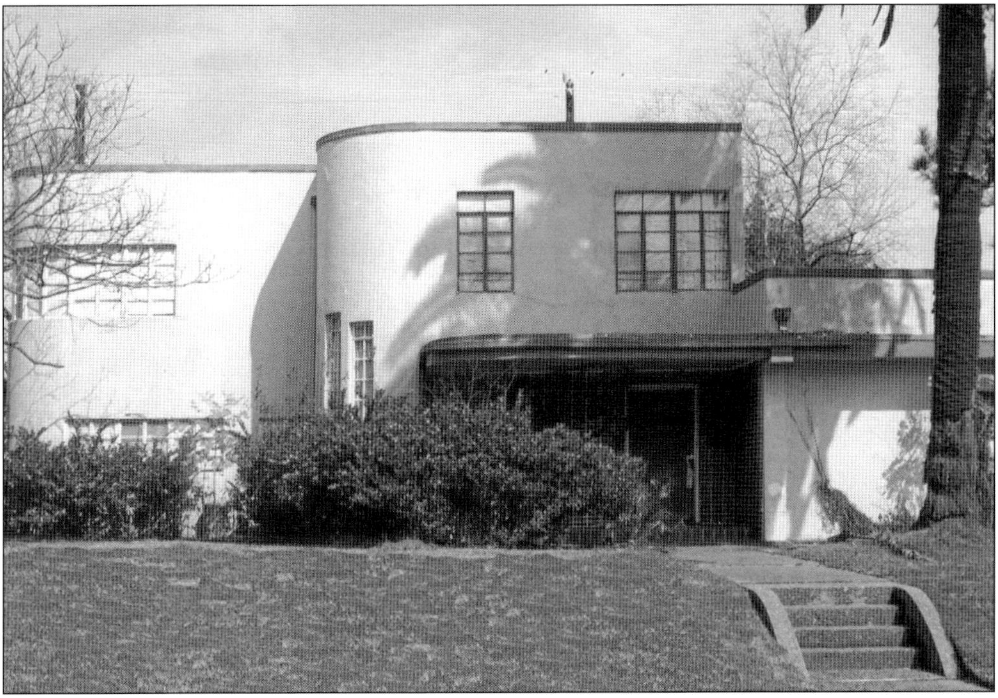

Architect Harry Grogan designed this home (above) at 3780 Gramercy Street for Harvey Houck Jr., the developer of the Braes Heights subdivision, located just south of Southside Place. Although not built until 1947, it was considered a classic example of 1930s Streamline Moderne, which was heavily influenced by the design of streamlined ocean liners, locomotives, and airplanes. The home fell into disrepair and was demolished in 2007. A sleek contemporary (pictured below) built in 2014 now occupies the lot. (Above, courtesy of Karen Lantz, AIA; below, Kris Holt.)

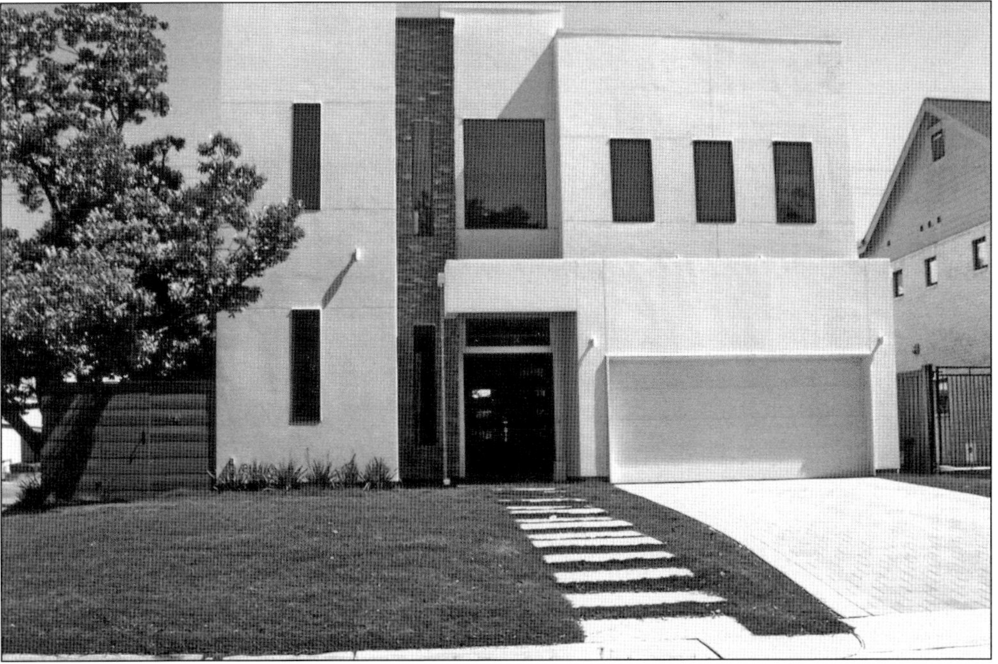

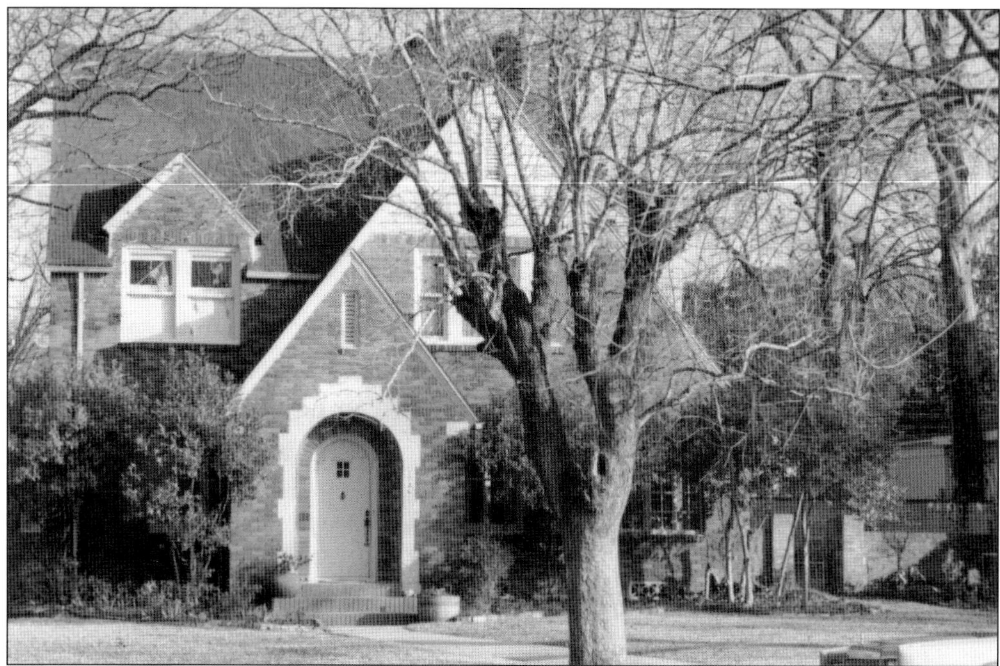

Once promoted as affordable for the working man, the neighborhood shifted over the years toward a more affluent demographic. Although bungalows and modest two-story homes were once the norm, today less than 18 percent of Southside Place's original housing stock remains. The oversized lots, low tax rates, and proximity to the Texas Medical Center and downtown attracted speculative builders who initiated a wave of redevelopment in the 1980s. The trend continues with the small, aging homes being razed to make way for larger, more modern dwellings. From a quaint three-bedroom, Tudor-style home built in 1934 (above) to a sprawling 6,500-square foot, seven-bedroom, Tudor-style home built in 2001 (below), the contrasting photographs of 3746 Darcus Street illustrate the swing of the real estate pendulum. (Both courtesy of Kris Holt.)

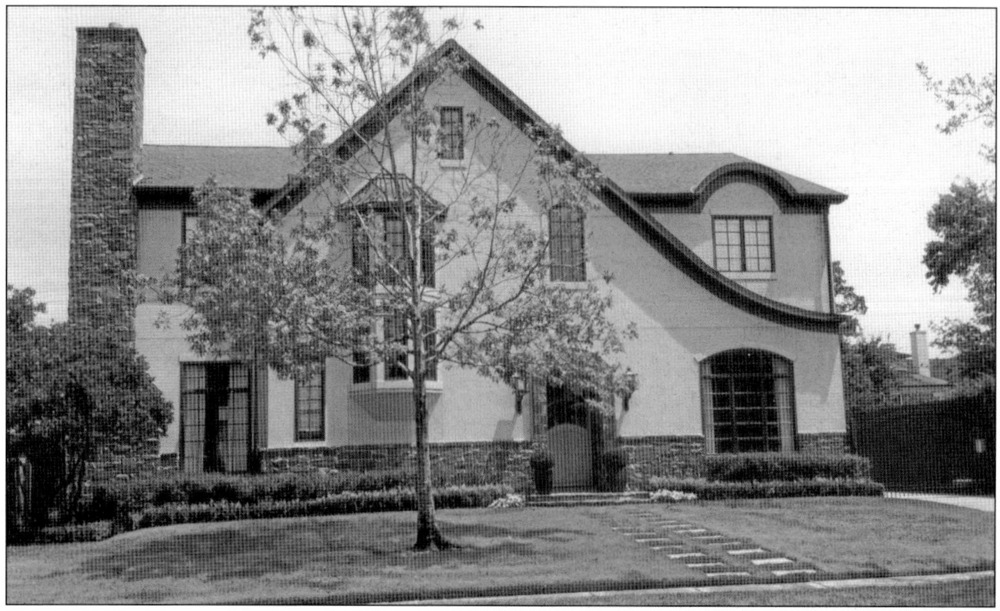

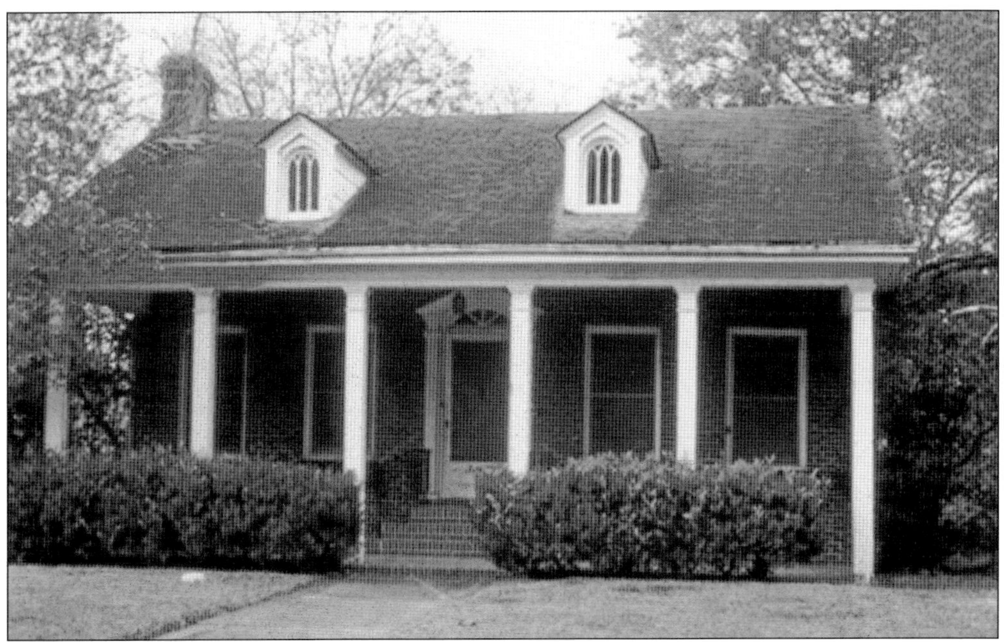

The original house at 3722 Farbar Street was featured in the 1920s subdivision sales and marketing material. Over the years, the house served its occupants well. During the Depression, the owners sublet to boarders and later housed extended family members. Periodically, the home was leased to renters. Outliving its usefulness, the home was demolished in 1999 and replaced with this custom-built, 7,100-square foot home, complete with quarters, a media room, and a three-car garage. (Both courtesy of Kris Holt.)

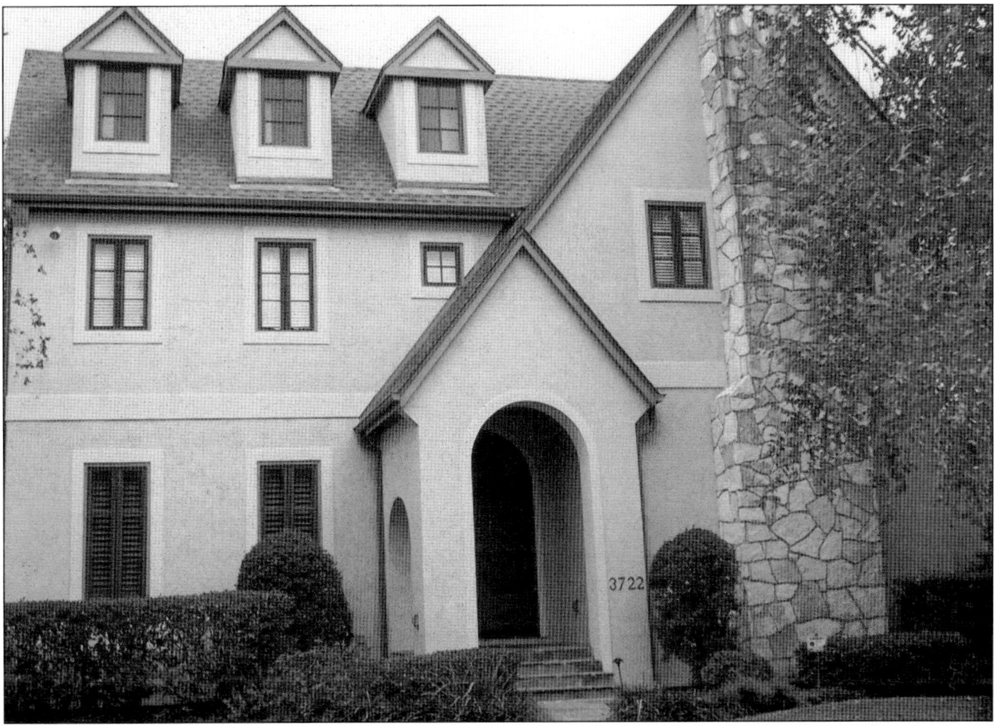

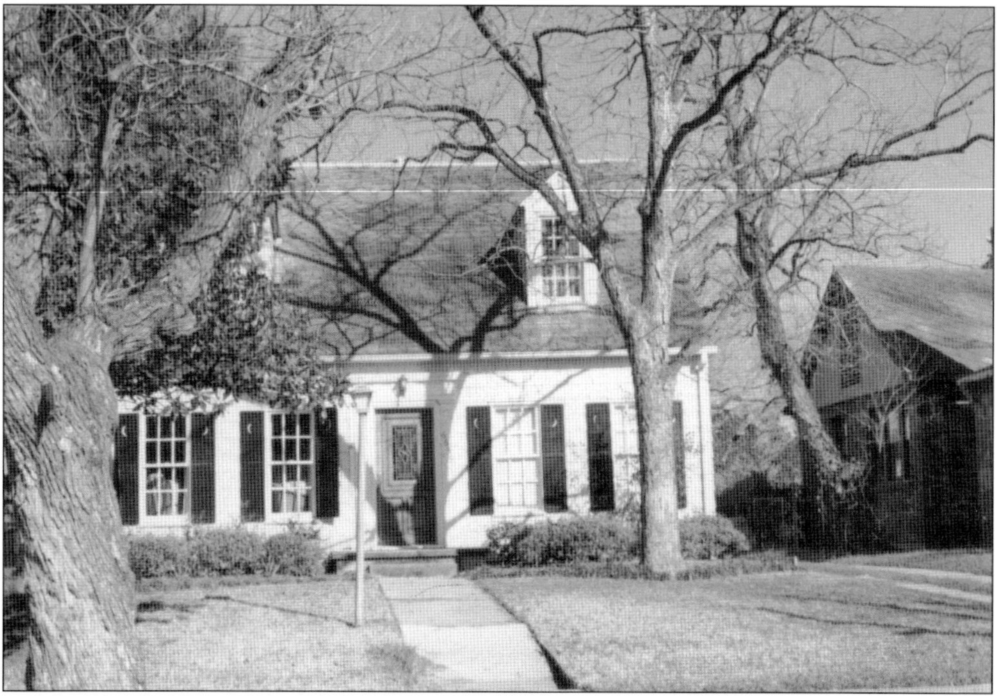

With fewer than 480 single-family homes, Southside Place is the smallest municipality in Harris County. Residents sense a personal, almost intangible connection to community. It is often the reason why many families remain or return to the neighborhood to raise families of their own. The wood-framed charmer (pictured above) at 6639 Edloe Street was torn down, and a new brick home (below) was built by a third-generation family member in 2010. (Both courtesy of Kris Holt.)

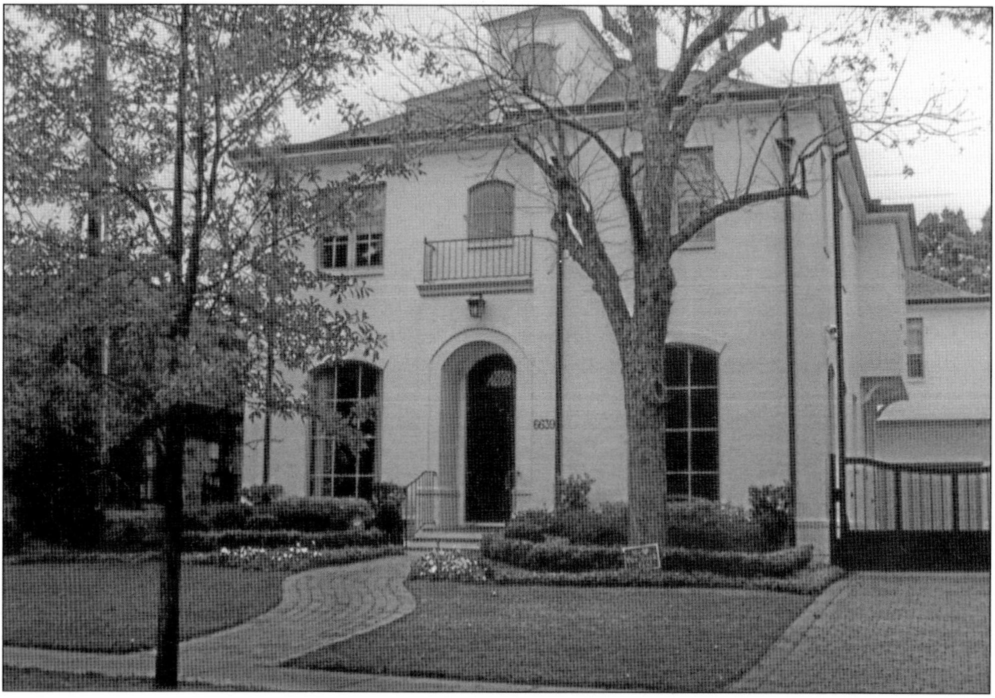

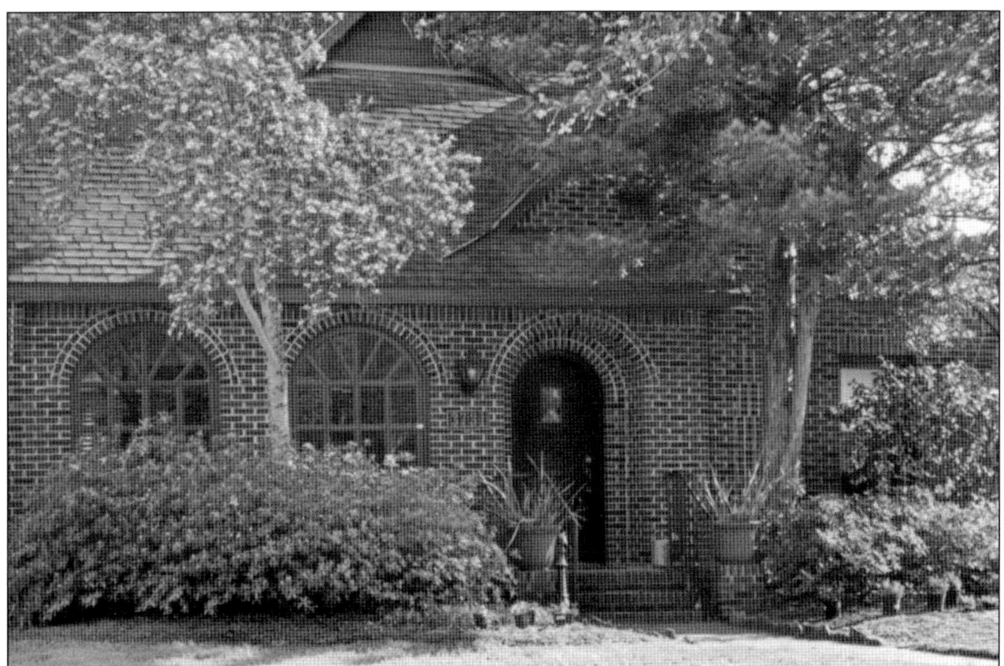

Some vintage properties in the city fare better than others in terms of sustainability and preservation. Ethel and Andrew Jackson purchased 3731 Darcus Street (above) in 1938 for $4,800. More than 75 years later, their grandson's family calls this brick bungalow home. Located on the corner of Ingold and Auden Streets, 3784 Ingold (shown below after a fresh snowfall in 1934) has undergone several additions and design changes yet still retains much of its original charm. (Above, courtesy of Jackie Duffie; below, Kris Holt.)

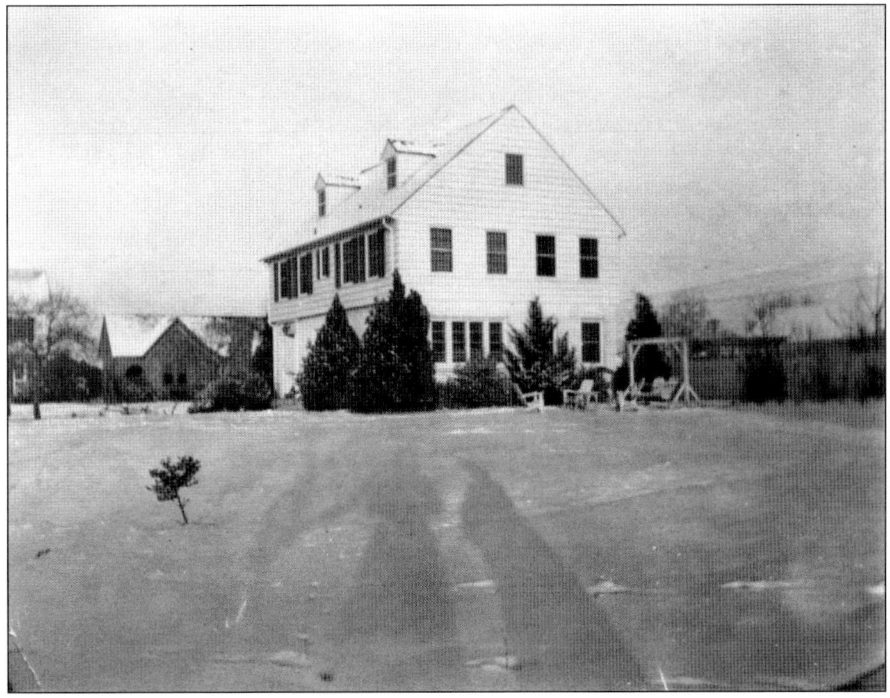

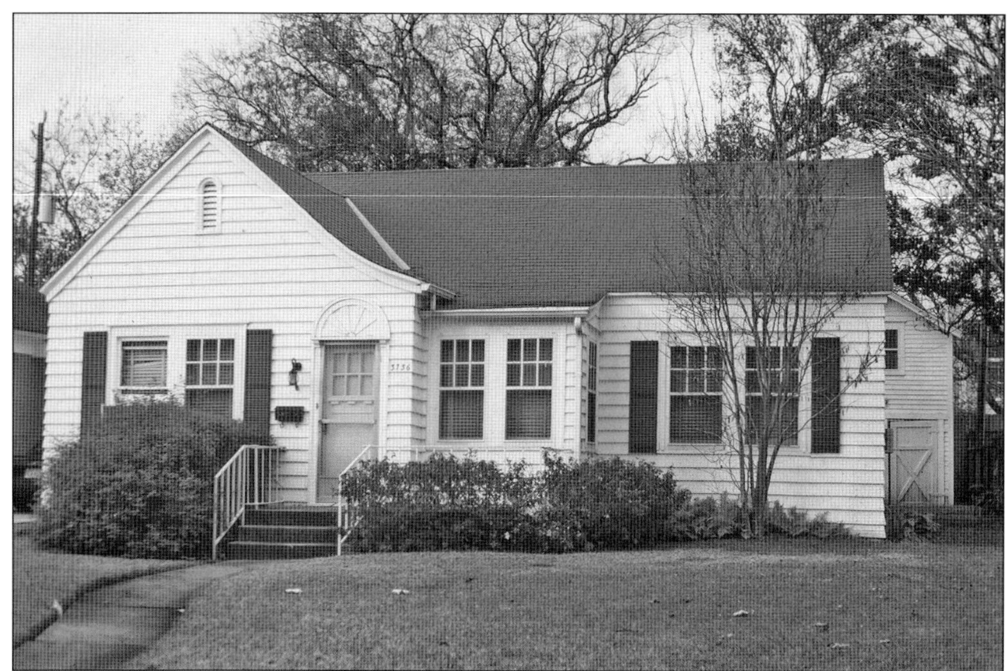

While many homes were torn down over the years, others got a second chance. These original Southside Place homes were salvaged and moved outside the city limits. The house at 3736 Jardin Street (above) was moved in 2000, and the home at 3727 Darcus Street (below) was moved in 2005. Appreciated for their charm and sturdiness, both homes took up residence in League City, Texas. (Both courtesy of Kris Holt.)

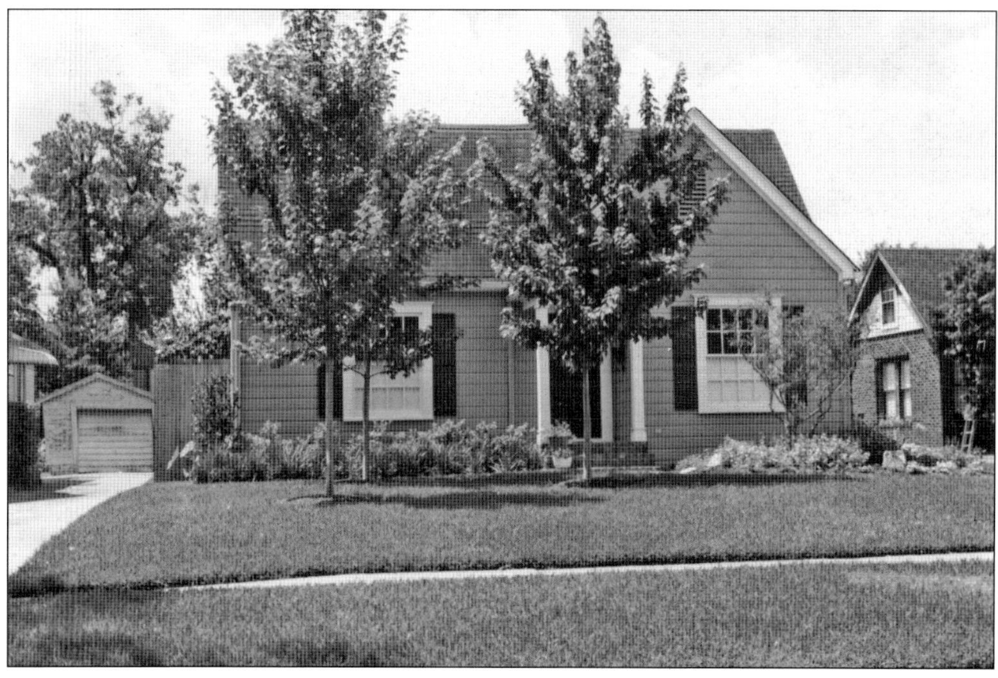

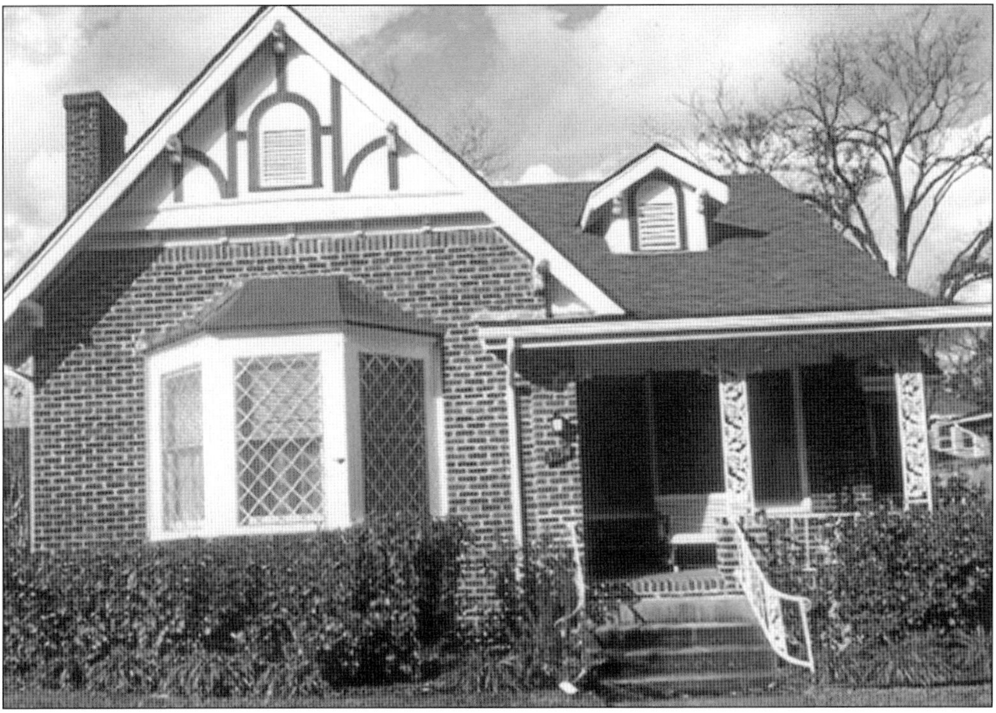

This home at 3734 Elmora Street was one of three original speculative houses built by E.L. Crain to open the neighborhood. When completed in 1925, the six-room, 1,200-square-foot home cost $8,200. It sold for its lot value for over $1 million in 2012. (Courtesy of Kate McCormick.)

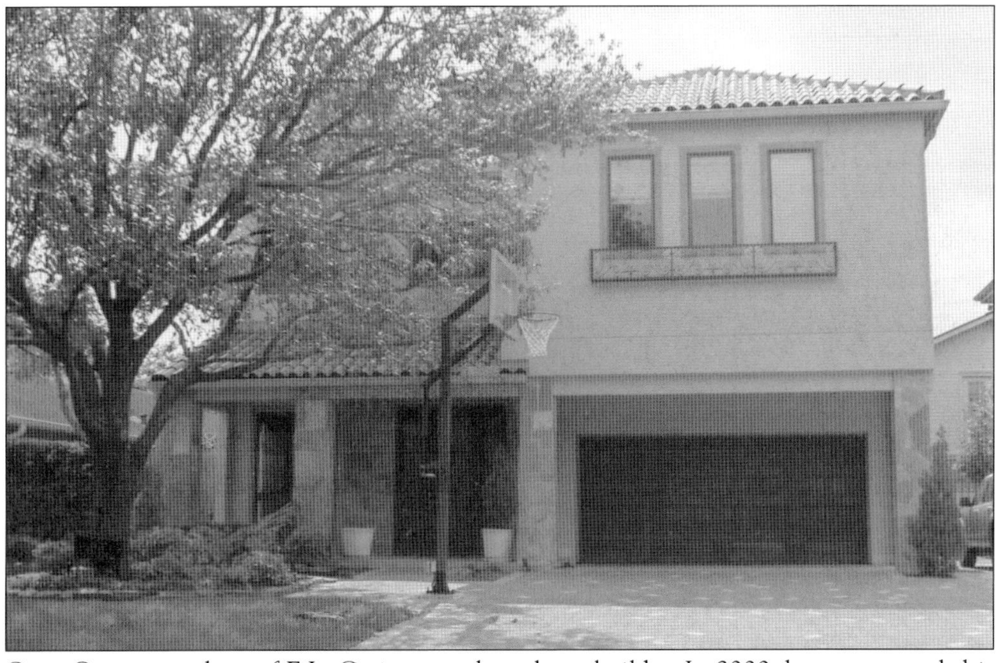

Gene Crain, grandson of E.L. Crain, was also a homebuilder. In 2000, he constructed this speculative home at 6710 Auden Street. At more than 5,200 square feet, this design is a far cry from the homes of his grandfather's generation. (Courtesy of Kris Holt.)

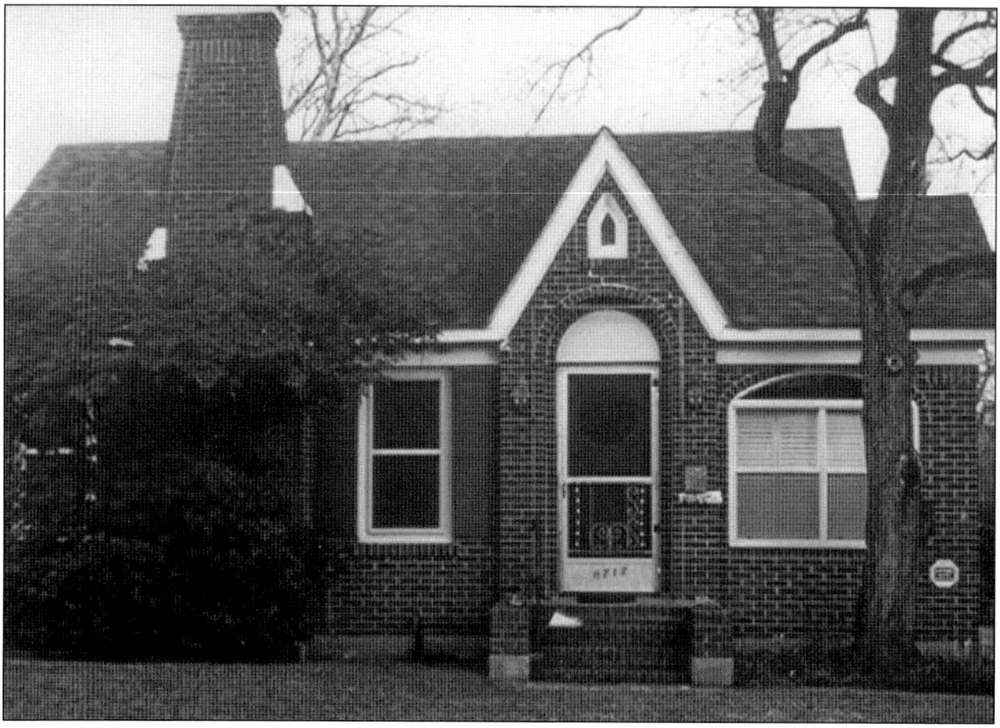

As of 2014, only a handful of Crain Ready-Cut homes remain in Southside Place: at 3757 Farbar Street, built in 1925; at 6717 Edloe Street (above), built in 1927; and at 3709 Garnet Street (below), built in 1924. Though diminutive in stature, all three loom large in the preservation of the historical record of Southside Place. (Both courtesy of Kris Holt.)

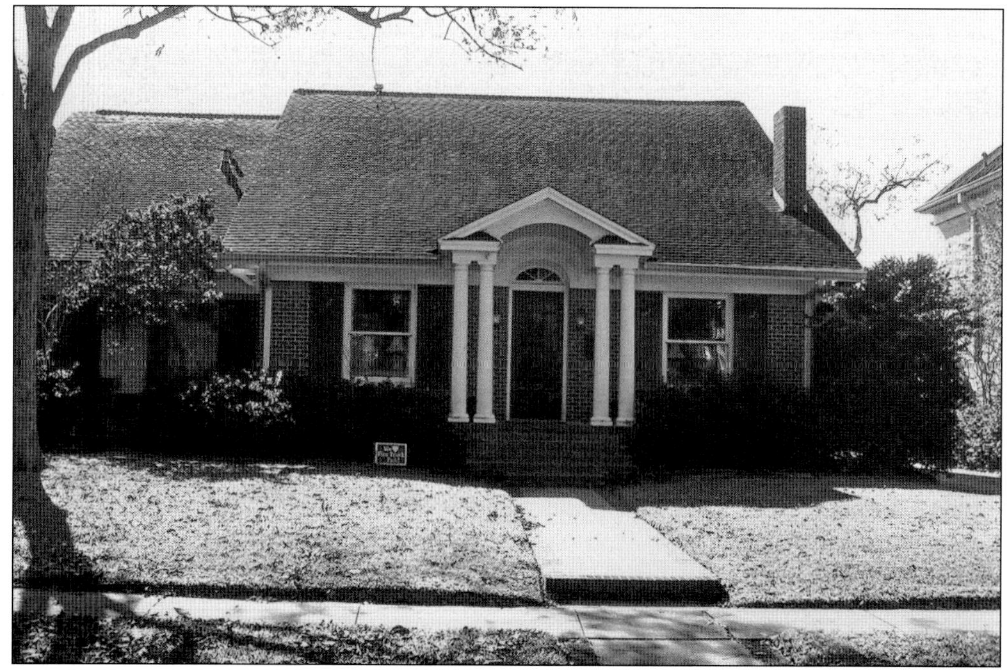

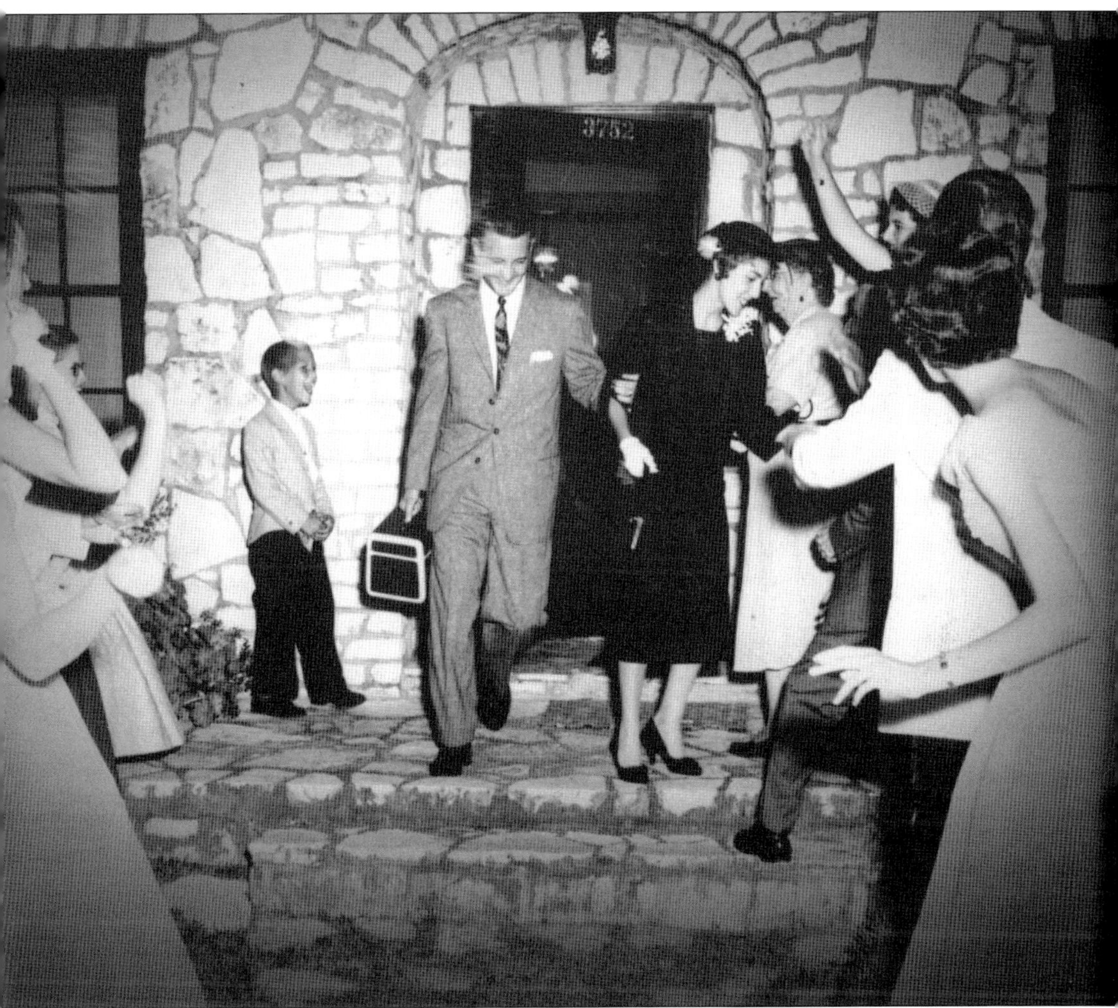

When families first staked claim 90 years ago in Southside Place, life was simple, and the homes were purposeful and unencumbered. Houses were largely single-story and less than 1,500 square feet. Two bedrooms housed large families, and air-conditioning consisted of a robust attic fan and open windows. As life evolved and the neighborhood grew in stature, so did the homes. Today, new homes average 5,000 square feet and sell in excess of $2 million. They are often three stories high with detached garage apartments above a two- or three-car garage. Despite these remarkable changes, a home continues to represent possibilities. Homes are where families are made, dreams are realized, and lives are defined. (Courtesy of Gayle Bowyer.)

Consistent with our mission to preserve history on a local level, this book was printed in South Carolina on American-made paper and manufactured entirely in the United States. Products carrying the accredited Forest Stewardship Council (FSC) label are printed on 100 percent FSC-certified paper.

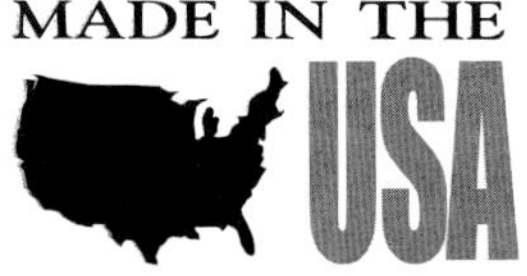